DON'T MENTION THE SCORE

Simon Briggs is the author of *Stiff Upper Lips and Baggy Green Caps*, and writes on sport for the *Daily Telegraph*. He grew up in Oxford, in a house full of academics, then studied history at Cambridge. But no-one has ever discovered which period.

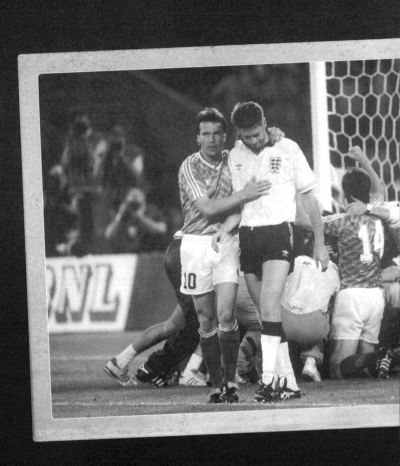

DON'T MENTION THE SCORE

A MASOCHISTS' HISTORY OF THE ENGLAND FOOTBALL TEAM

SIMON BRIGGS

Quercus

CONTENTS

Introduction   **7**

SECTION 1
Age of the Amateur   **10**

1 The Double-Barrelled Shooter   **12**

2 Hammered by the Scots   **22**

3 The Glory that was Corinth   **29**

4 Twilight of the Snobs   **39**

5 They Came from Central Europe   **50**

SECTION 2
Not-so-splendid Isolation   **62**

6 Don't Mention the War   **64**

7 Worst of British   **72**

8 Continental Drifters   **89**

9 They Might Have Been Giants   **109**

SECTION 3
World in Motion   124

10 Shock of Ages   **126**

11 The Hungarian Conquest   **146**

12 Broken Dreams   **164**

13 A Poisoned Chalice   **184**

SECTION 4
Forty Years of Hurt   210

14 Method Turns to Madness   **212**

15 Born to Run   **234**

16 Penance of the Pirates   **253**

17 Tears of a Clown   **277**

18 Golden Balls   **294**

19 The Sven Deadly Sins   **312**

20 The Wally with the Brolly   **335**

Index and acknowledgements   **342**

In loving memory of Julia Briggs
(1943–2007)

INTRODUCTION

'History started badly and hav been geting steadily worse.'
Nigel Molesworth, *Down with Skool!*

The French have a phrase, '*le vice anglais*', that denotes 'a perverse enjoyment of being beaten'. Masochism, to their eyes, is a peculiarly English trait. And anyone who follows the hyperventilating media coverage of the England football team might be tempted to agree.

Why do we insist on building up our boys as favourites to win every major tournament? Why do we portray moderate players as giants when it is so obvious that the whole thing will end in tears (or penalty shoot-outs, which is much the same thing)? Where is the sense of proportion, of self-deprecation, that is normally so much a part of our national culture?

Part of it is sheer commercial logic. To admit the truth – that the so-called 'golden generation' is made of iron pyrites – would hit sales of newspapers, replica shirts and St George bumper stickers where it hurts. But there are deeper and more mysterious forces at work here. In particular, there is the extra sense of expectation that comes with representing England, the country that invented the game.

The legend of England's lost footballing empire is built on the flimsiest of evidence – in effect, a dozen or so home wins between the wars (see page 92). Yet it is still pervasive enough to have left us with a raging superiority complex. The perception remains that we have not lost the Jules Rimet trophy, only leased it out for a little while.

The result is that when English footballers take the field, they are not just battling the opposition; they are competing with the ghosts of all the great names who went before them – the Mannions, the Lawtons and the Finneys. And when the national team qualifies for a big event (which is far from guaranteed these days), they are not just trying to win the Cup; they are trying to erase the disappointments of the last 40 years. No wonder the players look exhausted before the first match has even begun.

In the accelerated context of sport – where a player's lifespan consists of barely 10 years – the World Cup win of 1966 is starting to feel like an event from the Middle Ages. Hell, the Germans have won five major championships since then. Even the Spaniards, previously first-rate chokers, finally notched a title in 2008.

Are we wrong to expect more from our team? Are we wrong to believe that they should have managed better than a couple of semi-finals since 1966? Clearly, the idea that England retains some sort of *droit de seigneur* over the rest of the world is outdated and counter-productive. But that does not change the fact that 42 years without any silverware is a damn long wait.

Whenever England crash out of a major tournament, or make a horlicks of a qualifying campaign, it is always the track-suits who get the blame. Head coaches tend to roll, and quickly. Yet a more mature analysis might concentrate on the technical shortcomings of the players. By comparison with the rest of the football world, modern English players are underskilled and overindulged. A cushion pass, to their eyes, is what gets you into the VIP area at Spearmint Rhino.

The question has to be asked: why, when the best sides play pretty patterns and one-touch passing, has the England team reverted to a sort of siege warfare? Their idea of tactical sophistication is to lob the damn ball up there, as if it were a giant boulder, and pray to the Gods that it lands somewhere useful.

Such naivety is all the more frustrating when you consider that Englishmen have been playing some recognisable form of the game for over 150 years. So how did we waste such an advantage? Paradoxically, a head start can create problems of its own, as Sony famously discovered with Betamax videos. To invent something is rarely the same as to perfect it. As the journalist Bob Ferrier has written, 'Among the early [English] players there emerged the attitude that only by playing did the players learn the game and indeed train for it ... The business of being "taught" the game, of sitting down and rationalizing the game's problems, of thinking about them abstractedly, was simply not considered.'

The warning signs were there all the way back in the 1870s (see page 22). In their first few encounters with Scotland, the English team treated the football field as a battleground, a medium for the expression of all those manly traits – honour, pride and witlessness – that had been beaten into them at public school.

The Scotsmen had no truck with such dreary Freudian baggage. They had picked up the rules of the game, but not the self-sacrificing culture that surrounded it. As a result, their players were footballers rather than frustrated cavalrymen; and they relied on guile rather than force to put the ball between the sticks. Is it any wonder that they kept winning?

By the middle of the 20th Century, football had won converts all around the world, yet the essential story – from our Anglocentric perspective – had hardly changed. In 1960, Ferrier wrote that the Latin school was considered to be 'romantic', while the Central Europeans were 'lyric' and the Germans 'dramatic'. The English style, meanwhile, was still viewed as 'military', which shows how far we had come in almost a hundred years.

Not everyone involved in English football was a philistine. A generation of innovative English coaches had emerged between the wars. Jimmy Hogan (see page 101), the greatest of these, preached the virtues of playing in 'an intelligent, constructive and progressive, on-the-carpet manner'. But like so many visionaries, they were treated with disdain by the establishment, and most of them drifted abroad. At home, Football League managers were more likely to be men like Raich Carter (see page 121) – a great player in his own right, but an outspoken critic of organised coaching. 'They can either play or they can't,' Carter would scoff. 'Team talks won't make any difference.'

In January 2008, the FA went looking for a £30 million panacea in the shape of a European supercoach. After a few low-key friendlies, Fabio Capello's reign caught light with a dynamic 4–1 win over Croatia in Zagreb in September 2008 – a result that spawned a rash of 'Fab Four' headlines. Other observers pointed out that we had been here before, notably when Sven-Göran Eriksson's England thumped Germany 5–1 in Munich (see pages 317–18). A month later, they came within seconds of losing a vital World Cup qualifier to Greece.

For all Capello's ruthless efficiency (see page 338), he is likely to find himself struggling with the same problems that defeated his predecessors. He will still have little access to his players, because the Premier League clubs can see no benefit in English success. He will still lack ball-playing defenders, because English junior teams always go for the biggest and strongest lads at the back. And he will still have a shortage of creative, game-breaking forwards, because the whole system is so suspicious of anything out of the ordinary.

This, unfortunately, is our footballing culture. To change it, as Chris Waddle said in 1990, 'You'd have to start right back in the schools, right back at youth level. How would you do it? It would be like throwing a sponge against a wall.'

AGE OF THE AMATEUR

THE

AMATEUR

1872–1914

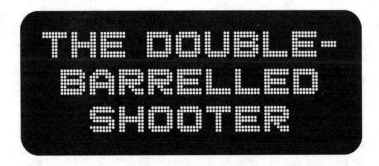

THE DOUBLE-BARRELLED SHOOTER

Think you're a whizz at football quiz questions? Well, you might know who scored the winner for Tottenham in the 1981 FA Cup final.[1] You might even know which Football League club has no letters in its name that you can colour in.[2] But you will be doing well if you can name the first man to score a goal for England.

The year was 1873, and the place was the Kennington Oval. England's emergent national team was confronting the Scots for the second time (after the first had produced a soggy 0–0 draw). Our knowledge of the game is a little sketchy: the newspapers of the day were more interested in angling and greyhound racing than they were in 'Association football', which was still seen as rugby's poor relation. But what we do know is that Leonard Howell kicked off for England, that the ball went straight into Scotland's half, and that the game was still barely a minute old when an underarm throw-in found Captain William Slaney Kenyon-Slaney advancing on goal.

So what happened next, as Sue Barker might ask on *Question of Sport?* Well, the unfortunate Robert Gardner produced the first of many Scottish goalkeeping howlers – an appropriately bathetic moment to open the 136-year tragicomedy of England's football team. Captain Kenyon-Slaney 'passed' the ball towards the goal, according to *Bell's Life in London*. But in the words of the *Glasgow Herald*, 'A few heavy showers previous to the start had made the turf slippery and greasy on the surface, and the ball at the outset was so wet that … it slipped out of the hands of the Scotch goalkeeper and passed between the posts.'

Worse was to come for poor Gardner, the Scottish captain. Soon after the change of ends that followed every goal in those early days, England's

1: Ricky Villa. 2: Hull City.

centre-forward Alexander Bonsor shot a free-kick towards him. This was not an especially smart move, as all free-kicks had to be indirect until 1903. But Gardner's reflexes must have over-ruled his brain, because he went to catch the ball, then tripped over, carrying it with him into the goal.

That made it two Scottish clangers in ten minutes – a rewarding start for the spectators who had gathered to watch this sporting successor to the battles of Bannockburn, Culloden and Stirling Bridge. The crowd numbered around 3000: small beer compared to the numbers that W.G. Grace – the most famous Victorian sportsman – could draw to county cricket, but still a record for a football match in London. The contemporary reports speak of hundreds of people climbing up the Oval's railings for a cheap view, while a marquee was erected for the ladies, who apparently 'showed up well on the occasion'.

> **'The microbe of football is more virulent and more persistent than any other of its kind.'**
> Alfred Gibson and William Pickford, authors of the 1906 classic *Association Football and the Men who Made It*, diagnose an early form of football fever.

As it was in the beginning ...

Perhaps we should pause for a moment and acknowledge that the football witnessed by those spectators had little in common with the football we know today. About the only thing modern fans might recognise would be the shirts: England in white, Scotland in dark blue. But the formations and play bore little resemblance to the intricate 21st-century game. When a player had the ball, he simply put his head down and tried to dribble upfield. When he didn't have it, he tore around trying to charge down the man who did. Seen from above (from an airship perhaps?), the shapeless bustle must have resembled particles in Brownian motion.

The original rules, too, would confound the Premiership's pampered multi-millionaires. Throw-ins were not delivered over the head, but rolled onto the field in the style of a ten-pin bowler. Some sphere-throwers mastered the art of hurling the ball up to the goal-mouth from the half-way line. The goalposts were connected by a length of tape, not a crossbar, and nets did not exist until 1891, prompting many arguments as to whether the ball had passed through the posts or not. Free-kicks had to be appealed for, like wickets in cricket. There were no penalty kicks.

It was a rough game back then. The level of physical confrontation was more akin to that of modern rugby, and pile-ups of bodies, known as bullies or scrimmages, often developed on the field. During the 1879–80 season, the lawmakers were forced to decree that 'No player shall charge his opponent by leaping on him.' But you could continue to charge the goalkeeper – even if he didn't have the ball – until 1893–4. In Gibson and Pickford's lengthy anatomy of the early game, *Association Football and the Men who Made It*, the authors reveal that 'Several cases of serious injury and two of death had occurred owing to the custom of one or more players "laying the goalkeeper out" so as to prepare the way for a successful attack.' As the bumper sticker has it, you don't have to be crazy to play in goal, but it helps.

> **'Our readers would get into a fog among the profusion of technical terms such as "crowding up", "backing", "banding", "hindering", and "dribbling".'**
>
> A contemporary magazine explains why it will not be publishing a report on the 1872 international.

Kenyon-Slaney: an officer and a marksman

Back at the Kennington Oval, two more goals followed in quick succession. Scotland opened their own scoring account through a breathtaking run and strike from Lieutenant Henry Renny-Tailyour – 'the difficulty of the final kick being such as to elicit loud applause from the spectators'. William Gibb then proceeded to equalise with a shot from behind a scrimmage. But England were not finished yet. Kenyon-Slaney notched a second with his left foot, and the resultant change of ends gave them the advantage of the wind. They kept up the pressure, and eventually C.J. Chenery settled matters, making the final score 4–2 despite some improved work from

Gardner, who 'had four or five times been successful in stopping the ball from passing between the posts'.

The players left the field to a rapturous reception, and both teams moved on to the Freemason's Tavern for dinner and endless toasts. Scotland had lost, but their honour had not been besmirched, especially as their football association had only found eight players prepared to travel the 500 miles down to London on the overnight train. Two more were recruited from the services (Renny-Tailyour being a case in point), while

They don't make 'em like they used to: the scorer of England's first international goal was William Kenyon-Slaney of Eton, Christ Church and the Grenadier Guards.

Arthur Kinnaird, a nobleman who would later preside over the English FA for 33 years, was a Scottish landowner who had put down roots in London.

All in all, it was a dramatic and auspicious day – far more promising, with regard to the future of football, than that scoreless draw the year before. As the *Bell's Life* correspondent concluded, 'There was sufficient evidence on this occasion to convince the most sceptical that football, if

ARTHUR KINNAIRD
Caps I (for Scotland)   Goals 0

T HE SCION OF A DISTINGUISHED Scottish family, Kinnaird was instrumental in organising the first internationals. A red-bearded half-back with a red-blooded tackling style, he used to turn out in long white flannels, a striped jersey and a blue-and-white quartered cricket cap – though opponents were ill advised to giggle. His mother used to complain that he would come home with a broken leg one day. 'Don't worry, my lady,' one of his friends replied. 'It won't be his own.'

only aided by fine weather, is a game that would take its place among the leading pastimes of the day.' His judgement would prove remarkably prescient (except that bad weather has never really become a problem).

The only misleading element of the match was the scoreline, which rather suggested that England would develop into an adventurous, thrill-seeking bunch of playboys. Such footballers would indeed emerge from the nation's playing fields, parks and council estates, but all too often they were ignored, mistrusted and even despised by the straitlaced administrators who ran the game.

A game for grandees

If he were around today, Captain Kenyon-Slaney would probably be known as Kenyon-Sloaney. An Old Etonian and a future member of parliament, he was hardly the sort of man we think of as a footballer. And neither was Mrs Kenyon-Slaney (*née* Lady Mabel Selina Bridgeman) the sort of woman we think of as a footballer's wife – though she certainly was Posh. Lady Mabel could trace her lineage back directly to William the Conqueror.

Run your eye down the England team-sheet for that 1873 match and you can almost smell the money. There are a couple of northerners and three military men, including Kenyon-Slaney himself, listed as 'Household Brigade'. But the telling signs are there in the presence of such clubs as Oxford University, Wanderers (the famous amateur side captained by Charles Alcock), and Old Wykehamists (former Winchester College schoolboys).

The explanation is simple. Football, like its great Victorian rival cricket, was a labourer's game organised and codified by toffs. And the evolutionary process started with those great British institutions, the major public schools.

> **'It is clear that one is a gentleman's game played by hooligans; the other is a hooligan's game played by gentlemen.'**
>
> Famous epigram on the difference between football and rugby, attributed to an unnamed chancellor of Cambridge University.

Many motives could be cited to explain the public schools' sudden adoption of organised sport in the mid-19th century: to encourage teamwork, promote health and fitness, or teach youngsters to deal with disappointment. But the author and historian David Winner argues that all these came well down the list. The prime consideration was the contemporary moral panic surrounding masturbation, which was viewed as a serious sin that could to lead to madness, imprisonment or even death. Headmasters such as the Revd Edward Thring, of Uppingham School, believed that the pursuit of violent sports, followed by cold showers, could purge such unnatural desires.

As Winner suggests in his fascinating study *Those Feet*, the predictable, constipated, safety-first style of most English national teams can be traced back to these origins: soggy afternoons on school playing fields, where impressionable schoolboys were sent to hack a football around – not for fun, nor for the expression of their innate creativity, but to stamp out their basest urges. Winner describes the sport that emerged from this pre-Freudian soup as 'a game imbued with manly, martial virtues played with heavy leather balls in thick, ankle-high boots in seas of mud'.

In adapting what was essentially an old folk tradition – the frenzied and often murderous pursuit of a trophy through fields, farms and highways – each school came up with different rules. At Eton, where Kenyon-Slaney learned his skills, the game would start with a bully or scrum. Players could defend by crawling on top of the ball, though they could also be battered off it. Such sado-masochistic practices live on today at Eton, where the Field Game and the Wall Game are still played. (The latter represents the pinnacle of English sporting sterility: no-one has scored a goal in the St Andrew's Day match since 1909.)

'Rather a friendlie kinde of fyghte than a play or recreation – a bloody or murthering practice than a fellowly sport or pastime.'

Philip Stubbes, author of the 1583 pamphlet *Anatomie of Abuses in the Realme of England*, offers a Krazy Gang-style definition of early football.

Westminster School used a system of Ups and Behinds, reminiscent of Gaelic football or Australian Rules. Harrow would double the length of the field from 150 to 300 yards if the score was drawn at the end of play (a fairer system, some might say, than the modern use of penalties). Cheltenham pioneered the use of offside, known by some schools as 'sneaking'. And at Charterhouse – perhaps the most influential of all the early football schools – the game was played in the cloisters, where the boys were allowed to dribble but not pass.

CHARLES ALCOCK
Caps 1 Goals 1

'LIKE A THREAD OF GOLD his career runs through the weaving of the story of "Soccer",' wrote one admirer of Charles Alcock. It's not unusual for retired sportsmen to go into administration, but Alcock was different: he played the game and ran it at the same time. Not content with inventing and organising the first knockout tournament, he went on to captain Wanderers to victory in the inaugural FA Cup final. Alcock must have had his eye on a similar triumph in the first international: he recruited the England team, and then … injured his leg, rather disappointingly, and was forced to travel to Glasgow as an umpire.

Football? It's a riot!

The schools may not have invented the concept of football, but they certainly made it respectable. Until their intervention, the very word 'football' denoted little more than a glorified riot. Some historians claim that the concept was born in Saxon times, when the heads of Danish invaders were kicked through the streets of Chester. Others refer back to the moment in Homer's *Odyssey* where a 'princess and her retinues threw their veils to the wind, struck up a game of ball'. Whatever its origins, the game soon developed an anarchic and often violent spirit. Throughout the Tudor and Stuart eras, various monarchs tried – and failed – to prevent hordes of drunken ruffians scrambling after a ball every Shrove Tuesday: the unemployable in pursuit of the inedible. You may have come across the Carling ad where a mob of bare-chested men hack a football through the entrance to a car park. Apart from being a smart bit of advertising, this clip is about as close as we are likely to get to the game's ancestral form.

Why Shrove Tuesday? Probably because the Easter holidays were a throwback to earlier pagan festivals of spring. And whether you are talking about Greeks, Romans, Saxons or Danes, ancient sports contained a strong ritual element. According to the writer Derek Hammond, the first ball games were nothing to do with subjugating sexuality; quite the reverse. They were magical fertility rites: as Hammond puts it, 'part of the original heathen, naturalistic British religions which were about the earth and the sun and killing and fucking and getting what you want'.

In many cases, these primaeval free-for-alls were played with anything except a ball. This is evident from some of the bizarre traditions that live on in the darkest corners of the English countryside. Two Leicestershire villages still contest the Hallaton Bottle Kicking and Hare Pie Scramble at Easter each year. Or take the Haxey Hood, in Lincolnshire, where the aim is to move a leather tube from pub to pub. It is staged every Twelfth Night and features a Lord, a Fool and 12 referees called Bogginses. Hammond links the tube to the leather hood found on a number of bog mummies and argues that the whole game is actually a watered-down simulation of a midwinter human sacrifice.

Left to themselves, the school codes would probably have remained just as disparate (if not quite as weird). But then their old boys went off to university, and discovered that everyone was talking different sporting languages. Cambridge University has given the world the X-ray and nuclear fission; in 1848, it also produced the first version of 'Cambridge Rules', which were pinned up on a lamp-post in the centre of the city. A second attempt followed in 1862, and provided the basis for the version adopted by the Football Association when it was formed the following year during a meeting at the Freemason's Tavern.

This was the moment when football – that mad, bad and multifarious game – began to coalesce into the rather more precise concept of 'Soccer'. The name is believed to have been coined in the late 1880s by Charles Wreford-Brown (see picture, page 32), who went on to captain England during the following decade. The Oxford undergraduates of the day used to add the suffix '-er' to every noun, so that a swot became a mugger, and the first Metropolitan policemen were Peelers (after their founder Sir Robert Peel). The story goes that Wreford-Brown was coming out of his digs, dressed in sports kit, when a friend asked him where he was heading. 'I'm off to play football,' he replied. 'Association or rugby?' 'Why, soccer of course.'

'Are we playing hacking, Arthur?' 'Oh, yes, let's have hacking!'

Famous exchange between Charles Alcock and Arthur Kinnaird, two of the game's founding fathers, during an especially rough match.

Wreford-Brown would also chair England's selection committee around the time of the Second World War, perhaps in the hope of reforming the tail-on-the-donkey approach he had been used to as a player. Take the example of poor Kenyon-Slaney: having orchestrated that famous victory in 1873, England's first goalscorer was promptly dropped for life.

HAMMERED BY THE SCOTS

North of the border, the two rival footballing codes found themselves at loggerheads from the very start. Forget England v Scotland, this was Rugger Buggers v Soccer Jocks. Rugby was the first sport to organise a full international, in March 1871, and when soccer moved to follow, several rugby clubs wrote an angry letter to *The Scotsman*, blustering that a team drawn from a minority had no right to represent a nation.

A decade later, the boot was on the other foot. Or, rather, it was being applied to the other kind of ball. From Dumfries to Thurlo, Scottish society had fallen victim to football's virulent microbe. The infection spread beyond the doctors, lawyers and accountants who played the game in England, reaching out to manual labourers on farms and shipyards. Many of these blue-collar converts jacked in their day jobs and migrated to Lancashire clubs like Bolton Wanderers and Preston North End, where they collected far more generous wages than they could have dreamed of at home.

Scotland's football explosion started with the annual international against England. Nothing sells a sport so well as success, particularly success against your nearest neighbours and most bitter rivals. The Stuarts may have sat on the English throne, but for sheer satisfaction, Scotland's footballing sovereignty through the 1870s and 1880s must rank right up there.

Kenyon-Slaney's goals were soon revealed to be the first of many false dawns for English sport. After that, results grew frighteningly one-sided, and bashing the Sassenachs became as much a part of the northern spring as bagpipes and heather blossom. Over the next 14 years, Scotland won the annual Tweed derby ten times and lost only once. Charles Campbell, their first great captain, played in ten of these games: the last man to mount so many destructive raids across the border was Ragnar Hairy-Breeks, a fearsome Viking warlord.

We should not be too surprised by England's total ineffectuality in this period. Frankly, they didn't give a damn. In the upper-class world of English football, it was considered manly to play ball games, but undignified to take them too seriously. As a result, selection was arbitrary. Only two members of the victorious 1873 side returned the following year, and a fellow might find himself deployed at left-back in one match, then shifted into goal for the next. In 1875 Billy Carr turned up 15 minutes late after being 'delayed on his journey'. Some might describe this attitude as nonchalance; others as complacency.

Scotland's footballers, by contrast, took as much pride in their work as Australia's cricketers of the same period. Every goal, every win, helped to remind the world that Britain extended beyond the Lake District. And how the fans revelled in their team's successes. In 1878, 15,000 spectators squeezed into Glasgow's Hampden Park, while another 5000 occupied the surrounding buildings. They were rewarded with a 7–2 victory – still the second-heaviest defeat ever inflicted on an England side.

Bell's Life in London reported feebly that 'luck, in the real and genuine sense of the word, was against England in this contest' – a claim based around the fact that the wind suddenly dropped off at half-time. An alternative explanation was supplied by a letter to the same paper, penned by 'A Disgusted Englishman', who complained that the visitors had 'played very selfishly … and not for the success of the side'.

> **'In the whole of sport there is no greater paradox than that which made an upper-class game, the rules of which were an amalgam of those of half-a-dozen English public schools, the fervent and abiding passion of Scotland.'**
> Bob Crampsey, historian, on football's class breakthrough.

The dribbling disease

All the newspaper reports from this period say the same things. They describe the English players as bigger and more imposing than the Scots, who are always said to be 'wiry' (more Gordon Strachan, by the sound of things, than Alan Hansen). Then they go on to slam England's forwards for their lack of 'combination' – the contemporary term for the passing game. Like our letter-writing friend, many correspondents end up by laying charges of selfishness.

Such accusations are understandable, if a little unfair, as there was a major cultural difference between the way the English and Scottish players learned their football. The contrast stems, once again, from the great English public schools. Football, as played there, was such a violent business that to carry the ball yourself was an act of chivalry and self-sacrifice – exactly the sort of stiff-upper-lipped conduct that school sport was supposed to encourage. There was no class in a pass; indeed, shipping the ball on to a team-mate represented a shameful cop-out. All of which may explain why speedy and powerful dribblers, like Charlie Bambridge and William Mosforth, were so highly prized in 19th-century English football.

The phrase 'schoolboy tactics' might be an insult today, but in the Victorian era, that was all England had to go on. *Bell's Life* describes a revealing moment in the 1876 match when 'Three of the English forwards … started a pretty run down on their own lines, and ascended the hill in a manner which called forth loud cheers. Hubert Heron led the van,

> **'[England] play each man for himself, ignoring his fellows … it is a style of play the consequences of which are suicidal … the consequences of which are the reverse of glorious.'**
> Robert Livingstone, secretary of the Scottish FA, despairs of English football.

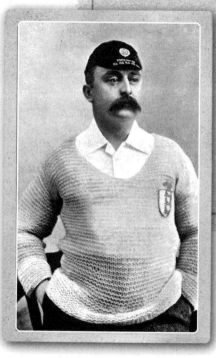

E.C. BAMBRIDGE
Caps 18   Goals 11

Had 'Charlie Bam' owned a guitar, he would never have stopped playing solos. He was the epitome of the amateur individualist, a man who saved his passes for the vicar's daughter. Mind you, he could be damn good to watch. During England's pulsating 5–4 win over Scotland in 1879, he scored what the journalist W. Unite Jones called 'possibly the finest goal ever seen in football … He ran practically the full length of the field and then put the ball past the lengthy Parlane'.

followed by Smith and Maynard, the two latter guarding their captain, who kept the ball at his feet till well up on the Scotch lines.'

With its wing-men and undeviating approach, this attack might sound reminiscent of Luke Skywalker's trench-bound assault on the Death Star. In fact, it is the sort of manoeuvre still used in Eton's Field Game. Heron's sidekicks were there to block off potential attackers, or to take the move on if he lost control of the ball.

The Scots had come up with a rather more scientific method, as befits the nation that gave us the steam engine, the bicycle and – perhaps most pertinently – the lawnmower. In Glasgow, the pioneering Queen's Park FC had been formed in 1867; it spent its first few seasons playing in-house games with lax offside conditions. The result, as Jonathan Wilson writes in his tactical history *Inverting the Pyramid*, was the 'pattern-weaving approach, characterised by strings of short passes zigzagging between the forward- and half-lines'.

There is a good example in one 1874 edition of *Bell's Life*, which describes John Ferguson winning the ball and making for the England goal. 'Angus MacKinnon soon shot out in front, and the pair, by magnificent "passing", piloted the ball clean through the English backs, until the only opponent was Welch, the goalkeeper.' You might already have guessed that MacKinnon scored, while Heron did not.

WILLIAM MOSFORTH
Caps 9   Goals 3

THE SHEFFIELD DODGER'S METHOD was to make for the left corner-flag and then fire the ball in, aiming not for a team-mate but for the goal itself. According to Gibson and Pickford, these 'eerie shots … came at all paces and in all manner of quaint curves, but they were all dead on the mark'. The same chapter recounts Mosforth's recollections of England's famous 1879 meeting with Scotland, which became acrimonious when the Scots thought they had taken a 5–4 lead with five minutes to go. The goal was disallowed, and one of England's great dribblers – either Mosforth or Bambridge – stole the match with a last-gasp winner. 'I don't know which of us it was,' Mosforth said, 'but I know that they carried me off the field afterwards.'

Two's company, four's a league

Cecil Rhodes once said 'To be born English is to win first prize in the lottery of life.' For a sportsman, it is also to wear an invisible target on your chest. This inescapable truth was brought home to England's footballers in the late 1870s and early 1880s, when Wales and Ireland formed national teams of their own. Over the next few seasons, the men in white shirts discovered the dual meaning of the phrase 'marked men'.

England's first encounter with Wales took place at the Kennington Oval in January 1879, while 'a cheerless mixture of snow and rain was falling'. One eye-witness claimed that the Welsh captain, Samuel Kenrick, was 'the heaviest charger the game has known', and that he 'bundled the English forwards about lustily'. Another report used the phrases 'fierce tussle', 'sharp struggle' and 'vigorous onslaught' in the space of 400 words. In the end, England crept away with a 2–1 win, thanks to a disallowed goal seconds from the end. The English referee's extraordinary

> **'Having broken his leg some weeks before a crucial match [Bambridge] outfoxed his opponents by turning up with a shin guard covering the sound limb and scoring the winning goal.'**
>
> D.J. Taylor on Charlie Bambridge, king of the English dribblers.

name – Segar Bastard – echoed the view of the visiting fans. (And, yes, he probably was wearing black, though in the form of a frock coat rather than the terylene training gear we are used to today.)

Three years later, Ireland entered the fray, showing equal commitment but rather less skill. As footballers, the Irish made a mighty fine hurling team: England notched 13 goals in that first match – a tally which reduced the home captain to tears – and maintained an average score of 6–1 for the rest of the century. In the words of James Catton, 'It was quite common for the sons of Hibernia to show all the dash and impetuosity of their character for the first twenty minutes of the match and then to fade away to a comparatively helpless lot.' Yet a summons to enjoy the easy pickings at Belfast's Bloomfield Park was often received with distinct ambivalence. It was not just Ireland's robust defending that put the players off; one administrator wrote that the Irish Sea crossing had to be made at least two days before the game 'to allow time for the ill-effects to wear off, for most good footballers are the worst sailors I've ever seen'.

In 1884, the annual Home Championship was launched. The first Anglo-Scottish clashes had been a bit of a jape, a battle for bragging rights between such eccentric amateur enthusiasts as Charles Alcock and Arthur Kinnaird. A decade later, the whole business was becoming far more serious and formal. Losing to Scotland was one thing; finishing in the basement of a league table quite another – a point not lost on the men who ran the game. The early 1880s mark the first watershed in English footballing history: the moment when the national team starts taking itself seriously.

The first step to recovery, as any AA member knows, is to admit the existence of a problem. Flick through the newspapers from this period and you will notice a shift in the national mood. Take, for instance, this peppery editorial from the 18 March 1882 edition of *Bell's Life.* 'The Scottish defeat was by no means unexpected,' the paper argued. 'But to be beaten by Wales; this is, indeed, decadence.'

In this infamous match, played at Wrexham on 15 March, England had lost Bambridge early on to a dislocated shoulder. Battling on with ten men, they still managed to score three times – but shipped five goals as well. The same article went on to suggest that 'the English players ... were beaten by the superior organisation of their opponents, as they have been before, and will continue to be beaten as long as there is such an evident lack of co-operation on the part of English clubs and players to make their own fixtures and individual gratification subservient to what ought to be the highest interest of the game – the international matches.'

If these remarks sound familiar, it is probably because you can still read similar laments in a Sunday broadsheet almost every week of the year. The Premiership clubs still operate at a far higher level than national teams, still use far too many foreigners (even if today's imports are just as likely to be Brazilian as Scottish) and still dominate the calendar to such an extent that England's players go into most internationals overworked and underprepared.

But there is one crucial difference between ancient and modern: in 1882, football was still fluid and unformed. Anyone could come along with a bright idea and shake up the established order of things. Which is exactly what a 33-year-old journalist named N. Lane Jackson proceeded to do.

THE GLORY THAT WAS CORINTH

'Show me a good loser, and I'll show you a loser.' So said Stu 'The Kid' Ungar, arguably the greatest poker player in history. His aphorism sums up the yawning gap between British amiability and American professionalism. Yet there have been exceptions to the rule – and never more so than in the golden age of the Corinthian football team. Here was a team that operated stricter ethical standards than the Pilgrim Fathers. And still, for much of the 1880s, they were just about unbeatable.

> 'With an intelligent nonchalance and in their tailored shirts and well-cut shorts they brought a quality and culture to the game.'
>
> The historian Edward Grayson admires the Corinthian style.

The Corinthians were founded in 1882 by N. Lane Jackson, a wealthy journalist who was fed up with watching the Scots make fools of England's best footballers every year. It was not ability that England were lacking, Jackson realised, with a flash of insight that would have delighted Miss Marple. It was teamwork. He also twigged that as long as the average England team continued to be drawn from seven or eight different clubs, they were never going to give up their debilitating addiction to dribbling.

Jackson unveiled his idea in 1882, during a meeting at the Football Association's offices. He envisaged a football club that was also a private club – a club, in other words, that only clubbable chaps could join. As he explained later, 'public school and university men provided most of the players for the English side, so I thought that by giving them plenty of practice together they would acquire a certain measure of combination.'

And so the Corinthians were formed – a team that boasted more Oxbridge degrees, handlebar moustaches and country estates than you could shake a shooting stick at. Despite the odd social anomaly (Tinsley

THE BROWN BROGUE
Caps 13   Goals 14 (while worn by Tinsley Lindley)

'IT'S ALL RIGHT: he's a gentleman: look at his boots,' declares a bystander of Professor Henry Higgins in the first scene of *Pygmalion*. The same test could apply to several of England's greatest gentlemen footballers, men who eschewed the conformity of the ankle-high bovver boot in favour of something lighter and more manoeuvrable. In the 1950s, that enlightened maverick Stanley Matthews enlisted a Yorkshire shoe factory to build a new kind of boot, based on the leather slippers he had seen Brazilian players wearing in Rio. Some 70 years earlier, Tinsley Lindley had gone looking for a cheaper solution, and came up with a pair of ordinary walking brogues. Nineteenth-century players would use any equipment they could lay their hands on, often cobbled together in a Heath Robinson sort of way. Shinpads had been invented in the mid-1870s by Samuel Widdowson, a fleet-footed English wing, who wore cut-down cricket pads outside his socks. And then there was W.N. 'Nuts' Cobbold, a hard-running forward and fierce shoulder-charger, who prefigured the modern quarterback by turning out 'swathed in rubber bandages and ankle guards'.

Lindley was the son of a Nottingham lace-maker made good), most members came from old money and possessed both athletic and aesthetic prowess. Anyone unable to translate Homer on sight need not apply.

Even the club's name was a learned reference to the Isthmian Games, a Greek sporting festival held in ancient Corinth. Given the sense of entitlement among these army subalterns and sprightly clergymen, they might as well have dubbed themselves the Olympians and have done with it.

> **'It is a standing insult to sportsmen to have to play under a rule which assumes that players intend to trip, hack and push their opponents, and to behave like cads of the most unscrupulous kidney.'**
>
> C.B. Fry – Corinthian footballer, England cricket captain and world-record long-jumper – laments the introduction of penalty kicks.

Nobody has ever played football quite like the Corinthians. They disapproved of penalty kicks, which were introduced during the 1890–1 season, because they implied the insulting possibility of deliberate foul play. On the rare occasions that a penalty was awarded against them, the Corinthian goalkeeper would lean insouciantly against one of the uprights until the kick had been taken. They also believed that the game should be played exclusively with the feet, which meant keeping the ball on the turf at all times. It was just about acceptable for a defender to hoof it upfield under pressure, but any forward who tried the same trick would soon find himself hoofed right out of the team.

The 1880s were a decade of rapid tactical evolution among English clubs – and about time too. On Lancashire's cramped and muddy pitches, teams of (mostly Scottish) professionals would circulate the ball as if it were a parcel at a children's party, searching for a clear sight of goal. The Corinthians were more dashing, emulating the Queen's Park technique with a style Jackson described as 'passing forward on the run'. They used the full width of the pitch, eliminating off-side by taking the ball up to the corner-flag. It would then be centered – along the ground, of course – for the centre-forward to stroke home.

For all their high-minded principles, the Corinthians made ferocious opponents. They favoured big men – the average weight of the players was

The not-so-dirty dozen: 12 members of the Corinthians line up, c. 1895. Charles Wreford-Brown, the man credited with inventing the term 'soccer', is in the foreground on the left.

a hefty 13 stone – and the historian Edward Grayson sums up their approach as 'healthy, robust, cultured play and good old-fashioned shoulder-charging'. They usually marmalised the tough northern League teams they came up against (always in 'friendlies', as the Corinthians' constitution forbade them from entering competitions), and some of their other exploits sound as though they have been torn from the pages of *Boy's*

Own. In 1892, for instance, Jackson issued a multi-sport charity challenge to all-comers. His men ended up taking on the Barbarians – a rugby union club with a similarly elitist ethos – and succeeded in beating them at their own game.

England's great sheikh-up: the discovery of 'The Pyramid'

Jackson's brainwave changed the culture of English football at a stroke. From the depths of a 15-year trough, the national team suddenly discovered the joys of continuity and combination. Corinthian players dominated selection for the next decade; in games between England and Scotland, they won 52 of the 88 caps available between 1882 and 1889. Little by little, results began to improve.

But selection was only half of it. In 1884, the same year that General Gordon began his famous defence of Khartoum, England's footballers finally began to pay attention to tactics. Back in 1872, they had gone into the first international with one back, one half-back, and fully *eight* forwards – a formation (1-1-8, in effect) that might best be termed 'the scattergun'. Or perhaps just 'the playground mêlée'. They soon switched to 2-2-6, and ran with that for another decade. But their adoption of a 2-3-5 pattern in 1884 represents a major technological advance. You could call it a moon-landing moment – a small step for the English selectors, a giant leap for football-kind.

Known as 'the pyramid formation', this alignment would dominate football at all levels for the next 70 years. The key advantage was the

> **'I was once accused of mistrusting men with waxed moustaches. Well, so, to a certain extent, I do. It often means vanity and sometimes drink.'**
> Robert Baden-Powell, founder of the Boy Scouts, on the Corinthians' preferred form of facial hair.

J O H N G O O D A L L
Caps 14   Goals 12

Goodall (see photograph page 44), was essentially a Scotsman, yet the accident of his birth in London allowed him to qualify for England. But for this fortunate detail, he would probably not have played international football at all, like so many other Scottish professionals of his era. Professional or not, Goodall was a genteel and dignified character; the journalist James Catton called him 'as quiet as an old sheep, but such a player'. His football was self-effacing too; despite an excellent goal-scoring record from inside-right, he preferred to pass the ball, and the limelight, on to more famous forwards such as G.O. Smith. In his time at Derby County, Goodall was a mentor to Steve Bloomer, the prolific striker who became known — ironically enough — as 'the hammer of the Scots'.

introduction of the centre-half, who became known as 'the pivot'. Matches were won and lost through the performance of this man in the middle. Ideally he needed to be a composite of Nobby Stiles and Glenn Hoddle — though preferably with Stiles's courage in the tackle and Hoddle's range of passing rather than the other way around.

England's reshuffle strengthened their hand: in 1884, they held the Scots to a single early goal, but could not score themselves. The following year they went one better, securing a 1–1 draw thanks to some timely interventions from a pair of young brothers at full-back. Known as 'the Meridians' because of their initials, A.M. and P.M. Walters meshed together like clockwork on the field. They were blue-eyed, deep-chested warriors who charged like bulls and kicked like siege guns, but still had the ball-skills to pass to each other 'with the accuracy of well-trained forwards'. As Gibson and Pickford wrote in 1906, 'It is doubtful if the game has ever produced a better pair of defenders … Previous to their time – say 1885 – combination amongst backs was practically unheard of.'

At the other end of the field, England had discovered a spring-heeled Jack-in-the-box named Tinsley Lindley. He may have weighed a measly 10st 4oz, but Lindley was famed for his almost supernatural sleight of foot. His dribbling technique was so perfectly honed that he even used it on the rugby field, where his team-mates claimed he could 'manipulate the oval with the same control and certainty as he did the globe'. A Cambridge graduate and professional barrister, Lindley was a renaissance man whose many and varied accomplishments typified the Corinthian principle, even if his bourgeois origins did not.

'Lindley was slightly built and skilfully elusive,' wrote his fellow Corinthian C.B. Fry. 'Half-backs seemed to be chasing a shadow. He had a pair of conjuring feet and a trick of timing a shot at goal from a crossing ball, after the manner of [Sussex and England batsman] Ranji's glance to leg.' On his international debut against Ireland Lindley immediately stood out from the scrimmage, earning repeated cheers for his 'neat performance'. He notched his first goal for England that day in 1886, and set off on a scoring spree that brought him 15 goals in 13 games – still one of the highest ratios ever achieved.[1]

The honourable Lindley wins his case

Whatever the deficiencies of English teams over the years, they have usually had the luxury of a top-notch marksman to aim for. Lofthouse, Greaves, Lineker: the baton has passed from generation to generation. And Lindley, far more than that one-hit wonder Kenyon-Slaney, can claim to be the first of the breed. He was England's centre forward and captain when they finally secured their first Home Championship, dethroning the Scots by a resounding 5–0 margin in 1888. He also opened the scoring with a rare header from a corner after 30 minutes.

Lindley's team were the first England side to produce what Ruud Gullit once called 'sexy football'. According to *The Field* of 24 March, 1888, 'The forwards played to one another with a grace and unanimity

---

1: Lindley's statistics are complicated by a disputed goal he may or may not have scored against Wales on 29 March, 1886. If we award him that goal, he scored in his first nine games for England – a record surpassed only by G.O. Smith's contemporary Steve Bloomer, who managed 10. Even without it, he still managed six games in a row.

'The Renton Ruffian.'

Soubriquet applied to Robert Kelso, a Scottish half-back who 'had many a severe bout' with England's W.N. 'Nuts' Cobbold in 1887.

worthy of all praise, and the defence was perfect.' Yet the newspaper also raised one important caveat. 'The golden offers of Lancashire [have] induced so many of the rising stars of Scotland to migrate southwards,' it explained, '[that] the talent at the disposal of the Scottish Association is limited and impoverished.'

A classic English mindset, this: after 15 years of hurt, you finally beat the bastards, and promptly decide that they must be rubbish. Lindley felt that England deserved more credit for their gradual improvement; he described his two previous appearances against Scotland (a 1–1 draw and a tense 2–3 defeat) as 'the turning of the corner'. But the Scots preferred to pin the blame on the hordes of young players escaping across the border. This exodus was hardly a new phenomenon; as we have seen, travelling footballers had been discreetly hiring out their bodies for years. But then, in 1885, the English FA took the bold decision to legalise professionalism. Suddenly the talent drain grew from a trickle to a gush.

The refugees went on to become the sporting equivalent of the feared Scottish mercenary soldiers who had rampaged around Europe in the 17th century. By the late 1880s – a time when Preston North End's 'Invincibles' often fielded seven Scots, and Bolton Wanderers as many as ten – these brawny labourers had taken the Football League by storm. With their

W.N. COBBOLD
Caps 9 Goals 6

WE CANNOT BE QUITE SURE why Cobbold was universally known as 'Nuts', though C.B. Fry suggested it was 'possibly because he was the very best Kentish cob quality, all kernel and extremely hard to crack'. Contemporary photographs show that he bore an uncanny resemblance to *Monty Python's* Graham Chapman in 'Stop that, it's silly' mode. His party trick was to 'shoulder his way through a whole crowd of the opposition, and emerge triumphant with the ball at his toe'.

G.O. SMITH
Caps 20   Goals 11

SMITH MADE HIS ENGLAND DEBUT two years after Lindley's swan-song, and immediately proved himself to be a worthy disciple. Like so many Corinthians, he was a sporting polymath, who scored a famous century in the 1896 Varsity cricket match. And like Lindley, he was more likely to baffle his marker than to barge him out of the way. A tall but slight figure, who suffered from chronic asthma, he was described by the journalist James Catton as 'the quietest, mildest man who ever deceived a pair of heavy backs and crashed the ball into the net'. His greatest asset was his head – not because he was good in the air (he once said that nothing would make him happier than headers being banned from the game), but because he was a brilliant strategist. His strike-rate of 11 goals in 20 games was not all that high by the standards of the time, but he was a master of the assist: football's first real play-maker. His approach reversed the 'head down, bollock on' philosophy of the olde English dribbler; as he put it in an early coaching manual, 'the individual credit of anyone should be subservient to the good of the side. A selfish player, however brilliant, should never be allowed to remain in any team.'

> **'I would rather keep goal against His Satanic Majesty than G.O.'**
>
> Jack Robinson, Derby and England goalkeeper, on G.O. Smith's striking prowess.

livelihoods on the line, they defended hard and fouled liberally; one typical Scottish anecdote describes R.S. McColl, the amateur Glasgow Rangers striker, encountering a burly half-back who told him 'I'm not here to play fitba'. I'm here to see that you don't play fitba'.'

Would such a rustic approach have prevented the likes of Lindley and Bambridge from whizzing about like rooks on an empty chessboard? It seems unlikely, given the Corinthians' glorious record, but then the theory was never tested. The Scottish FA took a tough stance on professionals, who were only admitted to the national side in 1893. Scots based in England had to wait another three years before the authorities finally caved in, their resolve crumbling under the weight of recurring defeats. Only in 1896 was the Tartan Army finally reunited, and the playing field levelled.

> **'He'd eyes all round his shirt, had G.O. ... No forward was ever more artfully adept at drawing his opponents before passing.'**
>
> G.O. Smith, as assessed by C.B. Fry, a defender who considered himself something of an authority on strikers.

TWILIGHT OF THE SNOBS

From our modern perspective, the amateurs of the Corinthian era have come to resemble the giant sabre-toothed cats and woolly mammoths that roamed the planet during the last Ice Age. They were exotic, romantic, fantastic – and all too soon archaic.

By the turn of the 20th century, amateur footballers had virtually disappeared from the England side. It was not quite an asteroid moment, but certainly a steep decline. James Forrest, of Blackburn Rovers, became the first licensed professional to play for England in 1885. Within five years, he was just one among many. A few survivors of the old order endured past 1900; men like G.O. Smith, whose freakish talent defied Darwin's law. But they were isolated exceptions. Like those oversized mammals, the amateurs' reign had ended almost as quickly as it began.

For our more nostalgic historians, the eclipse of the amateur marks the moment when English football lost its *joie de vivre*. D.J. Taylor laments their passing in his book *On the Corinthian Spirit*, where he damns the professional mindset as 'dogged resolve, niggling efficiency, mistrust of "style"'. For Taylor, the Victorian period represents a charming lost world of artistic individualism and waxed whiskers, its high-minded principles completely at odds with those of the multi-million pound businesses we know today.

Yet the Corinthians' legacy was not so quickly extinguished. The professionals had taken note of their freewheeling style, and by the early 1890s a pair of will-o'-the-wisp wingers named Billy Bassett and Fred Spiksley had emerged within the Football League, mounting lightning attacks that made them every bit as exhilarating to watch as Lindley or Bambridge. Bassett's favourite manoeuvre was to push the ball forward and then escape his marker by running *outside* the touchline. According to one contemporary, 'Bassett was invariably seen at his best in an international encounter, and if the opposing half-back did not know his

> **'His feat of running down the wing in a mackintosh during a League match, holding an umbrella, may never be repeated.'**
>
> Edward Grayson on Charles Athersmith, the Aston Villa speedster who succeeded Billy Bassett on England's right wing.

methods he frequently ran loose.' He is also credited with being the first winger to cross the ball accurately while on the run.

This cross-pollination between lords and labourers made the 1890s a uniquely fertile time in English football. At the start of the decade, everything came together to create England's first golden era: three seasons, nine successive wins in the Home Championship, and an aggregate score of 37–7. Amateurs and professionals both played their part; in the words of historian Brian James, 'It was as though six horses were pulling, and a tractor pushing, the waggon of English international football – two utterly different sources of power, harnessed to one end.'

The way of the dodo

Why did the amateurs fade away so quickly? The key factor was training – or, rather, lack of it. Bassett described his daily programme as 'a six-mile walk, a work-out with Indian clubs [wooden dumb-bells shaped like bowling pins], or a few laps around the ground'. This might sound gentle by the standards of today's Premiership, where midfielders regularly cover seven or eight miles in a game. But it was still enough to give him an edge over the average pipe-smoking amateur.

The typical Victorian gentleman was no lover of progress. Consciously or not, he seems to have perceived scientific practice as a challenge to God's natural order. All of which may explain why the Corinthians viewed any kind of pre-match preparation as the worst kind of caddishness – the sporting equivalent of shooting your enemy in the back.

The 1890s was a decade of massive structural upheaval within the game. To continue the Ice Age analogy, continents were breaking up and realigning themselves in roughly the order we know today. A modern time-traveller would find much that he recognised: by the end of the 1890-1 season, football had crossbars, goal-nets, linesmen, two-handed throw-ins and penalty boxes (or at least a penalty oval). And the crowds were changing too. There are few mentions in this period of the parasol-toting ladies who had tootled dutifully along to watch their sweethearts contest the earliest internationals. The flat caps had taken over the terraces, displacing the bonnets, bowlers and boaters to the nearest tennis, golf or cricket club.

There was a full-blown democratic revolution in progress – one that would transform a minority sport into a ravenous, world-bestriding giant. Football's founding fathers had envisaged their game as a way of moulding feckless youths into officer-class material; now, with the help of the social workers who used football to spice up their Bible classes, the game had caught the imagination of the working man. 'There was a great demand ... for something to bring to a Saturday afternoon a richness to alleviate the stifling drudgery of the rest of the week,' wrote Brian Dobbs in his in-sightful *Edwardians At Play*. 'Football, for players, and even more for spectators, came to fill this yawning gap as perfectly as if it had been invented for the purpose.'

> **'One is irresistibly reminded of the story of Mother Partington's attempt to hold back the Atlantic with a broom.'**
>
> Gibson and Pickford on the FA's efforts to slow the march of professionalism.

The game's attractions are spelled out even more clearly in a well-known passage from *The Good Companions,* J.B. Priestley's 1929 novel set in an imaginary textile town based on Bradford. A Yorkshireman himself,

W. J. OAKLEY
Caps 16   Goals 0

'GIVE ME "OAKERS" IN A ROUGH and tumble and you may have any other man in England except [rugby flanker] Sam Woods,' wrote the ever-quotable C.B. Fry. From this description, you might imagine Oakley as a thuggish amalgam of Tony Adams and Steven Seagal. In fact, he was an Oxford-educated amateur centre-back who relied on height and speed rather than brawn. But he was tough, nevertheless: at Parkhead in 1900 a collision with his own goalkeeper and a Scottish forward left him bleeding, concussed and briefly unconscious. He played on, like an automaton, and finished the match by asking his teammates who had won. Oakley's injury in that game was said to have 'unnerved' his great friend G.O. Smith (see page 37), who underperformed for the only time in his international career. Afterwards, Smith stayed on in Glasgow to nurse Oakley until he was well enough to return to Ludgrove, the prep school where they both worked under the headmastership of Arthur Dunn. When Dunn died suddenly in 1902 – the result of 'football strain', according to some accounts – Smith and Oakley retired from the game to run the school themselves.

Priestley fully understood the transformative power of sport within a beaten-down community. 'For a shilling Bruddersfield United A.F.C. offered you Conflict and Art', he wrote. 'Not only had you escaped from the clanking machinery of this lesser life, from work, wages, rent, doles, sick pay, insurance cards, nagging wives, ailing children, bad bosses, idle workmen, but you had escaped with most of your mates and your neighbours, with half the town, and there you were, cheering together, thumping one another on the shoulders, swapping judgments like lords of the earth.'

It is a marvellously vivid passage, though perhaps a little idealised. The other side of Priestley's shilling can be seen in the regular reports of 'bad language', 'disgraceful scenes' and 'free fights' in newspapers from the 1880s onwards. While the fictional fans of Bruddersfield may have thumped one another on the shoulders, real men aimed for the nose.

How Dunn's 'Old Crocks' socked the Jocks for six

Back on the field, England were turning the tables on their oldest rivals. In the early 1890s, their teamwork was so impeccable that Scotland's play was often described as 'disjointed' and 'individual' by comparison. Yet England's united façade disguised a deeply divided dressing-room: great unwashed in one camp, smug unpaid in the other. It seems remarkable that the likes of Lindley and the Walters brothers could exchange passes so freely with their professional team-mates when, off the field, the two groups refused to eat at the same restaurants, stay in the same hotels, or even travel on the same boats.

Perhaps such tensions helped to fuel creativity. Or, more likely, the 1890s simply produced a rich crop of talented English footballers, drawn

> **'The new football is a far more effectual arouser of the unregenerate passions of mankind than either a political gathering or a race meeting ... The multitude flock to the field in their workaday dirt, and with their workaday adjectives loose on their tongues.'**
>
> Charles Edwardes, writing in *The Nineteenth Century* magazine in October 1892.

from all strata of society. Between 1889 and 1896 England went 20 matches without defeat – a record that still stands today. Their selectors were confident enough to treat Wales and Ireland as junior sparring partners; for the first three years of the decade, these matches were staged on the same day, on different grounds, and with totally different XIs, yet still ended in comprehensive victories.

> 'The "Old Crocks" gave a display such as I have never seen ... perfect in conception, combination, and execution.'
>
> Journalist James Catton on England's much-maligned champions of 1892.

Age did not wither them: England's 'old crocks' defied the critics to demolish Scotland's finest at Ibrox Park in April 1892. John Goodall, himself a Scottish exile (see page 34), is the second figure from the left in the front row.

During this sequence of scintillating wins, England's finest (half) hour came against Scotland in 1892. This team was mockingly christened 'the old crocks' by the Scottish media – a rather mystifying judgement, in view of the fact that Arthur Dunn was not just the only amateur in the side, but the only player over the age of 30. Dunn's men soon settled the argument with four unanswered goals inside the first 25 minutes, including the first just seconds into the match. According to *The Field*, the disappointed crowd produced 'a storm of hisses and groans, which speaks volumes for the unsportsmanlike conduct of a portion of the Glasgow football community'.

'**I think I can now claim a certain superiority for English football.**'
Charles Alcock, football's founding father, enjoys England's dominant form in 1899.

The following year's rematch was even more dramatic. England were in difficulties with half-an-hour to go, 2–1 down against an experienced Scotland side. But then Bassett and Spiksley came alive with a series of daring raids down the flanks. Frederick Wall, who served 39 years as FA secretary, called this game the fastest of the whole series, and reported that by the final stages, the Scottish half-backs 'had no pith left in their legs and "couldna run"'. The final score was a crushing 5–2 and included a fine headed goal from R. Cunliffe Gosling, an Old Etonian banker whom Wall reckoned to be 'the richest man who ever played for England by the side of a professional'.

While Wall's judgement would probably have held true for most of the 20th Century, the advent of the Premier League has upped the stakes alarmingly. Even allowing for inflation, Gosling's personal fortune (£700,000) cannot possibly compare with that of David Beckham (£90 million and counting).

The curious tale of the half-cut half-back

> **'Even in his cups, to interrupt his singing of mournful Scottish ballads was to court disaster.'**
>
> Brian James on Jamie Cowan, Aston Villa's hard-nosed Scotsman.

There is one other Anglo-Scottish clash from this period that deserves a mention. The year was 1898: Scotland had finally welcomed back her professional exiles, and had even managed a couple of wins, so hopes were high among the crowd at Glasgow's Parkhead ground. But that was before the Scottish centre-half, Jamie Cowan of Aston Villa, had embarked on one of the strangest performances ever seen in an international. When England had the ball, Cowan kept missing his tackles; and when he finally won possession, he would invariably dribble into trouble. The cry of 'Whit are ye playing at Jamie?' went up around the crowd.

Cowan spoke to a reporter a couple of days after the game, which England won by a comfortable 3–1 margin. 'I had had a bad cold,' he said, 'and perhaps I was a bit excited as well.' He might as well have come out and admitted the truth; that he had sat up late the previous night working on a case of Scotch.

A vital cog in Aston Villa's strongest-ever side, Cowan was a classic hatchet-faced bruiser, the kind of midfielder who could turn his opponent's legs to jelly with a single glance. 'His affability was said to increase in direct proportion to his alcoholic intake,' one historian claimed. 'But even in his cups, to interrupt his singing of mournful Scottish ballads was to court disaster.' Perhaps that was the problem; if anyone had been brave enough to send the fearsome Cowan to bed, his international career might not have ended in the drink.

Double work with the crooked elbow

Judging by newspaper reports of early crowd behaviour, most Scottish fans shared Cowan's weakness for a 'wee dram'. The Tartan Army marched not

WILLIAM FOULKE
Games 1   Goals conceded 0

GOALKEEPERS OFTEN TALK ABOUT making themselves big – but 'Fatty' Foulke, the Sheffield United and Chelsea keeper, needed little help. He is believed to have been the first target of the crowd chant 'Who ate all the pies?' At a time when the dimensions of the average player were around 5ft 9in and 11 stone, Foulke's vital statistics were quite different: 6ft 6in and anything up to 24 stone, according to his own account. There is a classic team photograph of Sheffield United where he looks like a member of a different species, a capybara among guinea pigs. Foulke was a great crowd-puller: the fans loved it when strikers tried to bundle him into the net, only to rebound into the mud of the penalty area. And he was also a crossbar-puller: he liked to yank the beam down as opponents approached, so reducing their target area, and once accidentally snapped it in two. One of the many excellent Foulke anecdotes relates to his time at Chelsea, when 'he got into the dining-room before the rest of the team and polished off all eleven breakfasts. In response to the remonstrations of his team-mates he only replied: "I don't care what you call me, so long as you don't call me late for lunch."'

on its stomach, but on its liver. English crowds had their moments, of course, but they were a distant second when it came to what one journalist called 'double work with the crooked elbow'. For the England–Scotland international at Blackburn in 1891, there were more visitors than locals, and more empty whisky bottles than either.

We are lucky enough to have a vivid description of events in Blackburn that day, thanks to an intrepid reporter from the *Northern Daily Telegraph*. According to his hair-raising account, the first outriders of an estimated 5000-strong force arrived in town as early as 4 a.m., at which hour 'sleeping townsmen were alarmed by shrieking war-whoops and riotous singing, accompanied in several places with the crash of glass and the smash of door panels'.

Special trains had been laid on for the occasion, and as each one arrived, 'the porters had to clear out armsfull of whisky bottles ... It was apparent that many of the passengers were too far gone to walk.' By mid-afternoon, and the start of the match, our correspondent reports that 'the

> **'Nothing could better illustrate the vastness of this stadium than that 400 should drop through a hole and the rest remain in ignorance.'**
> The *Daily Mail's* reporter on the Ibrox disaster, 1902.

remarkable spectacle was witnessed of scores of Scotchmen, in all stages of intoxication, sprawling on the seats of the stands, either asleep or simply quarrelsome'. The article finishes with the equally bizarre image of visiting fans being released from their police cells just in time to sprint to the railway station and catch the last train home.

At Scotland's home internationals, the sheer size of the crowds threw up a different set of problems. The Parkhead ground struggled to accommodate the 45,000 who rolled up for the 1894 match (including two brothers who ended up in Glasgow's Royal Infirmary after a barricade fell on them). Two years later, some 60,000 squeezed inside the gates; as Sir

Henry Newbolt almost wrote, 'there was a breathless crush in the Close that night'. Despite the presence of 150 policemen, and as many Gordon Highlanders, some desperate fans were forced through the crash barriers onto the cycling track around the field. Their countrymen in the terraces responded with the grace and chivalry for which football crowds are known, sending down a hail of stones, cinders, oranges, empty bottles and flasks.

> **'Wallets, purses, caps and gloves were used to staunch wounds, and umbrellas and sticks made duty as splints.'**
>
> An eye-witness account of medical improvisation at Ibrox.

Regrettably, the authorities failed to appreciate that these stampedes would, sooner or later, produce a really horrible result. On 5 April, 1902, football suffered its first genuine disaster. England were the visitors at Glasgow's Ibrox Park, which had been rebuilt only two years earlier with soaring steel-and-wood stands to accommodate the masses. About 10 minutes after the kick-off, a 70-foot long gap opened in the floor of the Western terrace. Hundreds of fans fell several stories onto the ground. The final tally was 26 dead and almost 600 injured. But there was no thought of stopping the game. The majority of the crowd had no idea what had been going on, and a sudden interruption could easily have provoked a riot.

It was an ugly day in the game's history. The players left the field at the interval to discover their dressing-rooms filled with suffering humanity, yet were still instructed to go out and play the second half. As the journalist James Catton put it, they finished the match 'with the moans and the groans of the victims haunting their ears'.[1]

1: The 1902 match at Ibrox ended in a 1–1 draw but was later expunged from the records. A month later, a replay was held at Villa Park, producing a 2–2 draw this time. Gate receipts of £1000 were forwarded to the relief fund for the disaster.

THEY CAME FROM CENTRAL EUROPE

'No-one would have believed in the last years of the 19th century that this world was being watched keenly and clearly by intelligences greater than man's and yet as mortal as his own.' So runs the ominous first sentence of H.G. Wells's 1898 novel *The War of the Worlds*, in which Martian spacecraft land in the London suburbs and set about destroying civilisation with their heat-ray.

Aliens were a key concern for Englishmen of this period: not so much the little green men lurking in the Milky Way, more the power-mad Germans stockpiling dreadnoughts in the North Sea. The literature of the day was full of paranoid tales of plots and invasions. And sport, too, was soon to become a parade ground for national muscle-flexing. If ball games have ever been 'war without the shooting' – in George Orwell's famous phrase – it was in the lead up to the two great conflicts of the 20th century.

In 1899, the Football Association sent an expeditionary force – sorry, football team – to Germany and Austria for a series of unofficial internationals. It was a test of strength for the embryonic Continental clubs, which owed their very existence to the enthusiasm of British expats. In Austria, for example, Baron Rothschild's gardeners had sowed the first seeds, founding the Vienna Cricket and Football Club in 1894.

On the face of it, the FA's early tours were all about spreading the word – just one more example of the Englishman's penchant for the missionary position. But in the powder-keg that was pre-war Europe, sport took on a double meaning; any defeat could be used as evidence of racial weakness. In the words of historian Alan Tomlinson, 'It was as if nations wanted to reach out to each other for a handshake whilst simultaneously puffing out their chests in pompous self-satisfaction.'

Giving the game away

The players on that German tour of 1899 certainly gave their best for Queen and country. Having won the opening match 13–2, they performed even more courageously during the ceremonial drinking games that followed. According to one Berlin reporter, these 'drew to a close around seven in the morning'. And if the next day's rematch produced a slightly closer contest (10–2 this time), it was probably because 'most of the Britons were somewhat affected' by their heroic efforts in the bar.

Even with hangovers, the English passing game was far too slick for the German 'kick and rush'. A report in *Spiel und Sport* remarked on the way the Englishmen kept the ball on the ground, and 'very rarely kicked … with their toes, but nearly always with the inside and outside of their boots'. The star attraction was Billy Bassett, still embarrassing defenders in his final year of competitive football. At one point, he mocked his man-marker by leading him around the back of the goal and back onto the pitch.

> **'The imagined community of millions seems more real as a team of 11 named people.'**
> Historian Eric Hobsbawm on nationalism in sport.

In 1908, England returned to Austria-Hungary for their first recognised internationals outside the British Isles. They brought a full-strength side this time, including nine of the men who had just drawn in Scotland, and totted up an aggregate score of 28–2 from their four games. If football really had offered a guide to military prowess, the First World War would have been over in weeks.

Such landslide victories were bound to produce further chest-puffing back in Blighty. Especially as the doctrine of Social Darwinism, which stated that nations were destined to battle for survival like beasts, was then in vogue. The Continentals were confidently dismissed as either effete and lily-livered (the French and the southern Europeans) or mechanical and unimaginative (the Germans): both stereotypes that have endured until the modern day.

The Edwardians counted themselves great educators, yet even they could not have imagined how far their pupils would go. During the inter-

> **'There is no doubt that the class of men who are taking the control of the game upon the Continent, etc. are apt scholars and may not be content to remain in that position very long.'**
>
> The president of the Scottish FA glimpses the future, 1914.

war years, the home nations slumped back into isolation, while the central European powers embraced new methods of coaching, training and preparation. By the time Ferenc Puskás and his 'Magnificent Magyars' came to Wembley in 1953, the Hungarian football team had become a marvel of technical perfection. Puskás's famous 'drag-back' was so far ahead of anything seen in the Football League, he might as well have been using the Martian heat-ray.

Master of all he surveyed

Isaac Goldberg once wrote that the essence of diplomacy is 'to do and say the nastiest things in the nicest way'. If England footballers were to serve as ambassadors in short trousers, they needed a suitably adroit figurehead, a man who could lead the national team to victory while simultaneously charming the Continentals out of their lederhosen.

It was a daunting job specification, yet the FA found the ideal candidate in Vivian Woodward. The last of the great amateurs, Woodward possessed both Lindley's dribbling dexterity and G.O. Smith's tactical nous, not to mention the speed of a greyhound and a knack for using his spindly 5ft 10½in frame to outclimb defenders. As he put it, 'It is easier to escape your policeman when the ball is in the air, especially if you are a couple of inches taller than they are.'

An architect by profession, Woodward was master of all he surveyed. He scored 29 goals in 23 full internationals, and another 57 in 44 appearances for England's amateur team, which bore the brunt of the FA's foreign exchange programme. Even more remarkably, no-one had a bad word to say about him. Woodward's natural modesty made him hugely popular among his team-mates with England,

Spurs and Chelsea, while his stoical response to punishment won him the respect of the most hard-bitten defenders. Overseas, he was said to be the most famous Englishman on the Continent – just like Beckham today. 'Vich ees Woodward?' was a familiar cry on the European terraces.

Some might argue that Woodward's England record is distorted by the weakness of the emerging teams he often played against. But tours to such far-flung destinations as South Africa and Sweden certainly tested his ambassadorial skills. The Foreign

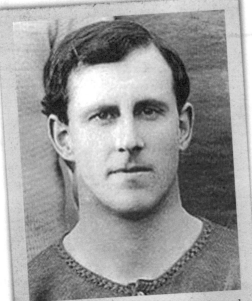

Last of the great amateurs: Vivian Woodward scored 29 goals in 23 full internationals and was arguably the most famous Englishman on the Continent in the early 20th century.

Office kept a close eye on events in Bohemia in 1908: Woodward's men won 4–0 in stiflingly hot conditions, but the fans turned threatening when the English referee awarded a penalty, and gave the unfortunate Mr Lewis a good hiding after the game. Contrary to popular belief, the Bohemians weren't all garret-dwelling artists and tubercular sopranos; some of them were old-fashioned thugs.

'They go for the man and not the ball.'

Ernest Mangnall, Manchester United's manager, slams Hungarian footballers after the club's 1908 tour to Budapest ended in a riot.

The World Cup that never was

Time for another quiz question. Which British national football team was the first to take on the world, and win? Chances are, you're already thinking about 1966 and Geoff Hurst's Wembley hat-trick. If so, you're five miles out on the venue and almost 60 years on the date.

In October 1908, Vivian Woodward led Great Britain into the first full-scale Olympic football tournament. Six teams contested the medals at the White City Stadium – a £60,000 development erected as part of a grand Franco-British Exposition. Standing on the plot now occupied by BBC Television Centre, this spanking new venue held up to 110,000 fans, and was surrounded by 140 acres of fountains, restaurants and gardens. (Definitely not Wembley, then.)

> **'The British press and public came to feel their "racial virility" was on trial.'**
>
> Historian Richard Holt on the London Olympics of 1908.

Woodward's team was effectively the same England amateur side who had been dishing out crunching defeats to Continental opposition for years. They played two qualifying matches, demolishing Sweden 12–1 and easing past Holland 4–0, on their way to a final against Denmark. The Danes were probably the best European side of the pre-war era (thanks to regular fixtures against Glasgow's Queen's Park FC, whose visits to Copenhagen suggested a taste for duty-free Carlsberg). Even so, they were not expected to bother the English too much. Denmark's reserve goalkeeper for the tournament was Niels Bohr, later a Nobel prize-winning quantum physicist, who was more likely to calculate the orbit of an electron than the flight of a sweetly struck shot.

To everyone's surprise, the final turned out to be a closely fought affair – almost as taut and tense as that of 1966. Woodward could hardly have been marked more closely if he had brought his butler with him, while his team-mates had an equally hard time escaping the Haralds, Bohr and Hansen, who marshalled the Danish defence. But then, towards the end of the first half, came the turning point. Denmark's first-choice goalkeeper, Ludvig Drescher, made a weak clearance that led to a soft goal for Frederick Chapman. The error changed the whole tone of the match, and Woodward clinched victory when he slipped his custodian for an instant and scored a vital second. The British – alright, the English – had struck gold. If only their descendants had qualified for Euro 2008, a full century later, we could have called it an omen.

It's just not on

More than a hundred years after its invention, the offside trap remains one of football's least edifying ploys. No-one pays gate money to watch the back four stepping up like a lumbering chorus line. But if you thought George Graham's Arsenal were bad, you should have seen England on their 1906 visit to Hampden Park. For the final 20 minutes, the Scottish forwards couldn't even leave their own penalty area.

Colin Veitch, the father of the offside trap, was not your common or garden clogger. A versatile midfield general with Newcastle United, he was also a composer, a playwright, a close friend of George Bernard Shaw, and a leading figure in the formation of the Professional Footballers' Association. You might have expected such a sophisticated man to have strong sporting principles. And perhaps he did – in the sense that he valued results above all else. Newcastle won the League three times in the early 1900s through the simple expedient of pushing nine men deep into the enemy's territory. It sounds barmy now, but in those days the offside rule applied anywhere on the field.

> **'The Englishmen had not played well against Sweden and Holland, and the Danes made them look a very ordinary eleven.'**
> *The Times* damns Great Britain's gold-medal winners at the 1908 Olympics, who had been weakened by a row between the FA and the majority of amateur clubs.

JACK ROBINSON
Caps 11   Goals conceded 11

THE GOALKEEPER RESPONSIBLE FOR barring William 'Fatty' Foulke's path to the England team, Robinson pioneered the art of the full-length dive. He once wrote 'Never on any account use your feet if it is possible to use your hands', and amazed crowds with his gymnastic saves. In his 1956 classic *Soccer Revolution* the Austrian emigré Willy Meisl described how Robinson had arrived in Vienna with the Southampton side of 1900 and 'showed for the first time how to tackle low shots by flying through the air with the greatest of ease. Until this day that type of save is called a "Robinsonade" in Austria and Central Europe. After the match … his goal was bombarded simultaneously with six balls and he blocked most of the shots.'

Manchester City's Frank Swift executes a textbook 'Robinsonade', 1948.

The 1906 England–Scotland game ranks up there with cricket's Bodyline series as an example of how sport should *not* be played. England's captain, Stanley Harris, was an amateur and Corinthian, though few would have guessed it when he motioned to Bob Crompton to drop back, while everyone else – including centre-half Veitch – took up their positions within 20 yards of Scotland's goal-line. The risk of a sudden breakout was reduced by the fact that, until 1925, a player needed *three* opponents in front of him to be offside.

England's desperate tactics did little to change the result. (Scotland were already 2–0 up before the switch, and still ran out 2–1 winners.) But they did prompt some emergency surgery to the rule-book. As the historian Brian James has written 'It may be coincidence that the brilliant if erratic Harris never played for England again. It is certainly no coincidence that before the year was up the International Board had altered the offside rule so that no player could ever again be offside in his own half.'

> **'Standing at 5ft 9¹/2 in, and weighing 12st 7lbs, he is splendidly developed, and a fine figure in shirt and knickers ... probably his punts are the biggest things in League football.'**
>
> Gibson and Pickford come over all dreamy in their profile of Bob Crompton, England's full-back and captain.

A marksman in a million

English football made a sticky start to the 20th century. At international level, crowds were dwindling and results sagging, to the point where Wales won the Home Championship in 1907. The League game seemed healthy by comparison, except that its players were developing a reputation as money-grabbing oiks who would shoulder-charge their own grandmothers for a bigger slice of the pie.

> **'I had no more chance of catching that shot than a snowball in Hades.'**
>
> Peter McBride, the Scottish goalkeeper, after Steve Bloomer's winning goal in 1904.

When Gibson and Pickford put out their famous 1906 overview, *Association Football and the Men who Made It*, they were able to report that 'The game of football is on trial. Hardly a week goes by but trenchant criticisms of latter-day developments are to be seen in the papers … What the player fails to realise is that by introducing fouls and despicable actions into his play he will in the long run certainly lower it in public estimation, and bring disgrace on … our grandest national game.'

If ever football needed some star quality, it was now. Fortunately, the League clubs had hit a rich seam of charismatic players. England had a commanding captain in the Blackburn Rovers defender Bob Crompton, the first footballer to own his own car, whose record of 41 caps would not be broken until the 1950s. Jack Robinson and Billy Meredith were dominant figures at club level. And looming over all of them was Steve Bloomer, the Derby County striker generally agreed to have been football's first superstar.

Despite his legendary status, Bloomer was not the sort of man who would shoulder-charge anyone. In fact, you might have backed his grandmother to win that particular bout. When he made his debut for Derby County, aged 17, one observer was amazed by his feeble appearance: 'pale, thin, ghost-like, almost ill-looking, he caused the Derby crowd to laugh when they first saw him'. But he had enough speed to cover 110 metres in 11.5 seconds and a knack for hitting the ball before the

> **'A man of action, a living force, a strong, relentless destroying angel.'**
>
> Steve Bloomer, as seen by Gibson and Pickford.

'And he ghosted in at the far post ...' The whey-faced Steve Bloomer, of England and Derby County, whose pale complexion belied his speed and athleticism.

goalkeeper had settled. As G.O. Smith put it, 'It was only necessary to say "Steve", and before his name had died on my lips the ball was in the net.'

Smith admitted that he did not particularly enjoy playing with Bloomer, who tended to lounge around the field, looking lazy and uninterested, until a chance arrived. Then he would spark suddenly into life, flashing past his bewildered marker, and closing in on goal. Bassett played in Bloomer's England debut, against Ireland in 1895, and wrote: 'At one point, having lost out again to Steve, I heard the Irish left-half remark "Oh well, let him have it," and he walked off the pitch and stood outside the touchline for a minute. He soon resumed but just for an instant he was in a most abject state of despair.'

BILLY MEREDITH
Caps 48 (for Wales) Goals 11

A SORT OF PROTOTYPE RYAN GIGGS, Meredith was the first Welsh lord of the wings and a great asset to Manchester United in their early years. He was born in Chirk, just 300 yards from the English border, and possessed all the Giggs attributes: great speed, deft control and a stinging shot. Like his contemporary Steve Bloomer, Meredith (adjusting shorts, left) seems to have hit the ball with his laces rather than the instep. He was a dedicated trainer with an ascetic lifestyle, which may explain why, in almost 20 years of football, he barely missed a dozen matches through injury. But he did miss the best part of two seasons because of an 18-month ban, imposed in 1904 for allegedly offering a bribe to Aston Villa's Alec Leake. Meredith played in the Welsh team that won the Home Championship in 1907, though he remained incensed that the referee had missed a blatant handball in the penalty area during the 1–1 draw with England. He had to wait until 1920 – and his final international appearance, aged 46 – before finally tasting victory over the old enemy. 'Afterwards, in the dressing room, they said that he wept unashamedly,' wrote his biographer John Harding.

'I nearly jumped out of the ground altogether when bang, bang, bang went revolver shots from behind me. There were two excited spectators firing shots into the air, a revolver in each hand and a merry dance on either leg.'

England receive a warm welcome from the Belfast crowd in 1904, as recalled in Steve Bloomer's memoirs.

Bloomer's eye for the main chance brought him 28 goals in 23 full internationals – the second-best strike-rate in England's history. The numbers are almost identical to those recorded by Woodward (29 in 23). Shirts bore no numbers in those days, and goal tallies were often disputed, so some Bloomer fans have argued that these two turn-of-the-century giants should be rated as equals. Yet their goal celebrations should have provided a clue. Woodward used to offer a regal wave, and a few handshakes, on his way back to the centre circle. Bloomer, ever the soloist, delighted in performing a cartwheel.

NOT-SO-
SPLENDID
ISOLATION
1914–1945

DON'T MENTION THE WAR

In football, as in most sports, the British regard for manliness has a way of regressing into mindlessness. And yet there have been exceptions: players with vision, seasons of success, moments of dash amid the drudgery. The England teams of the 1890s went about their business with flair and adventure. Late 19th-century strikers such as G.O. Smith and Steve Bloomer outstripped anything the competition had to offer. Vivian Woodward appeared in 70 matches for England,[1] and ran out on the losing side only four times.

> **'War is the noblest and most genuine sport, the sport *par excellence*.'**
>
> Carl Diem, the man entrusted with organising the Berlin Olympics of 1916, did not seem entirely disappointed by their cancellation.

So how did we English waste such a commanding position? As inventors of the game, our footballers had a head start over every opponent – including those pesky Scots. Even allowing for our natural tendency to value strength over subtlety, one might have expected us to keep up with Continental developments over the first half of the 20th century, at the very least. But the outbreak of war in 1914 had far-reaching consequences for the whole British game. Not only did this horrifying conflict rob England of an entire generation of young talent, it also drove the FA into their infamous decade of 'splendid isolation'.

Sport evolves through interaction, through the cut and thrust of attack and defence. If you shut yourself away from this ever-changing

1: Of Woodward's 70 internationals, 44 were for England's amateur team and three were unofficial.

process, you risk becoming an anachronism, a Neanderthal. And so it was with English football: in the absence of regular fixtures against European opposition, the game stagnated. Players and managers knew little of the quicksilver passing that was being honed by the Danubian School of central European nations. What is worse, they didn't care. The Edwardian myth of British supremacy remained pervasive: what could garlic-munching Frenchmen have to offer that Englishmen didn't already know? To quote a famously insular and possibly apocryphal *Times* headline from the 1950s, it was a case of 'Fog in Channel: Continent cut off'.

The greatest game of all

The First World War was a huge moment for muscular Christianity and its battalion of team sports. Remember, public school football had originally been conceived as a metaphorical approximation of battle. It was supposed to generate characterful young men, whose admirable qualities were defined by one headmaster as 'pluck, resource, self-control, good fellowship, and what-not'. And here was its ultimate test: a game with few rules and no time limits, contested by two determined teams on the muddy field that was Flanders.

> **'I think myself that [the footballs] did help them enormously. It took their minds off it.'**
>
> Major Irwin, Captain Nevill's commanding officer, on his famous wheeze.

Equipped with barbed wire, machine-gun posts and trench mortars, defences were so strong that forward movement was nigh-on impossible. Still, British pluck was not to be suppressed, even in the face of such terrifying odds. On 1 July 1916, General Haig sent his men out on the ill-fated Somme offensive that would cost 420,000 men. The Brits had *balls*, you see; it was only brains they were lacking. As if to signal this, Captain W.P. Nevill launched the advance of his regiment, the 8th East Surreys, by kicking a football into no-man's land. His bathetic gesture has passed into legend, one of those moments of doomed heroism which occupy such a central place in our national myth.

Nevill had planned his stunt carefully. On his last London leave before the big push, he bought two footballs, inscribing one with the words 'The Great European Cup-Tie Final. East Surreys v Bavarians. Kick-off at zero', and the other with the legend 'NO REFEREE'. (According to one regimental colleague, this was his 'way of telling the men they needn't treat the Hun too gently'.) Nevill is also reported to have offered a reward to the first platoon to kick a ball over the German trenches, but he never got to present it. He was shot in the head as he ran forward to encourage the men – just one of more than 19,000 lives lost on that first day of the attack.

> ## 'An English absurdity: football play during storm attack.'
> German caption beneath an illustration of Captain Nevill's eccentric raid.

Whether consciously or not, Nevill was echoing the sentiments of one of the most popular poems of the time. Sir Henry Newbolt's *Vitaï Lampada* describes a soldier rallying his comrades with the same

exhortation he had received from his cricket captain at school: 'Play up! Play up! And play the game!' But if there was ever a moment that killed off the reckless identification of war and sport in England's collective mind, it was the Somme offensive. The sense of disillusionment can be judged

'Play up! Play up! And play the game!' The famous football charge of the East Surreys at the Somme, as imagined by a contemporary illustrator.

'One human episode amid all the atrocities which have stained the memory of the war.'
Sir Arthur Conan Doyle on the Christmas Day football of 1914.

> **'This war [is] being won by our football heroes today. Our men have played and are playing the game. We are still in the scrum, it is true, but the ball is being carried forward, and we doubt not that in God's good providence the goal for which we are fighting ... will soon be won.'**
>
> Colonel Treeby addresses a regimental ceremony at Kingston Barracks to celebrate the recovery of Nevill's famous footballs, 1916.

from a letter home by one of Nevill's closest friends: 'When one sees the remains of a fine battalion one realizes the disgusting sordidness of modern war, when any yokel can fire a gun that may or may not – chance entirely – kill a man worth fifty of the firer.'

In all probability, such gallant talk of sporting values had always been more popular in the officers' quarters than among the salt-of-the-earth troopers on the Western Front. The infantrymen preferred real football to the kind played with artillery shells, as they showed during the well-known Christmas Day truce of 1914. The two sides' soldiers met in no-man's land in a heartwarming – and all-too-brief – moment of shared humanity. Games of football, played with tin cans if nothing else came to hand, broke out up and down the line, though the most famous was in the vicinity of Armentières. *The Times* reported that an unnamed British regiment lost 3–2 to their opponents, while the Lancashire Fusiliers' official history claimed that one of its companies had won by the same score.

Some of the English soldiers confided to their opponents that they were 'exceedingly thankful for the truce because they simply have to play football again'. But the Christmas Day détente proved to be a one-off. The following year, both sides stayed in their bunkers, too brutalised by the events of the previous 12 months to even consider fraternising with the enemy.

One of Captain Nevill's footballs survived the first day of the Battle of the Somme; 19,000 British soldiers did not.

A national scandal

Should the FA have been quicker to strike up sporting contact with Britain's wartime opponents after the war? Perhaps, but their reluctance is understandable, and not only because their president, Lord Kinnaird, had lost two sons in the conflict.

Germany was an international pariah at this time, as witnessed by the punitive 'War Guilt' clauses inserted into the Treaty of Versailles. Slogans used in the British general election of 1918 had included 'Hang the Kaiser' and 'Squeeze Germany 'til the pips squeak'. Even into the 1920s, propaganda posters drawn up by an alliance of British businessmen were still showing German soldiers bayonetting babies and abusing women. In such a climate, football could hardly rush back into bed with

LEIGH RICHMOND ROOSE
Caps 24 (for Wales)

There are plenty of rivals for the title of 'football's first superstar'. Vivian Woodward was one of the best-known Englishmen on the Continent, while Steve Bloomer possessed the deadliest shot in the country. But when it came to sheer celebrity, the Welsh goalkeeper Leigh Richmond Roose had them both covered. A tall, handsome, charismatic figure, Roose played for a

string of top clubs including Everton, Stoke City and Sunderland. He was that rare thing, an attacking goalkeeper, who used to bounce the ball all the way to the half-way line before releasing devastatingly accurate kicks and throws. As a direct result, the FA changed the rules to prevent keepers from handling outside their own penalty area from the 1912–13 season onwards. 'Get back in your box' was the general message. Even in his private life, Roose possessed the original pair of wandering hands. In 1909, he started being seen around London with Marie Lloyd, England's leading music hall singer. According to his biographer, Spencer Vignes, the affair raised Roose's profile to the point where 'Sunderland FC was inundated with fan mail from women across the United Kingdom wanting to marry, have sex with, mother or go on a date with the Prince of Goalkeepers.' Roose was awarded the Military Medal in August 1916 for his gallantry on the Somme, but six weeks later he was dead, the victim of another futile sortie into no-man's land.

the enemy, especially as the sport had already fallen into public disfavour for being insufficiently 'patriotic'.

Most of the damage had been done in the first winter, 1914–15, when the Football League kept running unabated despite the alarming events at hand. In the clubs' defence, they were only responding to the universal belief that the war would be over by Christmas. But as winter drew on, with no sign of a conclusion, opinion began to turn against them. In November, *The Times* suggested that the continuation of professional football was 'becoming a national scandal', and that managers were 'virtually bribing [the players] away from their country's service'.

The sport did its best to respond. Internationals were suspended until the Victory matches of 1919. The League also shut down, reducing even the biggest teams to local fixtures

> **'The "British team" is certainly on its way to Berlin; but in a very different sense from what was contemplated even so lately as in June last.'**
>
> Theodore Cook, Britain's leading Olympian, laments the cancellation of the Berlin Games of 1916.

contested by unpaid players. Thousands of volunteers joined the Football Battalion of the Middlesex Regiment, including two England internationals in Evelyn Lintott and the great Vivian Woodward. But none of this managed to salvage the game's reputation in the eyes of the great public schools. Those same institutions who had once nurtured football now damned it as grubby, mercenary and – worst of all – unpatriotic. Their collective disgust condemned well-heeled schoolboys to the agony of scrums and line-outs for the rest of the century. It would take football 70 years to regain its standing with the middle classes, in the post-Gascoigne revolution so skilfully captured by Nick Hornby's *Fever Pitch*.

Are past events better explained through the actions of individuals or the play of abstract forces? It is the historian's eternal dilemma, summed up in Blaise Pascal's question, 'If Cleopatra's nose had been shorter, would the face of the world be different today?' Or, to put it in a more modern context, 'If Johnny Rotten had never met Sid Vicious, would we all still be listening to *Tubular Bells*?'

Similar questions apply to the decline of English football – and, most particularly, to the grisly period after the First World War. In more than 130 years of internationals, the 1920s represent the bloodiest, sweatiest and most tearful decade of them all. In the Home Championship, England won just 11 games out of 31. They finished bottom of the table on three separate occasions – a fate that has never befallen them before or since. For a while, they massaged the figures with a few cheap results against the likes of France, Belgium and Sweden. But even that technique came unstuck in Madrid in 1929, when a shocking, unprecedented 4–3 defeat drove the *Daily Express*'s correspondent to confess 'I never thought I would live to see the day when eleven Spanish players humbled the might – more or less – of English soccer.'

What had happened to all those dashing amateurs and wily old pros? Where were the successors Vivian Woodward and Steve Bloomer? The obvious answer was that they had died on the fields of Flanders. Yet Austria, too, had seen thousands of potential Bloomers nipped in the bud – and that had not stopped her from emerging as the dominant power of European football. Something else was happening in England, something that Brian Glanville blamed on the 'conservatism and timidity' of the club game. 'League football, with the immense significance it gives to relegation, breeds cowardice,' he wrote. 'Managers are afraid to try unorthodox tactics on the field, and equally reluctant to introduce new methods of training.'

Glanville's comments, written in 1955, could pertain to just about any era of post-war English football, up to and including the present day. But they were especially appropriate for the 1920s, a decade when faceless teams played charmless football. As a spectacle, the League has never been so moribund. Ham-footed midfielders scuffled after the ball, mistaking enthusiasm for creativity. Lame-duck wingers fired in cross after cross, only for the lofty new breed of 'stoppers' to nod them all away.

If the sinuous Austrian side of the 1920s was known as 'the Wunderteam', England were turning into the Blunderteam. In 1924 the selectors recruited the following XI to face Northern Ireland in Belfast: Edward Taylor, Alfred Bower, Samuel Wadsworth, Harry Pantling, George Wilson, Thomas Meeham, Kenneth Hegan, Robert Kelly, Joseph Bradford, Harry Chambers and Frederick Tunstall. (If you recognise any of those names, you are either a devoted club historian or a potential Brain of Britain.) Somehow this ropey bunch contrived to lose the match 2–1, even though Northern Ireland had been refused access to several players by the Football League. According to *The Times*'s correspondent, the Irish were reduced to fielding 'Brown, the inside right of Tranmere Rovers, at outside right, playing him with Croft, of Queen's Island – a player new to international football. That this combination proved so successful against what was considered the English best team is very remarkable.'

It is conceivable that some alchemist of a manager could have turned such dross into a successful England side. But he would have needed a free hand on selection and tactics. (Ironically, this is exactly what Jimmy Hogan, a Lancastrian who had represented Fulham, was given when he took charge of Austria after the war.) Within England, though, no-one had even considered employing a manager as a strategist, rather than a booker of hotels and keeper of accounts. The FA did ask Herbert Chapman, Arsenal's cerebral mastermind, to accompany the team to Italy in 1933. But as Chapman had no say on the composition of the team, he might as well have donned a lion suit and entertained children from the touchline.

Even at this late stage, the word 'amateur' retained positive associations when it was applied to footballers. Not so selectors. England teams of the period were picked by the International Selection Committee – 14 amateur dunderheads, whose faddishness would have alarmed even the flightiest fashionista. In 1930, an *Athletic News* editorial explained that England had picked 145 players in their 33 Home Championship games since the war, before adding, in bristling italics, '*And 66 of them have still to gain a second cap*'. Even once selected, there was no guarantee of being allocated a familiar position. In one typical masterstroke, the committee deployed West Bromwich Albion's busy right-half Tommy Magee to man-mark the legendary Scottish winger and playmaker Alan Morton in 1925. 'I could catch him all right … except that I never knew where he was going,' lamented Magee, after Morton's delicate crosses had delivered two unanswered goals for Hughie Gallacher.

It is not difficult to find explanations for England's dire results during the 1920s. English players were trained to be fearful by the League, thrown into unfamiliar combinations by the national selectors, and sent out onto the field without so much as a word of encouragement. Surely this explains why they performed like half-drugged sleepwalkers for much of the decade? Well, maybe. But Pascal would probably bring our attention back to the question of Cleopatra's nose – or, in this case, Dixie's boot. Football may be a team game, but it only takes one player to spark an apparently hapless bunch into life. Dean did it briefly in the late 1920s, just as Stanley Matthews would in the mid-1930s, and Paul Gascoigne half-a-century later. These men succeeded because they were singular, driven talents who transcended the mediocrity around them. Yes, English football suffered from plenty of systemic weaknesses throughout the 1920s – but it also suffered from a shortage of independently minded players.

Football's back in Blighty!

Wins and losses were not the first things on the players' minds when football returned after the war. In the 'Victory international' contested by England and Scotland on 26 April 1919, only four free-kicks were awarded – making this arguably the cleanest fixture in football history. If 'peace is harder to make than war', as the French prime minister Georges Clemenceau once remarked, nobody had told the teams, who engineered the most honourable of 2–2 draws.

Like the Christmas Day games of 1914, this proved to be a brief outburst of chivalry. Within six months, the Home Championship was back – and so were the hair-raising tackles. Servicemen were well

> **'Modern forward play is in a bad way if Saturday's display may be taken as a criterion, for there were scarcely half-a-dozen decent shots made during the match.'**
>
> *The Times* on Scotland's 1–0 win over England in 1922.

represented in the England side: goalkeeper Sam Hardy had been a steward in the navy, while Sunderland striker Charles Buchan was a former sergeant in the Grenadier Guards. A versatile dribbler who earned comparisons to G.O. Smith, Buchan could blame the war for limiting his England career to just six matches over an 11-year period.

Hardened by their experiences, these men subscribed to the classic English belief that manliness is next to godliness. Take the example of Kenneth Hegan, another army officer, whose four appearances in the middle of the decade made him one of the last Corinthians to play for England. During an FA Cup tie against Millwall in 1930, Hegan suffered a broken tibia towards the end of the first half. He played on, no doubt dismissing the injury as a mere scratch, and was still on the field at the end of extra-time!

Jimmy Seed showed courage of a different kind after surviving a debilitating gas attack in the final months of the war. Swiftly dropped by Sunderland almost as soon as he returned home, he recalled feeling 'bitter, for the first time in my life', as he walked away from Roker Park. Seed was forced to go to the obscure Welsh club Mid-Rhondda just to get a game, but he fought his way up the ladder and eventually won five England caps as a right-sided forward. His story reads like an object lesson in the value of perseverance – though Sunderland might have inferred a different moral: 'Never let your Seed go to waste.'

WEMBLEY STADIUM

England Internationals: 223,
up until reconstruction

WHEN FOOTBALL CROWDS sing 'We're going to Wem-ber-ley', they are rather closer to the area's original name than they might realise. According to the authors Pete Tomsett and Chris Brand, the patch of land handed over to the Archbishop of Canterbury in AD 825 was described as 'Wemba Lea' – which translates to 'Wemba's clearing'. A little over a thousand years later, the railway pioneer Sir Edward Watkin attempted to build an English version of the Eiffel Tower there – but he ran out of money after the first stage. Then, in April 1922, work started on an ambitious stadium, designed to host the Empire Exhibition of 1924–5. This time, construction went swimmingly. The building was completed in 300 days – roughly one-tenth the time required for its modern makeover. The programme for Wembley's first match – the 1923 FA Cup final between Bolton Wanderers and West Ham United – boasted that it was 'the greatest Arena in the world – the largest, most comfortable, best equipped and holds more than 125,000'. But when the big day came, that figure was easily exceeded

by the 210,000 who were estimated to have fought or climbed their way in. The match only went ahead after the mounted policeman George Storey and his white horse Billy had calmly cleared the overspill off the pitch – which is why this game is now remembered as the 'White Horse final'.

Herbert Chapman and the beast with three backs

The year 1925 was a time of dramatic change within English football, and all because of one teensy little alteration to the rules. Previously an attacking player had been offside if – at the time of a forward pass being made – there were fewer than *three* opposition players between him and the goal. Now it was *two*.

Clearly, football's administrators were hoping to encourage free-flowing, attack-minded football. But the results were decidedly dubious. Yes, their adjustment did weaken the dead man's grip of the offside trap. And yes, the number of goals scored in the Football League did increase, from 4700 in the 1924–5 season to 6373 the following year. The downside was that the new rule proved to be a clogger's charter, encouraging a couple of forwards to hang way up the field while the rest of the team fed them long, high passes. As *The Times* commented in October 1926, 'the change has brought about an even greater looseness in the constructive art of the game … today every team is far more apprehensive in the matter of defence than used to be the case'.

No-one grasped the implications of this new 'Route One' football as quickly as Arsenal, who set themselves to play more in the spirit of George Graham than Arsène Wenger. They had made two key signings in the summer of 1925: the pioneering manager Herbert Chapman joined from Huddersfield Town, while Charles Buchan moved from Sunderland on a groundbreaking deal that earned his old club £2000 plus £100 for every goal he scored in his first season. (There were 20.) A pair of natural leaders,

> ## 'A mass-produced, unimaginative, cheap brand of soccer [which] became the weekly fare in Britain for many post-war years.'
>
> The Hungarian émigré Willy Meisl saw the 'third back game' as football's Great Fall.

> **'Alex was one of the fastest footballers over ten yards I ever came across. Whether he would have lasted for a hundred is highly problematical. Personally, I doubt it.'**
>
> Cliff Bastin on his Arsenal team-mate Alex James.

Chapman and Buchan came up with a tactical masterstroke – a reinvention of the traditional 2-3-5 formation that transformed Arsenal from relegation contenders to cocks of the walk. Unfortunately, the 'third back game' also proved to be mechanical and buttock-clenchingly dull.

The fundamental principle was the elimination of risk. 'If we manage to keep the opponents from scoring,' Chapman used to say, 'we have one point for certain.' To achieve that aim, he withdrew the centre-half from his playmaking role in the middle of the park, and told him to serve as the middle pin in a three-man defensive line – a third back, in other words. According to Bernard Joy, who filled this role in the 1930s, 'The secret is not attack, but counter-attack … We at Arsenal achieved our end by deliberately drawing on the opponents by retreating and funnelling to our own goal, holding the attack at the limits of the penalty box, and then thrusting quickly away by means of long passes to our wingers.'

Arsenal really hit their stride when they signed Alex James – a small, baggy-shorted Scotsman – for exactly this purpose in 1929. James had been knocking the goals in as an out-and-out striker with Preston, but Chapman got him playing like an American quarterback, standing just in front of his own penalty box and picking out wide receivers. The tactic proved so successful that Arsenal won the League four times in James's eight seasons at Highbury.

Even Chapman's critics admitted that there was an elegant simplicity to the Arsenal method, which had James strafing the opposition with precision passes, and left-wing Cliff Bastin bombing down the flanks.

Imitators at other clubs were not quite so polished. According to the Hungarian émigré Willy Meisl, they tended to rely on 'a standardized style of attack': 'Most passes to the forwards were made down the middle or out to the wingers whose passes came in rather high,' Meisl wrote. 'Why the opposition never insisted on keeping the ball low and on making precision passes to the middle along the ground, either on to the centre-forward's foot or exactly timed into the "empty space" before him confounded me, as it surely would confound most modern stoppers. After years of silent observation I hit on the only possible explanation, which had eluded me for so long because it was too simple: *they could not do it!'*

At a time when many European and South American teams were turning football into an art form, Chapman's more pragmatic, scientific approach would lead the English game down a concrete highway of mediocrity. He said he was only waiting for the rest of the League teams to catch up, and would then come up with something different. Sadly, he never got the chance: Chapman died on 6 January 1934, aged just 55. A football tragic in every sense, he contracted pneumonia after watching Arsenal's third team play Guildford City on a wet winter's night.

> **'Thirty years ago, men went out with the fullest licence to display their arts and crafts. Today they have to make their contribution to a system.'**
> Herbert Chapman defends the third back game.

The effect on the English game was far-reaching: had Chapman lived another decade or so, it would surely have been he, not Walter Winterbottom, who took over the England manager's job when it was finally created after the Second World War. Instead we are left with Brian Glanville's mournful obituary, 'It is ironical that [Chapman], the most progressive figure British football has yet produced, should have been largely responsible for the development of its most negative strategy.'

> **'In the first twenty minutes or so the display of some of the English forward players was one of the most painful I have ever witnessed. I felt at that moment that I ought to apologise to the world in general for having any connection with English football.'**
>
> 'Broadcaster', of the *Daily Express*, on the 1927 England v Scotland match – which England eventually won 2–1. Which of us has not echoed his sentiments at some time?

Dixie Dean and his titanium cranium

Few sportsmen can claim to have undergone surgery more often than the great Everton and England striker Dixie Dean (although Evel Knievel might have a shout). Over a 17-year-career, Dean needed 15 different operations – and yet he was hardly a fragile reed of a man. Indeed, Dean was as sturdy and stout-hearted as an oak – a player who never shirked a challenge or bemoaned his fate. 'The only thing I used to do, while I was laying there, was to say to the man who given me a broken rib or a broken shoulder blade, "Has this done you any good?"'

Dean is often described as a 'bustling' centre-forward, though this rather under-rates his gifts. He was certainly a physical player, who prided himself on his kangaroo leap and rocket-powered header. According to Matt Busby, who was then starting his own career at Manchester City, Dean's outstanding quality was that he could 'hit the ball with his head as hard and as accurately as most players could kick it'. He retained this unique talent even after a horrific motorcycle crash left him with a metal

> **'Don't forget that the ball we played with was much heavier than the balloons they have today. I suppose they've got to have them lightweight now because they play in bloody carpet slippers!'**
> William 'Dixie' Dean on football then and now.

plate implanted in his skull. When the news broke, Everton fans assumed that they would have to find a replacement, but Dean was back scoring goals within three months. 'Having broken bones can help,' he said. 'Those parts of my skull and jaw which were fractured and healed are much stronger as a result.'

Held together with bolts and stitches, Dean was English football's answer to the six-million dollar man – and remarkably chipper with it. But he did suffer one injury he could not laugh away. Playing for Tranmere reserves at the age of 17, Dean wound up the opposing centre-half by scoring twice. 'Tha'll get no more bloody goals today, you're finished,' his marker barked at him. At the next opportunity, the defender landed a solid kick in Dean's testicles – one of which had to be removed later in hospital. According to Dean's own account, this score was settled in a Chester pub almost two decades later, when a familiar-looking fellow sent him a pint across the bar. 'I thumped him and they took him to the hospital, so we're evens,' Dean would recall. 'It was the only time I ever retaliated.'

Dean's very excellence made him a target. If karate failed, defences would assign a tall 'stopper' of a centre-half – such as Arsenal's former policeman Herbie Roberts – to man-mark him out of the game. The Swedes used to call these players 'overcoats' because they clung so tight, but Dean would simply drop a shoulder and shrug them off.

When his England debut came, in 1927, Dean opened his account with 12 goals in his first five appearances. The best of them gave England a surprise 2–1 victory at Glasgow's Hampden Park – a notoriously intimidating ground where they hadn't won for almost 40 years. 'One defender came for him,' wrote 'Broadcaster' in the *Daily Express*, 'and then another, and then another. They all seemed around him, but although he did not seem to be travelling much faster than they were, he stuck to the ball like a leech, kept them off somehow, and, as the goalkeeper came out, slipped the ball neatly past him for the winner.'

Dean's spirits were only slightly dampened when an England selector came into the dressing-room after-

'I had broken bones, bones taken out of my ankles, broken ribs, broken toes and two cartilage operations ... Harry [Cooke, the Everton trainer] put the bones and the cartilage in pickle and when new fellows joined the club the first thing Harry did was to show them the jars.'

Dixie Dean on a rite of initiation for Everton newcomers.

wards and asked who he was. 'I told him my name but it didn't seem to register with him. "I'm the player who scored the two goals," I added. "Oh, yes," he replied. "But you didn't do much else did you!"'

> **'Dixie told me that before one England match he refused the soup of the day, which was consommé, at the pre-match lunch. He said: "I'm not drinking that dishwater." And they dropped him for the next game. That's how the FA worked in those days.'**
>
> *Brookside* actor Bill Dean, who took his stage name in honour of Dixie, and later became a close friend.

Wizardry and wild romance

The dark clouds seemed to be lifting when Dean's opportunism helped England share the 1926–7 Home Championship with Scotland – their best finish of the decade so far. They then mustered an aggregate of 20 goals in three games on a summer tour of Belgium, Luxembourg and France. In a prosperous year that saw dance halls springing up across the country, and racy young 'flappers' painting their eyes with kohl, English football was beginning to catch the optimistic mood of the times. Yet, as every Englishman knows, optimism has a way of presaging disappointment.

Back on Home Championship duty in the autumn of 1927, Dean's goal-rush suddenly dried up. The selectors' creativity, unfortunately, did not; they used 24 different players in the three internationals. The first match, against Northern Ireland, produced a stinging 2–0 defeat (though this disappointing result could be partly excused on the grounds that goalkeeper Ted Hufton had had his arm broken by a typically lusty Irish challenge after 20 minutes). The second saw Wales sneak home 2–1 in a game that *The Times* said 'did not produce much high-class football. A modern craze for doing everything in a hurry spoiled all efforts at combination at both sides.'

There was still one last chance to regain face. Scotland had been faring little better, taking only a draw and a loss against the Welsh and the Irish. No-one expected them to go to Wembley Stadium, the new home

ALAN MORTON
Caps 31 (for Scotland)   Goals 6

THE LEGEND OF the 'tanner ball player' has been a feature of Scottish football since the earliest days. The term denoted someone who has grown up playing with the cheap little 'tanner ball' that his dad might have bought him for sixpence. Alan Morton is a good example: as a child he spent hours in his backyard 'lobbing, chipping or driving the ball through a small hole in a cellar-door', according to one historian. A cricket fan might be reminded of Don Bradman, throwing a golf ball against the water tank behind his house and then hitting the rebound with a stump. Such home-grown footballers are usually masters of feints and trickery, and the 5ft 4in Morton, known as 'the Wee Blue Devil', was no exception. On his first appearance against England, the *Athletic News* reported that he had 'a peculiar dainty feinting zig-zagging style. He appears at every step to be about to dart inside, yet still holds his course.' More recently, Paul Gascoigne was described as 'the last tanner ball player', while Zinedine Zidane, who learned his mazy dribbling on a tough estate in Marseille, was a French master of the art.

of English football, and win – especially when they named a pint-sized forward line in which every man was 5ft 7in or smaller. The centre-half, Tom 'Tiny' Bradshaw, was a more formidable presence at 6ft 2in, but he had never played in an international before, and was being asked to mark Dean. 'Fears have been expressed that one or two of the men of experience have perhaps too great a burden of years upon them,' said *The Scotsman*, 'while the recruits will be severely tried in this exacting test.' Captain Jimmy McMullen expressed the same feeling more succinctly when he told his players to 'go to your bed, put your head on your pillow and pray for rain'.

The Scots got their wish: the next day brought torrents of the stuff. Not only did the slippery conditions nullify England's greater height, weight and speed, but the ball whizzed over the slick turf, rewarding Scotland's superior passing technique. And the Blue Devils could thank their stars again in the third minute, when English left-wing Billy Smith fired a shot onto the post. The rebound fell to McMullen, who passed to Alex James – then playing his first international. After some neat midfield combinations, the ball was shipped out to Alan Morton on the wing, and his perfect cross invited Alex Jackson to deliver the *coup de grâce*. Scotland's ball control seemed almost supernatural – which explains why this team would go down in history as 'The Wembley Wizards'.

The England defenders held on for a while, if only through the primitive method of barging the dainty Scotsmen off the ball. At the interval, things could have been worse: they were only trailing 2–0. But the second half was humiliatingly one-sided. According to *The Scotsman*, 'the big Scottish section

> **'In one movement – and it was typical – the ball went eleven times to a Scottish player without touching an English boot or head.'**
> The *Daily Mail*'s J.H. Freeman on the Wembley Wizards.

of the 30,000 crowd were jubilant … they never knew whether to cheer or laugh. They were uproariously amused one minute, cheering themselves hoarse the next. To borrow an expression from the golf links, it was "daft stuff".' Despite a late consolation from Robert Kelly, who nailed a 40-yard free-kick, the final score was 5–1. *The Times* reckoned it would have been more if the Scots had not indulged 'in the artistic pleasure of playing with the mouse rather than killing it outright'.

Scotland's tribal gathering

Reports from London on the evening of 31 March 1928 reveal a post-match party of bacchanalian proportions. At King's Cross Station, a series of traditional Scottish reels broke out all over the platform, pitching one over-enthusiastic reveller onto the track. And it wasn't just the visitors who were enjoying themselves. 'The Scots' success was splendidly received by English enthusiasts,' wrote the *Glasgow Herald*. 'In the city in the evening,

The greatest victory since Bannockburn? Fans escort James McMullan – captain of Scotland's 'Wembley Wizards' – from the pitch after a 5–1 pasting of England, 31 March 1928.

throughout the streets, Scottish visitors were cheered and praised, and in the big popular restaurants and hotel lounges, bands generally rendered programmes of Scottish songs.'

What price could you get on such scenes being played out in Glasgow after an English win? The idea is laughable, and not just because of the lack of any worthwhile English anthems. Passion always runs higher among the underdogs. The highs are higher, and the lows – especially in Scotland – are positively subterranean. As P.G. Wodehouse had it, 'It is never difficult to distinguish between a Scotsman with a grievance and a ray of sunshine.'

There was rather less fervour among English fans, who seemed more concerned with the snakes and ladders of the Football League than the fate of the national team. After all, the local League team played every week, while it was hard to identify too strongly with England when no-one knew who would be turning out in any given match. Just look at the crowd figures: an estimated 210,000 fans squeezed into Wembley for the famous 'White Horse Final' of 1923, but the average attendance in the Home Championship was a fraction of the size.

Nevertheless, there must have been real anger among the 80,000 who had turned up at Wembley that afternoon. There certainly was in the press-box, judging by the recurring use of words like 'ludicrous' and 'pathetic'. Not only was this the heaviest defeat England had suffered for almost half a century, it was also the first time she had ever lost all three matches in the Home Championship. For a précis of the prevailing mood, we can turn to that other great idol of the 1920s, Noël Coward, and his script for *Brief Encounter*. 'I had no thoughts at all,' Coward's heroine declares in the final scene, 'only an overwhelming desire not to feel anything ever again.'

CONTINENTAL DRIFTERS

There is something about English football after the war that puts one in mind of an awkward adolescent. Outside the bedroom door, a whole new world is opening up. But our hero prefers to skulk at home, popping his pimples and venturing no further than the neighbours' garden (i.e. Belgium). He is the Adrian Mole of the international game.

Over the course of the 1920s, England turned down invitations from Austria, Germany, Hungary, Italy, Spain, Switzerland and the Irish Free State. At first, such sulky behaviour could be explained as the legacy of conflict. But as the decade wore on, those traditional English vices of ignorance and arrogance loomed ever larger. The Football Association pulled out of FIFA twice

> **'Our Continental friends respect us more when we lick them than when they lick us.'**
>
> Long-serving FA secretary Frederick Wall, in his 1935 memoir.

during the decade, and on the odd occasions when an English representative did bother to appear in Paris, he was usually there to complain.

A future of friendlies against Luxembourg and the Low Countries was never likely to set the blood racing. Thankfully, it never came to that. Searching for a new way to promote British interests (and preferably one that did not involve strafing tribesmen with a machine gun) the Foreign Office chose this moment to take an interest in football. The diplomats had spotted the potential of the most addictive drug ever to come out of England. Colombia has her white powder; we have our white ball.

With a few skilful nudges, the people at the FO persuaded the people at the FA to look beyond the end of their own cigars. Gradually, the fixture list took on a more cosmopolitan air. Cities like Prague and Berlin joined such familiar haunts as Glasgow and Belfast. If you exclude the Home Championship, England played 28 internationals against 16 different opponents during the 1930s. Admittedly, they did not attend the first World Cup (held in Uruguay in 1930) nor the later events in Italy (1934) or France (1938). But the barriers were breaking, the Brighton Wall coming down.

Some observers took a dim view of the Foreign Office's intervention. In the winter of 1928, the *Daily Express* got hold of a message from Thomas Preston, a consul based in Turin, demanding that nothing other than 'the strongest and best professional combination' should be sent to play in Italy. The story appeared under the hysterical headline 'Football by order of the FO: English teams *must* win abroad'. In an accompanying editorial, the newspaper performed what mathematicians call a *reductio ad absurdum*: 'The view of the Whitehall mandarins seems to be that [if England lost] British prestige would receive an irreparable blow, the peace of England would be endangered, and Sir Austen Chamberlain would have to do whatever Herr Stresemann told him.'

A catchy column, perhaps, but also a rather disingenuous one. Nationalism and sport were already regular bedfellows, as the *Express* must have been well aware. All the way back in 1908, the first London Olympics had degenerated into a tetchy showdown between Britain and the United States. Now, as the Great Depression of the early 1930s hit home, Fascist leaders like Adolf Hitler and Benito Mussolini were determined to make political capital out of their athletes.

Before the start of the 1934 World Cup, *Il Duce* found some unorthodox ways to motivate the Italian players. If they won, they would receive Alfa Romeo cars and exemption from national service. If they lost … what is the Italian equivalent of Coventry? The Cup was duly delivered, by a bunch of wall-faced ruffians who looked as though they had been plucked from a police line-up. But this was not sport as the purists imagined it. In the words of John Langenus, the great Belgian referee, 'a certain spirit brooded over the whole Championship. Italy wanted to win, it was natural, but they allowed it to be seen too clearly.'

'**Could anything be sillier or more futile? It does not matter in the least whether we beat the Germans at "Soccer" or are beaten by them. But it does matter a great deal that we should be free and willing to meet them in "friendly strifes and rivalries of peace".**'

The *Daily Express* scoffs at the Foreign Office's sudden interest in football.

Illusions of grandeur

Even after all the traumas of the 1920s, English fans retained their unshakeable belief that England had the finest footballers on the planet. Perhaps this was not so strange for a sports-mad people who revered Wembley, Twickenham and Lord's as their holy trinity. What *was* strange was that many other European countries agreed. Clearly they had not witnessed the recent Home Championship matches, which left one reporter wanting to 'apologise to the world in general for having any connection with English football'.

Still, perception is often more powerful than reality, and 60 years before the formation of the Premier League, the English game was already developing a successful export industry. Just as Vivian Woodward had won overseas fame at the start of the century, so the likes of Dean, Matthews and Bastin gained a keen following on the Continent. Speaking in the late 1930s, one Yugoslavian claimed that if you 'ask any schoolboy in Belgrade: "Who is Bastin?" … he will reply at once: "Outside left for the Arsenal, the greatest forward in the world." But ask him: "Who is Winston Churchill?", and he will say: "I am sorry, I do not know that player."'

Many autobiographies of this period feature a moment where the hero steps down from a train in Rome, Vienna or Madrid and finds himself submerged under a crowd of well-wishers. And similar mêlées would often be repeated on the field, only this time with studs showing. Celebrity came at a price, because it made England's stars a target for aspiring rivals and ambitious dictators. Thanks to Mussolini's close interest, the Italians' visit to Highbury in 1934 turned into one of the most bloodcurdlingly violent matches ever played. It was not autographs being hunted this time, but scalps.

> **'I have found that when England lose abroad, they are damned categorically; when they win, it is taken for granted.'**
> Cliff Bastin.

Playing with bounties on their heads, England were bound to slip up a few times in Europe – and slip up they did, losing seven of 20 games in the 1930s. At home, though, they retained their old imperial swagger. Eight Continental teams came to visit during the decade, and eight went away defeated. Some of the scorelines were tight; the Austrian side of 1932 were widely reckoned to have had the better of their match at Stamford Bridge, despite losing 4–3. But the defensive line held, and the Englishmen's home remained their castle.

Here lie the seeds of the chronic over-valuation that has afflicted English football ever since, inflating expectations and causing solid international players like Bryan Robson or David Beckham to be rated as Gods. It might seem illogical, but England's unblemished home record – together with the FA's refusal to appear at any of the first three World Cups – allowed them to pose as emperors of the game. As the historian Stephen Wagg has written, the 1930s laid 'the foundation for a powerful post-war myth of England … as the game's unofficial world champions'.

It is about time that this myth was exploded, because it remains a dead weight on all our shoulders. England doesn't just expect; she expects the impossible, and this places both players and managers under near intolerable strain. 'Names and faces change,' as Wagg puts it, 'but the essential story does not: if England, who devised and exported the game, are beaten, then the man in charge of the England team is not doing his job properly and he must be replaced. Other countries, in this bizarre and ultimately racist conception of the international football world, play only walk-on parts.'

He's from Barcelona, you know

What is it about the Continental goalie that brings out the Anglo-Saxon sceptic in us? English commentators are never happier than when ridiculing a visiting keeper's vulnerabilities ('they call him Dracula because he's allergic to crosses') or pointing out that his flamboyant dive made a save look harder than it actually was.

One size fits all, as far as this hoary old stereotype is concerned. Its incarnations have been many and varied: Fabien Barthez, the French champion; René Higuita, the Colombian who invented the 'scorpion kick'; even Pope John Paul II. But no-one has played the role more convincingly than Spain's great inter-war keeper, Ricardo Zamora.

Described by one historian as 'flashy but safe', Zamora was respected enough for Real Madrid to sign him from Barcelona at a cost of £6000. Any accusations of faint-heartedness were exploded by Spain's epochal win over England in 1929, when he played much of the match with a broken sternum. But two years later, when Spain travelled to Highbury for the return fixture, Zamora left something vital at home: Mrs Zamora. The Spanish FA's refusal to let partners go on the trip was a nasty shock for a man whose wife was his talisman – and also his food-taster. (Alright, so he was a bit of a weirdo.)

> **'Our isolation was in no sense splendid. It was a matter for regret and a constant cause of difficulty.'**
> Stanley Rous, FA secretary from 1934 to 1962.

If Zamora felt anxious before the match, you wouldn't have known it. A bizarre scene developed as the players took the field, and Dixie Dean asked the band to play something Spanish. They responded with the march from Bizet's *Carmen*, whereupon – in the words of Dean's biographer John Keith – 'Zamora, to the dumbstruck reaction of the spectators, responded by goose-stepping to his goal and bowing to the crowd. He then proceeded to leap acrobatically around his goalmouth during the kick-in to produce a series of grossly over-spectacular saves. And while this was going on Dean turned to his Everton and England team-mate Charlie Gee and bet his six pounds international fee that they'd put more than five goals past Zamora, a wager Charlie accepted.'

> **'Most of the match, I was a Rose between two yawns.'**
>
> Henry Rose, football correspondent of the *Daily Express*, delivers a withering verdict on the 1938 England–Scotland international at Wembley.

You can probably see where this is going. Zamora had a dreadful match. Apparently fazed by the Highbury mudbath, he failed even to move when Tommy Johnson essayed a hopeful shot for England's second goal, and the ball limped into the net. The final score was 7–1, and after the match, a crestfallen Zamora addressed Dean, his tormentor-in-chief, through an interpreter: 'Zamora says tonight in Madrid he is nothing.' Dean's reply was heartless. 'Tell him that he's nothing here either.'

An admirable figure in so many ways, Dean comes out of this story looking small-minded and xenophobic. Zamora was a fellow pro, and a good one at that; for all his Fawltyesque antics, he deserved better than to be treated like a court jester. But then, Zamora was also a foreigner. For Dean, as for so many Englishmen of his generation, that was the biggest crime of all.

> **'What's Za-mora with you?'**
>
> Caption on a cartoon in the *Liverpool Echo*, showing Dixie Dean rounding the Spanish goalkeeper.

Missing his missus: Spanish goalkeeper Ricardo Zamora, deprived of marital support, let in seven goals in the Highbury mudbath, December 1931.

The Italian job

In the lead-up to England's notorious showdown with Italy in 1934, Britain's arrogant press-men lumped the Italians in with the rest of the Europeans. Cheese-eating surrender monkeys, the lot of 'em!

The Times painted Italy's prolific centre-forward Giuseppe Meazza as an effeminate fancy dan: 'Close marking … usually damps his ardour, for he is not over fond of rough and ready encounters.' The *Daily Express* came to a similar conclusion, suggesting that the Italians 'can "work" the ball delightfully and shoot well. But I do not think they will stand for the full 90 minutes the pace that England are likely to set.'

Such reporting was not only jingoistic but painfully ill-informed. Only five months earlier, the Italians had beaten Czechoslovakia in the World Cup final, where they proved themselves to be a supremely well-drilled unit. Though the Eastern European teams produced the silkiest football of the tournament, Italy overcame them in the end, compensating through what Brian Glanville called 'greater forcefulness and … excellent physical condition'. Mechanical and remorselessly pragmatic, they were the international equivalent of Herbert Chapman's Arsenal.

> **'Mussolini had offered them such terrific incentives if they beat us that their play deteriorated, in their over-eagerness, to a patchwork series of clever moves and questionable tactics.'**
>
> Cliff Bastin on Italy's infamous display at the 'Battle of Highbury', 1934.

For their visit to London in 1934, Italy were also highly motivated. The match had an obvious subtext: a crushing England victory would undermine the World Cup and expose its champions as mere pretenders. It was a crude bear-trap, none-too-subtly laid by the FA, but Mussolini insisted the tour should go ahead. Victory, he argued, would do wonders for Italy's international prestige.

The tone of the contest was set in the second minute. After a juddering collision with English striker Ted Drake, Luisito Monti had to retire with a broken foot. 'He kicked me deliberately!' Monti moaned. Now the challenges came flying in from all directions. Eddie Hapgood, England's captain and left-back, had his nose splattered by a flying elbow. Drake was grabbed around the throat, then punched on the chin, and finally forced off by a high tackle that left blood pouring from a deep wound in his calf. As a country, Italy is justly renowned for its artistry and style. But these boys looked as though the Renaissance had passed them by.

'For the first quarter of an hour there might as well not have been a ball on the pitch as far as the Italians were concerned,' wrote Stanley Matthews, then just a wide-eyed Stoke winger in his first international season. 'They were like men possessed, kicking anything and everything that moved.' But England had a few battle-hardened warriors in their own trench. Wilf Copping, their left-half, was a coal miner turned shin breaker. And as Copping would recall years later, 'It was dirty trick after dirty trick until me and [centre-half] Jack Barker showed them what tackling was all about.'

Already 3–0 down by half-time, Italy received a stern team talk from their manager Vittorio Pozzo. He 'ordered his players to stop brawling', according to the historian David Winner, 'reminded them that they were world champions, and sent them back onto the field with a firm handshake'. Most of the play in the second half was one way. Meazza scored twice, and England were lucky to hang on for a 3–2 win.

The aftershocks took weeks to abate. Drake, like his Elizabethan namesake Francis, would be revered at home and reviled on the Continent. The Italians claimed an unlikely moral victory, pointing at their second-half resurgence, and dubbing their players the 'Lions of Highbury'. The English, by contrast, saw the match as the 'Battle of Highbury', an example of foreign depravity that could be dug up whenever Italy rolled back into town. One newspaper printed a report 'by our war correspondent'. Another argued that matches against European teams should be suspended altogether.

> **'The true verdict of the match, in spite of appearances, is that England is still supreme in a game essentially her own.'**
>
> The Times offers a one-eyed summation of England's 3–2 win over Italy, 1934.

Protestations of English innocence were largely based on that old playground cry 'They started it!' Clearly there was not much to recommend the behaviour of Attilio Ferraris, who deliberately broke

WILF COPPING
Caps 20   Goals 0

THE VINNIE JONES OF HIS DAY, Copping deliberately used to refrain from shaving in the lead-up to a match, believing that a five o'clock shadow made him look more intimidating. In truth, he didn't need much help. Ken Jones, who played under Copping's supervision at Southend, described him as 'the archetypal British football hard case ... he taught tackling from the top down, "forehead in first", and stressed the importance of numerical superiority.' These tactics came in especially handy during the 'Battle of Highbury' in 1934, when Copping had three Italians seeking running repairs in the space of ten minutes. As the Arsenal right-half Jack Crayston quipped to his manager the following day: 'If we play Italy tomorrow, there's only one half back line to put out: Copping, Copping and Copping.'

Hapgood's nose with his elbow and then laughed in his face at the post-match banquet. But was he so different from Copping, who used to boast that he had 'got three of the bastards off in ten minutes'? A stench of double standards hangs over the match, bringing to mind Evelyn Waugh's great one-liner from his novel *Scoop*. 'Other nations use "force"; we Britons alone use "Might".'

'The first man in a tackle never gets hurt.'
The terrifying Wilf Copping, England's hard-case hero of the Battle of Highbury.

'Mozart' and the Viennese Whirl

If the Italians were the Mafiosi of the world football scene, the Austrians were the maestros. Their fluid, interchangeable formations, dreamed up in the coffee-houses of Vienna, provided the inspiration for what the Dutch would later call 'Total Football'. Rather than sticking to their slots in an imaginary grid, the Austrians moved freely around the field, taking advantage of whatever space they could find. Someone soon came up with the term 'Danubian Whirl' – an excellent moniker, as it sounds more like a dance than a diagram.

On 7 December 1932, the Austrian 'Wunderteam' met England at Stamford Bridge. They lost 4–3, but earned far more favourable notices than Mussolini's Italians. Bastin wrote that England's win had 'really been more than we had deserved', while the *Daily Sketch* described the visitors' display as 'first-class Corinthian with a kick in it, and played at twice the pace'. Perhaps the Austrians' only problem was that they were too artistic: like the Arsenal team of recent times, they wanted to walk the ball into the net, rather than taking their chances from medium or long range. With apologies to George Orwell, they played football without the shooting.

The best player on the Stamford Bridge pitch that day was Matthias Sindelar, a slightly built centre-forward who has variously been described as the 'Paper Man' and the 'Mozart of football'. As the Austrian émigré Willy Meisl wrote in his great polemic *Football Revolution*, Sindelar 'was truly symbolical of Austrian football at its peak period: no brawn but any

MATTHIAS SINDELAR
Caps 43 (for Austria)   Goals 27

Surely the finest footballer of the era, Sindelar (above, right) was at the heart of all of Austria's greatest performances during the 1930s, notably the 5–0 thrashing of Scotland in 1931, and the long-awaited 2–1 win over England in Vienna five years later. But on 23 January 1939, he was found dead in his Vienna flat alongside his half-Jewish girlfriend Camilla Castignolla. The pair had suffered an overdose of carbon monoxide, apparently from a faulty heater. Marked down as a dissident in the Gestapo's files, Sindelar had been a dedicated opponent of the Nazis, and repeatedly refused to play for Sepp Herberger's united German team after the *Anschluss* of 1938. To this day, no-one really knows whether his death was an accident, a suicide or a murder. But it was an appropriately grim way for the glories of the 'Wunderteam' to be snuffed out.

amount of brain'. A similar verdict was delivered by the Austrian theatre critic Alfred Polgar, who compared Sindelar to a chess grandmaster, 'inexhaustibly devising tactical feints which were followed by the true attacking move that his deception had made irresistible'.

A genuine virtuoso, Sindelar was so effortlessly elegant that his gifts seemed innate. Yet this could not have been further from the truth. In fact, he and his Austrian team-mates had learned their technical mastery from the most comprehensive coaching programme in the world. And who was leading that programme? An Englishman, ironically enough. A retired striker from Burnley, Lancashire, to be precise, whose name was Jimmy Hogan.

Hogan's run across the Channel

Today, England has a massive balance-of-trade deficit in football managers. Back in the 1930s, it was the other way around: teams from Europe and South America kept snapping up England's smartest ex-players, largely because they couldn't find a job at home.

Amazingly, practising with the ball was still frowned upon in England. There was a theory that it should be kept away from the players during the week, so as to keep them hungry for possession when match-day came around. This atavistic attitude filtered down all the way from the boardroom, where club chairmen were prone to shout things like 'Just get the ball in the bloody net.' Dick Turpin showed more respect for coaches.

Hogan was different. In one of his first matches for Burnley he spooned a shot over the bar, then went looking for Spen Whittaker, the team manager, to ask what he had done wrong. The question seemed to flummox Whittaker, who responded feebly that a striker just had to keep trying, and that a return of one goal from ten attempts was all anyone could expect. 'From that day I began to fathom things out for myself,' Hogan said. 'I coupled this with seeking advice from the truly great players. It was through my constant delving into matters that I became a coach later in life. It seemed the obvious thing, for I had coached myself as quite a young professional.'

Hogan's pioneering techniques included tactical lessons with a chalkboard, wholesome diets full of fruit and vegetables, and long hours of skill drills. He coached all over the continent, in Holland, Switzerland

'People abroad laugh at me when I express the opinion that the British footballer is still the most natural in the world, but his love and talent for the game have been sadly neglected, and he has not progressed with the times ... The foreigner, with far less talent, is being taught and is a most willing pupil.'

Jimmy Hogan, the Englishman who created the Austrian 'Wunderteam' and laid the foundations for the 'Magnificent Magyars'.

and Germany. But it was his work with the 'Danubian School' of teams (primarily Austria and Hungary) that would prove most influential. These countries developed their passing, anticipation and running off the ball with quicksilver precision, to the point where their free-flowing formations were as far removed from the increasingly static and stereotyped English game as Ultimate Frisbee is from the World Wrestling Foundation.

Hogan was just one of many talented English coaches working on the Continent at this time. Fred Pentland, once of Blackburn Rovers, had had the bittersweet pleasure of watching his Spanish team upset England in 1929. And George Raynor – formerly an unheralded clogger with Aldershot – would enjoy a similar experience with Sweden at Wembley three decades later. 'Perhaps I was too helpful,' mused Stanley Rous, secretary of the FA, who had originally got Raynor the job.

But Hogan was the pre-eminent example – not that you would have known it from his reception in England. On the two occasions when he did take up a post at a Football League club, he was treated like a skivvy. Fulham actually went as far as to sack him in the mid-1930s, after just 31 games, with the explanation that 'seasoned profes-

> **'As they know all about it in this country, there is no room for me, here. Our young players prefer not to be taught.'**
> William Hibbert, a former England centre-forward, is forced to emigrate in search of a coaching job in New York, 1923.

sionals do not need coaching'. In a list of great historical oversights, this canard must rank up there with the story of Decca Records, who famously rejected the Beatles' demo with a letter explaining 'Groups of guitars are on the way out, Mr Epstein.'

The Hungarians were among the many nations who worshipped Hogan's memory: in the words of Gusztáv Sebes, coach of the 1953 'Magnificent Magyars', 'When our football history is told, his name should be written in gold letters.' According to the author Jonathan Wilson, Hogan was 'the most influential coach there has ever been'. Yet today, sad to say, his name is all but forgotten in his home country.

When in Berlin ...

Adolf Hitler was not much of a sports fan; certainly less so than Mussolini, who enjoyed such combative disciplines as fencing, boxing and shooting. But he was well aware of sport's potential as a propaganda tool.

When Berlin hosted the notorious 'Nazi Olympics' of 1936, Hitler made sure that the city had its best face on. Interpreters were posted on every street corner, Jew-baiting posters were pulled down, and the Fascist newspaper *Der Angriff* instructed its readers that 'We must be more charming than the Parisians, more easygoing than the Viennese, more vivacious than the Romans,' and so on.

In May 1938, Berlin returned to the sporting map through the visit of an England football team. The timing is intriguing: from our modern perspective, it seems amazing that England should have agreed to visit just two months after Germany had forcibly swallowed up Austria (including

In the tyrant's den: the players take the field for England's notorious match against Germany in Berlin, May 1938. England captain Eddie Hapgood (white shirt) is carrying one of the match balls.

> ## 'All I know is football. But t'way I see it, yon 'Itler fella is an evil little twat.'
>
> Bert Sproston, England's full-back, as recalled in Stanley Matthews's autobiography.

'**When play was restarted we could hear all round the ground shouts of "Viva Ribbentrop" and "Viva Göring".**'

Tommy Lawton describes the crowd reaction in Milan, May 1939, after German referee Dr Bauwens had awarded Italy a dubious goal.

its glorious football team). But the Foreign Office were fully behind the fixture, and they gave the players strict instructions: the Nazi salute must be performed during the pre-match rendition of *Deutschsland Deutschsland über alles*. As Sir Nevile Henderson, British ambassador to Berlin, explained to FA secretary Stanley Rous, 'When I go in to see Herr Hitler I give him the Nazi salute because that is the normal courtesy expected … And if I do it, why should you and your team object?'

Six years later, England's captain Eddie Hapgood would come up with a memorable indictment of this crass decision. 'I've been V-bombed in Brussels before the Rhine crossing, bombed and "rocketed" in London, I've been in a shipwreck, a train crash, and inches short of a plane accident

… but the worst moment of my life, and one I would not willingly go through again, was giving the Nazi salute in Berlin.'

The salute has often been described as one of the darkest moments in English sporting history. Some have even seen it as an important link in the chain of events that led to the Second World War. (If it hadn't been for Britain's craven attempts to build bridges with the Third Reich, Hitler might not have been so quick to invade Czechoslovakia.) But to Stanley Rous, the FA secretary of the time, the whole tawdry affair was just 'a bit of fun'.

In his memoir *Football Worlds*, Rous claimed that he had given the players the chance to refuse, merely pointing out that their decision would determine 'whether the game was held in a friendly or hostile atmosphere … All agreed that they had no objection, and no doubt saw it as a bit of fun rather than of any political significance.' But this laughably offhand account stands at odds with the recollections of Hapgood and Matthews, who both claimed they had received a straight order. It is worth noting

'PONGO' WARING
Caps 5   Goals 4

TOM 'PONGO' WARING SOUNDS like he must have escaped from cocktail hour at P.G. Wodehouse's fictional Drones Club, where he would presumably have been playing darts with Tuppy Glossop and Oofy Prosser. The truth, sadly, is a little more prosaic. Waring was a Scouse striker who began his career at Tranmere Rovers – like his contemporary Dixie Dean – and went on to became one of Aston Villa's most prolific goalscorers. Some sources suggest that his nickname derived from his stinky feet, though others point to a cartoon serial that was popular at the time. Waring even had a second nickname: the Villa fans used to call him 'the gay cavalier', before the term took on a second meaning.

BRYN JONES
Caps 17 (for Wales)   Goals 6

ALEX JAMES'S SUCCESSOR at Arsenal was Bryn Jones, another diminutive inside-forward who harried England mercilessly in the Home Championship. Wales ran neck-and-neck with her vaunted neighbours over the 1930s, with four wins to match against four defeats – a feat which was largely down to Jones and his playmaking skills. And these results were all the more impressive when you consider the many obstacles that the English FA had placed in the way of her British rivals. From the start of the decade, Scotland, Wales and Ireland needed to give three weeks' notice if they wanted to recruit any players who were operating in the Football League – and even then, the relevant club still had the right to refuse. In the words of historian Brian James, 'Wales, year after year, had no idea of her team often until the morning of the match ... often even League clubs' reserve team players were refused their chance to play.' As for Jones, he smashed the world record for a transfer fee when Arsenal paid Wolverhampton Wanderers £14,000 for him in 1938, yet his own share was just the standard £10 signing-on fee, plus the maximum wage of £10 per week. When he objected, Arsenal's autocratic manager George Allison reacted like the master in *Oliver Twist*, turning purple with rage and threatening to 'make sure that you'll never kick another ball'.

that Stan Cullis, who had signalled his outright refusal to comply with Henderson's request, was quietly ditched from the team.

Hitler was not actually present at the Olympiastadion that day, as he had just returned from a trip to Rome. And this may have been fortunate for his team, who were comfortably outgunned – metaphorically, of course – by an angry and frustrated England side. The visitors took the match 6–3, and at least two of those goals were absolute crackers: a 60-yard run and strike from Matthews, and a spectacular 25-yard volley from Len Goulden, which Hans Jakob could not have saved in all the thousand years of Hitler's imaginary Reich.

England's performance was undeniably impressive, even if this was a fairly ordinary German side. The magazine *Football Woche* announced that they were the 'world champions of football after all', while the *New York Times* found space for the headline 'England conquers German Eleven, 6.3'.

> **'Muenzenberg ... would like to think of himself as a wily old fox. Yet against this Matthews he was at his wit's end.'**
> The German magazine *Fussball* on the one-sided battle between left-back and right-wing, 1938.

Looking back at the match, some 40 years later, Rous went so far as to draw parallels with the larger conflict to come. 'I was amused,' he wrote, 'at the contrast between Sir Nevile Henderson, sitting there wearing a shooting-hat with a hawk's feather and an old pullover, and Hermann Göring beside him glistening with medals and military magnificence. Henderson had a large pair of binoculars slung round his neck and each time we scored he would proffer them to the unsmiling Göring, saying, "What wonderful goals. You really ought to get a closer look at them." Perhaps there was a hint here of how British humour and improvisation would win out in a more important contest against the disciplined efficiency of the Germans.'

THEY MIGHT HAVE BEEN GIANTS

'Hobbits are an unobtrusive but very ancient people,' wrote J.R.R. Tolkien in 1954, 'They could, when put to it … survive rough handling by grief, foe, or weather in a way that astonished those who did not know them well.' In Frodo Baggins and his indomitable cousins, Tolkien created a caricature of Englishness. His story of the home-loving 'little people' who toppled a remote tyrant was clearly rooted in the events of the Second World War.

So many aspects of England's self-image date back to the 1940s: the stoicism, the resourcefulness, even the fondness for queuing. Many survivors experienced a strange sense of nostalgia for the Blitz, despite all the privations they had been forced to endure. They considered those years to be a time of national triumph, when the country pulled together in the face of overwhelming odds.

On the football field, the war was certainly a time for heroes (as they like to say in Hollywood). This country has never struck such a rich vein of talent. With Tommy Lawton leading the line, Stanley Matthews pirouetting up the wing and Stan Cullis orchestrating the backs,

'There are two things to be done – to fight the Germans and keep the mass of people at home from worrying.'

Viscount Montgomery, long-time president of Portsmouth FC, addresses the England team before a match.

England assembled a team to beat any 'Master Race' you could care to mention.

From a blinkered footballing perspective, it seems entirely typical that war should have broken out just as England uncovered a truly golden generation, far superior to the counterfeit version we are used to today. But the players – to their credit – could see the bigger picture. 'Not for one moment did I bemoan what I might have lost – like more England caps,' said Cullis later. 'I came home from the war in one piece and that was something to be grateful for. We all know that a lot of young men were not so lucky.'

By comparison with 1914–18, football had a good war. Afraid of air-raids and bad publicity, the FA rushed to suspend the League programme in September 1939. But regional competitions started up again within a few weeks, and carried on in front of ever-growing crowds. Despite Josef Goebbels's claims that the *Luftwaffe* had 'smashed' English football, the nearest the bombers came to a direct hit was when a doodlebug struck kennels near Wembley Stadium in 1944.

'The truly remarkable fact is how *little* the game was disrupted,' wrote Simon Kuper in his revealing book *Ajax, The Dutch, The War*. 'Crowds numbering tens of thousands were allowed to gather in grounds in the midst of the Blitz; teams travelled long distances to matches while official posters urged "DON'T TRAVEL UNLESS IT IS ABSOLUTELY NECESSARY" and … new kits were provided, if less often than before.'

This time around, the message to the people was clear: go out and enjoy yourselves while you can. Winston Churchill and King George VI went so far as to be seen regularly at matches. As Eddie Hapgood wrote, 'The Royal Box was nearly always crowded when we played a charity international at Wembley during the war. At one match there were seven Cabinet Ministers present.'

Why this dramatic shift in attitude? Probably because England's wartime leaders were trying to ingratiate themselves with the masses. Knowing that the war could never be won without popular support, they hit upon football as a means of reaching out to the man in the street – or, more specifically, the man on the terrace. (More recently, Tony Blair performed a similar manoeuvre when he claimed – unconvincingly – to have watched Jackie Milburn score from behind the goal at St James's Park.)

The result was that football, so often a bonding agent for fathers and sons, found itself performing the same function on a far grander scale. As Kuper suggests, the game 'entered the communal British soul during the war as it never had before'.

Ball-playing battles of Britain

As the proverbial storm clouds gathered over Europe, a formidable group of footballers were gathering too. Given cushy wartime employment as 'Temporary Sergeant Instructors', these players were stars with stripes. The 1942 World Cup, had it happened, would have provided a suitable stage for their talents. But instead they had to settle for pulping Scotland and Wales in a series of unofficial internationals.

The first signs of greatness could be spotted a few months before the conflict started. On 15 May 1939, Eddie Hapgood led a team containing the novice striker Tommy Lawton up to Hampden Park for a game that few expected England to win. The conditions could hardly have been less appetising. Torrential rain hammered down, and forced the visitors – who had not brought any spare kit – to change into the unfamiliar hooped strip of Queen's Park at half-time. They were already 1–0 down by this stage, and – in the words of John Macadam in the *Daily Express* – 'it looked if Scotland were going to have a runaway win'.

> **'A display comparable with the old masters, and every Scotsman I spoke to after the match agreed.'**
>
> Frank Coles, in the *Daily Telegraph*, on England's 1939 win at Hampden Park.

In his autobiography, Lawton described the thrill of hearing the Hampden Roar for the first time: 'I thought to myself, what a noise ... that is when I *could* think. The noise echoes and eddies round the giant bowl,

and smashes back into your eardrums.' But he would silence the crowd in the second half. First Lawton threaded a short pass through to Pat Beasley, who hit it into the roof of the net. And then, with just three minutes to go, Stanley Matthews got the ball.

A breathless Macadam described the finale: 'Matthews has been running riot and McNab and Cummings are sold out chasing him … [He] has it in marvellous control and the roar is a tornado of sound now. Matthews belts it right across true as an arrow to Tom Lawton's head. Lawton crashes it into the net and the game is won – and lost.'

This was England's first win at Hampden for 12 years, and a welcome fillip for an anxious country. (One of the jokes going around in the lead-up to the match had been 'What about the international situation?' 'Terrible, I can't get a ticket for love or money.') For the players in the England dressing-room, it also delivered respite from a decade of Scottish jibes.

'I had been brought up with people like [Scotland inside-forward] Jimmy Dunn about, always hammering us with how good the Scots were, how we'd never come to be as good as that famous Wizard team of Wembley,' recalled Joe Mercer. 'Now at last we'd shut them all up with that one goal – Hampden Park was like a grave – and never again until I finished playing did I feel the Scots were anything so very special in soccer.'

The Methuselah of football

If Fulham had erred in sacking Jimmy Hogan in 1934, what about Stanley Matthews and Stoke City? Matthews was 32 when Stoke offloaded him to Blackpool, whose manager reckoned he might have another couple of years

> **'The man who taught us the way football should be played.'**
> Pelé on Matthews.

in him. As it happened, Matthews had another couple of decades in him. He was 50 when he finally retired from the game.

Matthews's longevity was no fluke. The son of a professional boxer, he was an anomaly within English football, a dedicated trainer who could be found practising his sprinting at 6 a.m. every morning on Blackpool beach. As Bolton's Roy Hartle recalled, 'Stanley was light years ahead of everyone, wasn't he? Training on his own, taking all the orange juice and pills. But no-one copied him. Everyone thought he was strange.'

With the ball at his feet, Matthews was probably the most elusive dribbler that this country – or any other – has ever produced. He was not a pure sprinter, like Ryan Giggs, who could simply turn on the afterburners and leave defenders for dead. Matthews was more like a mosquito, buzzing up and down the touchline and evading all attempts to slap him down. His favourite trick was to show the full-back the ball, like a conjurer holding up a card, and then whip it away at the last possible moment.

Like most pioneers, Matthews had to put up with the carping of lesser men. He was accused of ball-hogging, showboating and excess vanity. Even the smallest gesture could be misinterpreted: during England's 1948 thrashing of Italy in Turin, he dribbled the ball to the corner flag, then paused and smoothed down his hair. The rumour spread that he had used a comb.

Famously unassuming off the pitch, there was something merciless about the way Matthews repeatedly humiliated his opponents. Cullis remembered one occasion when, with the full-back sitting helplessly on the ground, Matthews put his foot on the ball and waited for his unfortunate victim to get up, only to beat him all over again.

> **'Playing Stan is like playing a ghost.'**
> Manchester United defender Johnny Carey.

The wizard of dribble: Stanley Matthews toys with Scottish defender James Stephen in a 1944 wartime international at Wembley.

'On one occasion I headed one of [Matthews's] crosses, and later remarked to Stan that the lacing on the ball had caught my head a bit sharpish. He replied "Sorry Tom, it won't happen again"... I swear he had the ability to cross the ball with the lacing in the right direction, because never, after this incident, did I have similar trouble.'

Lawton on Matthews.

If he was ever challenged on this point, Matthews would reply that it was as important to break a team's spirit as it was to beat their offside trap. 'Eddie Hapgood once said I dribbled for the sake of dribbling,' he explained. 'This is not true. I dribble to get on top of the defence, hoping to destroy their confidence.'

The two Stanleys

There were actually two great Stans among England's wartime giants – not that many remember it today. While Stanley Matthews has been canonised as the patron saint of dribblers, few now think of Stan Cullis as anything but an irascible manager of Wolverhampton Wanderers.

JOE MERCER
Caps 5   Goals 0

Every great team has a player like Mercer, the sort of tireless grafter who ends up being denigrated as a 'water-carrier' or worse. Someone has to man the supply lines, after all. While Matthews and Lawton stole most of the limelight after England's famous win at Hampden Park in 1939, it was Mercer – unshowy as ever – who did the donkey-work. 'He was back in defence, first on one side then on the other,' wrote John Macadam in the *Daily Express*, 'always fishing the ball from a danger spot and pushing it through to his own forwards.' For most of the war, Mercer formed an imposing half-back partnership with Stan Cullis, a boyhood friend from the back-streets of the Wirral. The two men shared a feverish work ethic, and also a mature sense of perspective. 'In one way I ought to be sick when I think back to those years,' Mercer once said. 'For certainly the best years of my career were used up during the war ... But on the other hand this was a wonderful bunch to play with. I was lucky to be around at the same time. I have never played with a team so eager to do well. In those matches everybody fancied himself a bit, everybody wanted the ball. Every time you gave a pass, you made nine enemies. The spirit was as keen as that.'

As a player, Cullis's career was as neatly swallowed up by the war as any of his team-mates'. Since 20 of his England appearances were unofficial, he was left with just 12 full caps to his name – the same as Trevor Sinclair. Which is a travesty when you consider his huge stature as a creative centre-half. Three decades later, Tommy Lawton wrote that he had yet to see a better player in this pivotal position. 'Neil Franklin, Billy Wright, Bobby Moore and Germany's Franz Beckenbauer all deserve their world-class ranking, but I reckon Stan had them all beat.'

At a time when most centre-halves contented themselves with snuffing out attacks, Cullis was a throwback to an earlier, more adventurous era. He was bold enough to sell dummies on the edge of his own penalty area, before setting off upfield in his distinctive crouching stance, elbows pumping and balding forehead thrust out, like some footballing

> **'The most classical centre-half of his time.'**
> Ferenc Puskás, the immortal Hungarian striker, on Stan Cullis.

version of Rodin's *Thinker*. As Eddie Hapgood said of him, 'He goes his own way, always looking for the opportunity of the crack down the middle.'

Nicknamed 'the passionate puritan' by the commentator John Arlott, Cullis was a natural choice as England's wartime captain. He had grown up in poverty on the Wirral, but attended night classes until he was fluent in Esperanto and as comfortable discussing surrealist art as selection policy. When Monty Python picked the squad for their famous philosophers' football match, they had Beckenbauer playing alongside Kant and Plato. They could just as well have used Cullis.

Ever the patriot, Cullis volunteered for the army as early as September 1939. But his recruitment stalled when a doctor declared him medically unfit on the grounds of a low pulse. You might as well have discharged Don Bradman for having defective eyesight. In the end, Cullis wound up at the army's Physical Training Corps in Aldershot, where he became a 'Temporary Sergeant Instructor' alongside the likes of Tommy Lawton, Joe Mercer, Wilf Copping, Stan Cullis and Denis Compton.

One unintended consequence was that Aldershot, previously a modest third division side, suddenly became the football equivalent of the

Lancashire's M and Ms: Stanley Matthews and Stan Mortensen (right) were team-mates for England and Blackpool. The 1953 FA Cup final became known as 'the Matthews final', on account of a mesmerising exhibition of dribbling, despite Mortensen's hat-trick. When Mortensen died, 38 years later, one contemporary quipped 'I suppose they'll call it the Matthews funeral.'

Harlem Globetrotters. In a South London league that also included QPR and Crystal Palace, they were comfortably the strongest team. 'It was almost as though you would stand at the barrack gate, shout out for a centre-forward, a full-back, whatever, and out would come an international,' said their manager Bill McCracken. 'I was like a kid let loose in a chocolate factory.'

Compared to the average man in the Western Desert, Cullis and Co. had a thoroughly cushy war. But football, in its own small way, remained a hazardous business. During England's 4–0 thrashing of Scotland in April 1943, a brawl broke out after Clyde inside-forward Dougie Wallace reached down and grabbed Cullis's testicles *à la* Vinnie Jones.

> **'Sometimes I've fumed in the middle of the field when Stan has gone away on a mazy dribble, pattern-weaving his way down to the corner flag. But I've lost my irritation when [he] laid on a pass that is perfection itself.'**
>
> Tommy Lawton on his friend and England team-mate Stanley Matthews.

This was one injury that the man with the bucket and sponge could do little for. 'I must have leapt two feet in the air,' said Cullis. 'I had to wear a special bandage for two years after that, from morning to night.' His torn and blood-stained shorts were later used as evidence by the English FA, and Scotland made sure that Wallace never played for them again.

Make that the *three* Stanleys

There was, in fact, a *third* Stanley who helped engineer England's golden run through the 1940s. This was Stanley Rous, the FA secretary who had taken such a relaxed stance on the Nazi salute in 1938. Despite his error of judgement – which probably looks far worse now than it did at the time – Rous was that rare beast, an enlightened football administrator.

One of the war's happier consequences was Rous's conversion into a modern-style England manager. He picked the team and enforced discipline, even if tactics were usually left to Cullis to sort out. For the players, used as they were to the capricious tyranny of the FA selection committee, this was a huge relief. In the words of Joe Mercer, 'it gave us all the feeling we were being dealt with by someone who knew us, not by a committee of people we might never see'.

> '**As soon as Stan got the ball we just ran up the field, because we *knew* it would come across. He so rarely if ever lost the ball to put your team under pressure.'**
>
> Bill Perry, Matthews's Blackpool team-mate.

The benefits of continuity showed up most clearly in a ten-match sequence of fantasy football at the end of the war. Between September 1943 and VE-Day, England played 10 games, notching nine wins and a draw, with a goal difference of plus 31. But the really striking thing is that only 29 players appeared – round about the same figure that Sven-Göran Eriksson would trot out in a single friendly.

This free-scoring run began in controversial fashion. As England prepared to host Wales at Wembley, Cullis heard a whisper that Matthews would be double-marked, and instructed the team to give the ball to left-winger (and Middlesex and England batsman) Denis Compton instead. The score was 8–3 to England – enough, you might think, to quell any tactical second-guessing. But you would be wrong. 'The newspapers gave me a right rollicking,' Cullis recalled, 'and asked how I'd dared treat Stanley Matthews like that. They insisted the spectators had gone to watch Matthews, not me, and demanded that I be forced to give up the captaincy.' By this stage, Matthews had become such a celebrity that even the things he didn't do were news.

If Cullis felt the backlash, then what about Scotland? When England ran out for their next international, at Wembley four months later, it was almost as if the players over-compensated, because the ball kept being drawn magnetically to Matthews. Again and again, he jinked his way up the touchline, confounding angry defenders like a matador swirling his cape. He finished the game with a hypnotic dribble, taking the ball from the half-way line, around the goalkeeper and into the net to seal England's

R A I C H   C A R T E R
Caps 13   Goals 7

RAICH CARTER, christened Horatio, was an inside-forward with a deft touch, an arrogant manner, and a deep disdain for coaches. It is typical of English football that he should have ended up as a club manager in the 1950s and the 1960s. 'Maybe Raich was such a good player that he didn't understand how things that came easily to him might be difficult for other people,' said Jack Charlton, who played under Carter at Leeds. 'The only training we used to do at Elland Road in those days was to run down the long side of the pitch, jog the short side, sprint the long side, and so on.' In his heyday, Carter liked to be the centre of attention at all times, which caused problems when Matthews came along.

'The trouble playing with Stan,' he once said, 'is that he gets the credit. You give him the ball, he beats his man, centres, and Lawton heads a goal. They forget all about *you*.'

8–0 win. Although the match was unofficial, it remains the biggest margin of victory in the history of the series.

'I have yet to see such perfection in movement, unselfishness or team spirit as England showed that afternoon,' said Frank Swift, England's redundant goalkeeper. 'It was Stanley's match in particular ... When he scored the eighth and final goal, entirely on his own, the crowd cheered for minutes on end. Even some of the Scottish players clapped.'

Fun and (war) games

Matthews's crowd-pleasing style was in tune with the whole tenor of wartime football. Games ceased to be a metaphor for battle – there was more than enough of that to go round – and became playful exhibitions of flair and chutzpah, a means of bringing a smile to thousands of pinched faces. As players experimented with half-forgotten tricks, the average number of goals per game doubled, from three per match over the 1938–9 season to six in the first few months of the war.

> **'Fuck a ya Weenston Churchill and fuck a ya Deexie Dean!'**
>
> Outburst from an Italian soldier, captured in Africa during the Second World War, as recalled by the actor Patrick Connolly.

It is tempting to draw a correlation between such free-flowing club football and the success of the national team. Especially as writers like Willy Meisl would soon be blaming England's postwar slump on a lack of 'originality, individuality and adventurous spirit'. In truth, though, we shouldn't make too many claims for the wartime game, which was haphazard at best. Teams often arrived short-handed, having hitch-hiked their way from a distant barracks. Brighton were beaten 18–0 by Norwich, after turning up with only half their players. Charlton once fielded their milkman by mistake.

Such was the backdrop for one of the quirkier events in England's footballing history. During a match at Wembley in 1943, Wales lost their left-half Ivor Powell to a broken collar-bone. So, at half-time, England made an unprecedented concession: their 12th man, Stan Mortensen, would play the second half in Powell's place. The offer was both gracious and ground-breaking: substitutes would not make their first official appearance until the 1966–7 season. Mind you, England might not have been quite so forthcoming without the 4–1 lead they held at the break.

Then still uncapped, Mortensen went on to achieve many great feats on the pitch – including the striking of England's first World Cup goal in 1950. But he was lucky just to survive the war. When his Wellington bomber crashed into a tree, the pilot and the bomb aimer were both killed outright, while the navigator lost a leg. Mortensen, who had been operating the wireless, crawled away with head injuries that would confine him to the ground for the remainder of the conflict. But he fought his way back, just like Dixie Dean after that motorbike crash, and wound up with 25 full international caps. Tough creatures, these hobbits.

'You cannot even argue about this. This was a great England team ... Scotland had no chance.'

Bill Shankly, Scotland right-half and later Liverpool manager, on the England side of 1943.

WORLD IN MOTION

MOTION

1945–1966

SHOCK OF AGES

The summer of 1950 was a pivotal moment for the English game. After all those long years of 'splendid isolation', the FA's party-poopers had finally agreed to send a team to the World Cup. It was the beginning of a great romance – but, as with any new relationship, the protagonists had little idea what they were getting themselves into. Few would have guessed what a heart-breaking, stomach-churning, knee-trembling affair this would turn out to be.

Brazil was the venue for the 1950 tournament; virgin territory for a team that had never travelled beyond Europe. Yet, as the date of departure loomed, there was little planning and no fanfare. Billy Wright and his men prepared themselves with a few desultory practices at the Dulwich Hamlet ground in south London, as blind to their fate as the Bourbon kings before the Revolution. Some five miles away, in the FA's offices at Paternoster Row, a space was being cleared for the Jules Rimet Cup. Destiny, it seemed, was calling.

Well, destiny certainly was calling – but not quite in

> **'The only Brazilian I'd ever heard of was the Hollywood star Carmen Miranda, who jumped around in films with fruit piled up on her head.'**
>
> Eddie Baily, England's inside-left, reveals the depth of research that had gone into the 1950 World Cup campaign.

the way anyone expected. There have been many embarrassments along the road of the England football team (and a good thing too, for the purposes of this book). But none can compete with 25 June 1950: the day the Yanks beat us at our own game.

Has there ever been a more definitive instance of hubris and nemesis in the annals of sport? Remember, England had spent the past 50 years posing as unofficial world champions. In the absence of any concrete evidence, these madams of football had primped and preened for all they were worth. In the summer of 1950, they made their belated debut at the event of the year, blithely expecting to upstage a bunch of global footballing *arrivistes*. They soon discovered that, in sport, reputations count for nothing.

> **'The United States of America was also competing, but this was regarded as little more than a joke in doubtful taste.'**
>
> Brian Glanville on the 1950 World Cup.

England 0, USA 1. It is the starkest scoreline of them all. The unlikeliest upset. The first great wake-up call. Not that everyone was ready to hear it. Back in London, the receipt of a cabled newsflash was met with disbelief. 'When the "flash" result was passed to a sub-editor,' writes the former *Daily Mirror* correspondent Ken Jones, 'he smiled – understandably assuming an error in transmission; he reached for a pen to correct the score – surely, England 10, USA 1. Still smiling, he turned to a colleague and said "England defeated by the United States. Now, that *would* have been some story."'

What happened that day in Belo Horizonte? The Americans were a bunch of semi-professionals whose ranks included a postman, a mechanic, and – aptly enough – a hearse-driver. So how did the mighty, mighty England manage to lose to this half-arsed bunch of cloggers and scramblers, a team that few people even knew existed?

On one level, the result was just a massive, screaming fluke. A freakish spin of the coin, of the kind that football, more than any other

'I still cringe when I look back on that game. I take absolutely no satisfaction whatsoever in being able to say I took part in the soccer sensation of the century.'

Tom Finney on England's loss to the USA.

team game, has a habit of throwing up every now and again. No-one would claim that the Americans had the better of the play. England battered the woodwork, missed a whole bus-full of sitters, and were denied the most blatant of penalties. As Brian Glanville put it, the game turned into 'the waking equivalent of an anxiety dream, in which it was impossible to do the one essential thing, the thing which should have been so farcically easy – score goals'.

Yet there was another sense in which England brought misfortune on their own heads. Not so much the players – they could never be accused of lacking effort, especially after Joe Gaetjens's lucky goal, deflected in after 38 minutes, had opened Pandora's box. It was the FA's blazered buffoons who had sold the team short. Complacency and inertia lay behind the failure to scout out the venues, the opponents, or even the hotels. As the England coach Walter Winterbottom put it, 'We went to Rio pretty well unprepared. We had a couple of weeks together, but we were immature by the standards we had to face.'

Such negligence might seem strange to modern fans, but in 1950, England's priorities still lay with the Home Championship. If the FA deigned to send a team to Brazil, it was not because they had woken up one morning and glimpsed the diversity and splendour of the world game. They were simply trying not to fall out yet again with FIFA. The nation as a whole saw the World Cup as a tinpot tournament; like playing football at the Olympic Games, only without the medals.

Walter Winterbottom, footballing prophet

Rewinding a little, to the immediate aftermath of VE-Day, we find Stanley Rous fighting a battle of his own. After his illuminating experiences during the war, Rous realised that England needed a proper manager. The blueprint for success was simple: one man, one plan, one sole selector. The trouble was, he couldn't get anybody to listen.

Rous thought he had found the ideal candidate in Walter Winterbottom, a physical training graduate from Oldham. Here, surely, was a man who ticked all the boxes. Winterbottom had spent a couple of seasons as a centre-half for Manchester United, while his wartime role as a wing commander in the RAF showed that he could handle a G&T. The one thing he didn't have – and this would become an issue later – was any experience of club management.

English football had reached one of those *Sliding Doors* moments, when the future direction of the national side stood poised on a knife edge. If only Rous's bumbling colleagues in the FA's hierarchy had heeded his advice, they could have catapulted the team out of the Dark Ages. Instead, they went to the opposite extreme: the International Selection Committee was reformed.

Winterbottom still got to take charge of the team; it just wasn't the team he wanted. As Rous would put it, the FA 'gave Walter the responsibility, but saw to it that they retained the power'. He had the

> **'You just cannot tell star players how they must play and what they must do on the field in an international match. You must let them play their natural game, which has paid big dividends in the past.'**
>
> Even Stanley Matthews had a few blind spots on the value of coaching.

longest tenure of any England manager – 16 years, 139 matches and four World Cups – yet he spent most of it trying to educate the League chairmen in the virtues of team-building and player loyalty. It was a thankless task; you might as well set your Gran up on Facebook.

'One bad game and the selectors would throw a man out,' Winterbottom would recall. 'Or even if he did well he wasn't safe … Towards the end I would present my team and then let them try to argue me out of it. The trick of it was to stick to the men who were most important, and to make concessions to the committee where it didn't matter so much. If I felt losing "A" because they wanted "B" was not significant I would agree, so that "C", "D" and "E" might get by with less argument.'

The English game did its best to reject Winterbottom, just as a heart-transplant patient often tries to reject the very organ that might keep him alive. To the administrators, he was a righteous bore who was always banging on about the technical deficiencies of English footballers, when any fool could see that they just needed to *get stuck in.* To the players, he was a tiresome, schoolmasterly fogey – a walking vindication of the theory that those that can't, coach. Still, he kept beavering away, and we have him to thank for such innovations as Under-23 teams and 'B' internationals.

Looking back, Winterbottom can be seen as a sort of footballing John the Baptist. It was his voice crying in the wilderness, preaching the merits of healthy diets and finely honed ball-skills. And it would be his disciple, Tottenham and England right-back Alf Ramsey, who went on to become the nation's sporting messiah.

A panel of shopkeepers

The International Selection Committee consisted of a dozen club chairmen, described by Stanley Rous as 'retired butchers, greengrocers, builders, motor dealers, brewers and farmers'. Most of them took pride in shoehorning their own players into the England team. Unless, of course, they had a big League match to play that same weekend.

'It has never ceased to astonish me,' said Stan Cullis years later, 'that we went back to the old way of having a selection committee chopping and changing. It wasn't that they didn't know … they had been told the value of the system we had stumbled on by accident because of the war. It was a great opportunity lost.'

> ## 'Excuse me! Which side of the net do you want me to put the ball?'
>
> A sarcastic rejoinder from Len Shackleton, the 'clown prince of football', after Winterbottom had outlined a complex interpassing movement through midfield.

Still, things could have been worse for Winterbottom and England. Austerity Britain is usually associated with hardship and rationing, but in the mid-1940s, English football was churning out an apparently limitless stream of talent. As Cullis, Mercer and Carter reached the end of their terms, players as good as Neil Franklin, Billy Wright and Wilf Mannion were queuing up to replace them. Even a druid with a dowsing stick could have picked a winning team.

The most valuable discovery of all was Tom Finney, a plumber-turned-goalpoacher from Preston. Tommy Lawton, not a man given to exaggeration, called Finney 'possibly the greatest all-round player of them all ... [he] could hit 'em with his left foot, he could hit 'em with his right foot, he could head a ball, he could score and make goals, he could tackle'. There was only one problem: Finney's preferred position was outside-right, and Matthews – that doyen of wide men – was nowhere near ready to retire.

Here was a conundrum to test even the most far-sighted selectors (and, as we have seen, the International Committee suffered from chronic myopia). Though Finney and Matthews were good mates, and often roomed together on tour, the press portrayed them as bitter rivals. The debate developed into one of the first great selection controversies, a primitive forerunner of Hunt v Greaves or Lampard v Gerrard.

Winterbottom finally stumbled across a solution in 1947, halfway through a week-long tour of Europe. England had just gone down 1–0 to a superbly organised Switzerland side, whose defence resembled a Swiss watch more than a Swiss cheese. As the team licked its wounds, the manager called Finney to one side. 'We've got a bit of a problem,' he said. 'Bobby Langton's injured. Would you like to play outside-left?' Finney accepted at once, even though outside-left was his least favourite position. 'You play anywhere if it's for your country, don't you?'

WILF MANNION
Caps 26   Goals 11

THE WM FORMATION COULD have been named after Wilf Mannion, arguably the finest exponent of the inside-forward's art there has ever been. But like so many of his contemporaries, Mannion was a victim of football's archaic employment rules. Clubs would invest many thousands of pounds in transfer fees, yet the players themselves were limited to the pitiful £12-a-week maximum wage. At the peak

of his powers, Mannion sat out eight months of the 1948–9 season because he wanted to leave Middlesbrough. It was a battle he could never win as long as the clubs had absolute control over their slaves – sorry, players. Mannion made two points with his strike: firstly, that the chairman is always right, and secondly that England were an ordinary team without him. Even when they smashed Northern Ireland 6–2 in October 1948, the *Daily Mail* commented that 'the link Mannion provided between forwards and halves is missing – the twinkle-toed genius … of being able to alter the course of a match with one quick pass.' Known as the Golden Boy, Mannion was a diminutive figure with white-blond hair who ran with his arms outstretched and his palms facing the ground. He was loved and admired by his team-mates, who invariably benefited from his lethal passes. 'When I watched Pelé,' said Nat Lofthouse, 'I thought of Wilf.' One of his finest performances came in Great Britain's 6–4 win over the Rest of Europe in 1947, when the great Italian defender Carlo Parola spent most of the match yelling 'Man-e-yan, Man-e-yan'. It didn't help; Mannion still scored a hat-trick.

Victory in Europe (again)

Matthews on the right flank, Finney on the left. The new formation emerged for the first time in May 1947, on a trip to Lisbon, and immediately took wing. Under the gleaming new marble stands of the glorious Estádio Nácional, Lawton and Mortensen each scored four times, burying the Portuguese under a 10–0 avalanche. The final goal, tapped in by Matthews himself after a 40-yard dribble, prompted Neil Franklin to quip 'Stan is just the man for a crisis!'

The scoreline might give the impression that Portugal were mere lightweights, but in fact this was a seasoned team, stronger than the Swiss on paper, with a world-class goalkeeper in João Azevedo. The Portuguese tried everything – changing the ball to a schoolboy size after the first few minutes, switching Azevedo for his deputy as the score mounted, even replacing the man marking Finney (all this in the days before substitutes, of course). But England were quite unstoppable.

> **'His style is so graceful and so courtly that he wouldn't be out of place if he played in a lace ruffle and a perruque.'**
> Donny Davies, in the *Manchester Guardian*, on 'Golden Boy' Wilf Mannion.

England's triumphant forward line that day – Finney, Mannion, Lawton, Mortensen, Matthews – has a strong claim to be the finest they have ever fielded. As the writer Nick Varley has pointed out, both Matthews and Finney had been linked with an inside man who 'brought out the best in them and contributed plenty of attacking options themselves. Mortensen could give the simple ball to feet that Matthews thrived on, but could also use his bursts of pace to act like a second, deep-lying centre forward; Wilf developed an instant understanding with Finney, strong enough for both to know when to use the other as decoys. Lawton, meanwhile, apart from clinical finishing, was creating the spaces for all his fellow attackers by intelligent running off the ball.' For all the technical advances of the last 60 years, few modern teams can boast such seamless teamwork.

By now, England were coming into far more regular contact with their Continental rivals. A year later, they travelled to Italy – a country where both Finney and Mannion had served during the war. As if to make that point, the plane flew in over Anzio, the site of the Allies' landing in 1944. Lawton was surprised by England's hostile reception. 'With some of them, when you walked down the street it was, "*Inglese*" and they'd spit.'

Already smarting from military defeat, the Italians had no intention of losing further prestige on the football field. The manager, Vittorio Pozzo, whisked his men off to a three-week training camp, up in the hills above the Turin, and offered a win bonus of 100,000 lire each. From the moment the whistle blew, the *Azzuri* seemed to be camped on the edge of England's penalty area. But then Wright stole the ball and fed Matthews – who, uncharacteristically, chose to punt it up the right wing.

Mortensen outsprinted the defence, dribbling upfield until he had nearly run out of room. Then, as the goalkeeper stepped forward to cut out the anticipated cross, Mortensen unleashed a venomous, swerving shot that flashed in at the

'DEATH TO POZZO.'
Headline in Italian newspaper, the day after England's 4–0 win in Turin.

near post, right at the angle between post and crossbar. It was one of the great England goals. According to *Times* football correspondent Geoffrey Green, 'The Italians could hardly believe their eyes. It was some mirage surely. That huge crowd, packed tight in shirtsleeves like a white cloud in the shimmering light, grunted, caught its breath – and fell silent.'

The Italians came roaring back like poseurs on Vespas. Romeo Menti had two goals disallowed for offside, and goalkeeper Frank Swift was the busiest man in the England side. As the pressure mounted, left-half Henry Cockburn confronted the elusive Matthews, shouting 'Get yourself in this bloody game. We're chasing shadows here!' Matthews obliged with another incisive pass to Mortensen, who made as if to repeat his dazzling opener, before cutting the ball back to Lawton. England 2, Italy 0.

The battle remained fierce until midway through the second half, when Finney scored twice in the space of two minutes to complete England's emphatic 4–0 win. As Finney himself wrote in his memoir, 'It was what today's pundits might call "the ultimate professional display" and, aside from the 1966 World Cup victory, it had a very good claim to be the high point of the English game.'

And he marched them down again ...

Had there been a World Cup in 1948, rather than the London Olympics, England would have been very hard to stop. But two years is a long time for a football team. Like the Grand Old Duke of York, Walter Winterbottom had marched them up to the top of the hill. Unfortunately, he had got there a little too soon.

England were losing key personnel at both ends of the field. The Italy match was Lawton's last victory in an England shirt, while the long-serving full-back partnership of Laurie Scott and George Hardwick had also broken up. Even Frank Swift, a giant goalkeeper whose hands were said to resemble huge hams, was on the verge of a swift decline. Together with the 1943 thrashing of Scotland, Turin had represented one of the twin peaks of a glorious decade for English football. But now, with typically sadistic timing, this 'Team of the Century' was beginning to creak.

In at least two cases, England's wounds were self-inflicted. Despite the fact that Lawton was only 30 at the start of the World Cup, he had gone to play for Notts County in the Third Division (South), which took him right out of the selectors' orbit. He was lured by the promise of a day job, which boosted his earnings a long way above the £12-per-week maximum wage. But the fact that he called his autobiography *When the Cheering Stopped: The Rise, The Fall* suggests some regret in later life.

> **'In seven days, I have known what it feels like to be humiliated, relieved and proud.'**
>
> Billy Wright on England's 1948 tour of Switzerland and Italy, the first to involve air travel.

> '... and I assure you that, if elected, we shall do our utmost to bring back Wilf Mannion and Tommy Lawton.'
> Cartoon caption showing politician on the stump, 1949.

Neil Franklin, who had succeeded Cullis in the pivotal centre-half position, had even grander ambitions. In May 1950, a Sunday newspaper revealed that Franklin was among a group of players – nicknamed 'the Bogota Bandits' – who had been offered terms by clubs in Colombia. 'My wages would be £120 per week,' he admitted afterwards. 'It hurt me to think that I was unlikely again to pull on an England shirt, but I'd seen plenty of terrific players reach the end of their time with little to show for it but memories.'

Franklin, too, would rue his impetuous decision. He lasted barely two months at Santa Fe, where political riots had prompted a 6.30 p.m. curfew, and soon dropped out of the game altogether. The impact on his former team-mates – who had lost their pre-eminent defender less than a month before their flight to Brazil – would be just as far-reaching. 'Neil won everything in the air, tackled with superb timing and when the ball was at his feet possessed the nous to pass it with all the guile and intelligence of the most cerebral of inside-forwards,' wrote Matthews. His departure left a hole that would not be satisfactorily filled until Billy Wright moved to centre-half during the 1954 World Cup.

Going it alone

'Has there ever been a more dramatic meeting in the long series stretching back to 1872?' asked the *Daily Mail*'s Roy Peskett in the week leading up to England's visit to Hampden Park in April 1950. 'Hanging on the match is the biggest-ever "bonus" any international team has ever been offered. And that goes for Mussolini's Italian team and Hitler's regimented Nazi eleven. The Scots officials have in effect said to their players: win or draw at Hampden and you go to Rio – with an eight-week holiday trip to South America including two fourteen-day boat journeys plus the possibility of six international games at £20 a time in the World Cup play-offs. If you lose, there is nothing.'

Scotland's attitude to the 1950 World Cup summed up the 'Sceptred Isle' complex that afflicted British football as a whole. The top two teams in the Home Championship had both been offered entry to the tournament, but the Scottish FA peevishly announced that they would only go if they finished first – a decision that looks even more pig-headed now than it did at the time. With a certain dramatic inevitability, the whole tournament came down to that final game at Hampden Park, where Chelsea's Roy Bentley scored his first goal for England. It would earn him a certain notoriety as 'the man who robbed Scotland of Rio'.

After a couple of days in Brazil, the England players might have questioned the *Daily Mail*'s definition of a 'holiday trip'. Everything was different and disconcerting; even the journey out, which took 31 hours and five hops in a propeller plane, had introduced the unfamiliar concept of time zones and jet-lag. On arrival, Winterbottom was alarmed by the state of the Hotel Luxor on Copacabana beach – a glitzy resort that was totally unsuited to the needs of a professional sports team. The lobby was swarming with journalists, and the noise from the highway kept everyone awake. England's first visit to the World Cup was turning into *Mr Bean in Brazil.*

'When I inspected the kitchens I was almost sick,' Winterbottom recalled. 'The smell went up into the bedrooms, the food was swimming in oil and it was practically impossible to arrange suitable meals. Nearly all the players went down with tummy upsets at one time or another.' In the end, Winterbottom resorted to doing the cooking himself – another dogsbody role for a man who was a martyr to the cause.

Further tummy-flutters resulted from the players' trip to see Brazil thrash Mexico 4–0 in the curtain-raiser at the vast Maracanã Stadium. Matthews may have been the toast of Turin, but he was stunned by the level of technical expertise on show. The interpassing of Brazil's front three was stylish and economical. Even their one-word nicknames – Ademir, Jair and Zizinho – seemed to come freighted with an instant mythology. As Matthews himself explained in his autobiography, 'The fluidity with which

Brazil took the game to opponents had a controlled grace and style about it I had not seen before. In England, teams loved to attack but in comparison to the Brazilians, our style came across as hell-for-leather running and chasing.'

Matthews's point was underlined the very next day. Chile were England's first opponents in what turned out to be a dour old game. When set alongside the dancing feet of the Brazilians – who had virtually performed the *Macarena* at the Maracanã – England appeared to be wearing lead boots. Their midfielders were particularly off-colour, showing all the distribution skills of baggage handlers at Heathrow's Terminal Five. But at least the forwards retained the traditional English instinct for finding the net. A header from Mortensen gave them the lead just before half-time, before Mannion added some insurance with an angled drive.

Charles Buchan, writing in the *News Chronicle*, delivered a verdict of unwonted enthusiasm. 'On their display in the second half at any rate, England can win this trophy. I have no doubt now that they will beat Spain and the US and win the Group Championship.' Little did he know that England's goalscoring knack was about to desert them, in the most spectacular style.

> **'I was so excited and there was so much I wanted to tell my boys about the fine England play that I dashed back to Brazil long before I meant to return. The English play great football. They are formidable rivals.'**
>
> Brazil's manager Flávio Costa scouted out the Home Championship match at Hampden Park in April 1950. There was no such homework from England.

> **'I'm sticking to the bananas. What else can you do in a hotel where the food is so bad that even the dustbins have ulcers?'**
> Stan Mortensen enjoys the Brazilian experience.

Beautiful horizon, my arse

Portuguese for 'beautiful horizon', the city of Belo Horizonte is known for its grand plazas, its theatre festival and the footballing artists of Cruzeiro, who won the Brazilian treble in 2003. Cruzeiro's home ground, the Mineiro Stadium, is now a grand edifice that holds 72,000 fans. But in 1950, its predecessor was a rutted field scattered with stones and grassy tussocks – the sort of place you would expect to take a metal detector rather than a football team.

Winterbottom was so alarmed by the quality of the facilities that he arranged for the players to change at the Minas Athletic Club, ten minutes away. It was an unsatisfactory arrangement, especially as their nerves had already been shredded by the precipitous journey along the mountain road from the team's base at the Morro Velho gold mine. As Matthews (or his ghost writer) put it, the local bus driver 'commanded the wheel with all the calm and mental stability of Caligula'.

Matthews himself would take no part in the match. The victim of a typical bout of selectorial ping-pong, he had been summoned at the last instant from an FA tour of Canada, only to be left out of the Chile match on the whim of Arthur Drewry – the only member of the selection panel who had accompanied the team to Brazil. His treatment seemed to underline the point made by Tomas Mazzoni, a local football writer: 'The Englishman considers a player that dribbles three times in succession is a nuisance; the Brazilian considers him a virtuoso.'

Winterbottom wanted to reinstate Matthews against the USA, arguing that he 'might be just the man to unsettle a team that had very

> **'It was like leaving Wellington on the bench at Waterloo.'**
> Journalist Norman Giller on the omission of Stanley Matthews against the USA.

little international experience.' But his wishes, as usual, went unheeded. 'Never change a winning team,' insisted Drewry, a Grimsby fish merchant who later rose to become president of FIFA.

As kick-off approached, no-one could have imagined that such hairline decisions would matter a jot. Least of all the Americans, many of whom went out dancing till 2 a.m. the night before the game, and turned up at the ground with hangovers. They had lost 9–0 to the Italians in a warm-up match, and their most notable – or possibly notorious – contribution to previous World Cups dated back to Uruguay in 1930, when their trainer knocked himself out with his own chloroform and had to be carried limply off the field.

Still, the rules of football make no allowances for moral victories or past records. You cannot win without getting the ball into the net, and that is precisely what England could not seem to do. Within moments, the first chance had been wasted by Jimmy Mullen, the Newcastle left-winger who had been preferred to Matthews. Every miss from then on only added to the nightmarish feeling of futility. Mortensen hit the post – the first of 11 attempts to come back off the woodwork, according to the man from *The People* – while American goalkeeper Frank Borghi, formerly a minor league baseball catcher, made a series of last-ditch saves. England were like Wile E. Coyote chasing the Road Runner: they kept manoeuvring themselves into position, lining up their sights and … hey, where'd that damn bird go?

When assessed individually, each of the English forwards had more attempts on goal than the whole of the American team, who were reckoned to have mounted just two threatening attacks in the whole match. But that proved to be enough. On 37 minutes, a long

> **'It would be fair to give them three goals of a start.'**
> The *Daily Express* previews England v USA.

1950 WORLD CUP BRAZIL

Round One:

England 2 – 0 Chile
Mortensen 39
Mannion 51

England 0 – 1 USA
Gaetjens 38 (below, right)

England 0 – 1 Spain
Zarra 48

England's most shocking defeat of all time brought an ignominious early exit for Walter Winterbottom's squad, which included such luminaries as Stanley Matthews, Billy Wright and Stan Mortensen.

BERT WILLIAMS
Caps 24   Goals conceded 34

Bert 'the Cat' Williams was the man who conceded the only goal in England's epochal defeat to the USA, not that he could have done much about it. More gratifyingly, he also pulled off an astonishing save at Hampden Park to keep Scotland out of the same World Cup. The ever-lyrical Geoffrey Green described it elegantly in his 1953 book *Soccer: The World Game*. 'Imagine that searing shot, volleyed as only [Billy] Liddell can volley – those who have seen him shoot in this sort of mood will understand – and Williams's instinctive reflex action. It was a breathtaking moment. It was an answer as quick as thought itself, with Williams creating a picture of infinite grace as he leapt sideways and upwards as swift as a cat's leap, his yellow jersey lit by the fading sun, in a jack-knife action. One-handed he touched the searing ball over the white bar, finally to come to rest, a yellow splash against the green background. They talk about it still at Hampden.'

throw came in from the right, Walter Bahr shot towards goal – more in hope than in expectation – and Haitian centre-forward Joe Gaetjens sent a cruel deflection past Bert Williams (see left). There has been plenty of debate since then about whether the goal was intended. While the Americans credited Gaetjens with a brilliant diving header, other observers claimed that he wasn't even looking at the ball when it happened to cannon in off the back of his skull.

England upped their tempo after the interval, but their anxiety levels were rising as well. Mullen saw a header cleared from what seemed to be behind the goal-line – a foretaste, perhaps, of the Wembley controversy of 1966 – while Mortensen was brought down inside the penalty area by a tackle that one American defender cheerfully admitted was straight out of the NFL. 'Charlie bulldozed him all the way,' said American right-back Harry Keough. 'They both were at the penalty spot when they stopped. [Mortensen] was mad as hell – as anybody would have been.'

> **'Boy, I feel sorry for these bastards. How are they ever going to live down the fact we beat them?'**
> Harry Keough, the American right-back.

The Americans fell back and ran out the clock, helped by delighted Brazilian fans who passed the ball around mischievously whenever it was booted out of play. Eventually the whistle went, and the torture was over. 'Newspapers blazed all over the tiny stadium,' wrote Brian Glanville, 'a funeral pyre for English football.' Mannion expressed the feeling in the England camp most pithily. 'Bloody ridiculous. Can we play them again tomorrow?'

> **'The criticism was poured on us like boiling oil.'**
> Billy Wright on the reaction to England's World Cup flop.

If the American team thought their win would transform the status of the game back home, they were

> **'In affectionate remembrance of English Football which died in Rio on July 2, 1950. Duly lamented by a large circle of sorrowing friends and acquaintances. RIP. NB: The body will be cremated and the ashes taken to Spain.'**
>
> Mock obituary notice in the *Daily Herald*, after England crashed out of the 1950 World Cup.

disappointed. But it certainly raised Gaetjens's profile. Having begun the tournament as a restaurant dishwasher, he was able to parlay his moment of fame into a brief professional career with Arles and Racing Club de Paris. He then returned to Haiti, where he disappeared suddenly in 1964 – one of thousands of victims of 'Papa Doc' Duvalier and his Tonton Macoutes death squads. There are worse things, after all, than losing at football.

The final throe

That was not quite the end of England's World Cup. Dejected as they were, the players had one last chance to extend their campaign. If they beat Spain, back at the Maracanã, they could still qualify for a play-off to reach the second round.

Drewry finally agreed to reshuffle the team, calling up Matthews on the right wing and the pacy Jackie Milburn at centre-forward. The rumour was that Spain played a flat back four and could be vulnerable to the through ball. And so it proved when Milburn headed into the net after 14 minutes. Unfortunately, the linesman disallowed the goal for offside – a crass decision, in light of the fact that newsreels later showed a Spanish defender ahead of him.

England were almost as disgusted with the officiating in Brazil as they were with the hotel food. Winterbottom reckoned that Italy's Generoso Dattilo – who had refereed in Belo Horizonte – was so bad he should have been 'suspended for a lifetime'. For the Spanish match, they were allocated Giovanni Galeati, another Italian, and another libertarian. In the words of Eddie Baily, England's novice inside-left, 'the referee allowed an unbelievable amount of obstruction and shirt-pulling. I remember Alf [Ramsey], who had this thing about fair play, being furious.'

> **'England, it was thought, could win wearing bowler hats, carrying umbrellas, without raising perspiration.'**
> Geoffrey Green in *The Times*.

Referees remain one of football's imponderables, as do the performances of opposition goalkeepers. Having already suffered at the gloves of Borghi, England now ran into a brilliant display from Antonio Ramallets – 'the cat of Maracanã' – who showed all of Zamora's flair without the faultlines. Five minutes after half time, Telmo Zarra headed the only goal of the match, quite against the run of play. England's improvement had come too late to save them from ejection. They had been unfortunate, perhaps, but then ill-fortune has a habit of pursuing the ill-prepared.

> **'We were the better gentlemen, they were the better players.'**
> Stanley Rous after England's World Cup exit.

As Finney put it, in a typically clear-eyed assessment, the World Cup 'gave us an insight into how good the South American countries were. They were very skilful players and it was obvious you had little or no chance of playing against those sides in those days. We were by no means the best in the world. That was not true at all. The only reason you were probably thinking that was because you never played these sides, never saw anything about them because they were so far away.'

THE HUNGARIAN CONQUEST

Perversely, the fall-out from Belo Horizonte proved just how powerful the myth of English supremacy really was. England had just been spanked by the Yanks – a big enough shock, you might imagine, to splinter their international reputation into pieces. Yet the distances involved, plus the hostility of the conditions, allowed the FA quietly to gather up the fragments and glue them back together.

The football establishment applied the post-code rule – that favourite of unfaithful travellers around the world. If it happened in a different country, the rule states, it didn't happen at all. But this was always going to be a short-term solution. Sooner or later, a 'foreign' team was bound to succeed where Hitler's *Luftwaffe* and Philip II's Armada had failed, and score a decisive victory on English soil.

That day arrived soon enough. On 25 November 1953, England hosted Ferenc Puskás and his immortal Hungarian side at Wembley. The match was a rout: England lost 6–3, and were lucky to get that close. Their defence was cracked open like an oyster. Puskás's own first goal, fired in at the near post after some dazzling trickery, was the shot that was heard, if not around the world, then certainly around the nation.

The impact on the English game was crushing. Unlike the unseen Americans, Hungary had exposed England's failings in full view of every pundit, reporter and committee-man. Walter Winterbottom had spent the last few years trying to warn the FA's bigwigs that his team was falling behind. Only now did they finally believe him.

It was fitting that the Hungarians should have been the ones to burst England's bubble of complacency. Hungary had, after all, been among England's very first Continental opponents on Vivian Woodward's groundbreaking tour of 1908. They had learned from English coaches like Jimmy Hogan and Tottenham's Arthur Rowe. And they had grown into one of the greatest, most electrifying teams ever to play the game. According to backdated Elo rankings, Hungary's results over the early 1950s make them the pre-eminent side in the history of international football.

There should have been no shame in losing to a team this good, this imaginative, this inspirational. But what was embarrassing was that England went into the game with their eyes closed. If they had done their homework, they might have found out about the deep-lying centre-forward who acted as Hungary's attacking fulcrum. Instead, they fell back on the same hoary old tactics (if the application of studs to kneecaps can be dignified by such a title). Trouble was, they couldn't get close enough to land a kick.

The *Daily Mail*'s Brian James summed up the situation with his usual insight. 'Until now foreign footballers had been those

> '**Since the World Cup, I think we have shown that there isn't a great deal wrong with our game. Foreign teams still fear us.**'
>
> Billy Wright, in 1953, delivers a familiar-sounding mantra.

tricky clowns who did amazing things with the ball, but who couldn't shoot, wouldn't head the ball and didn't tackle.' Not any more. The secret was finally out – these foreign chappies could play a bit.

From denial to débâcle

Let's return to Brazil for a moment, and another opportunity missed. A sense of denial had been palpable from the moment England's defeated players trooped out of the Maracanã's half-finished changing-rooms. Excuses piled up like dead leaves. Referees, keepers, pitches, goalposts, hotels, even the damn bus drivers – everything had conspired against those plucky Englishmen. Really, it was a wonder they had collected any points at all.

> 'The sorriest feature in this drama is that the English, with very few exceptions, cannot get themselves to recognise what has happened. In their self-satisfaction and conceit they still fancy themselves the first in the football world and their defeats sheer accidents.'
>
> Ceve Linde, a distinguished Swedish writer, nails the English mindset.

For Stanley Matthews, the whole experience highlighted the narrow-mindedness of the English game. It wasn't so much the results that worried him; more the eagerness to pile onto the first plane home. 'British football could have learned much from the Brazilians and even the Uruguayans,' Matthews wrote, 'but the sad thing was that those in authority in our game didn't want to learn. I believe that had a detrimental effect on our game at all levels for a decade or more.'

Even the British pressmen, whose papers had paid some £750 to send a special correspondent to Rio, took no interest in the final stages. 'Could you imagine Britain's leading film critics leaving Cannes International Film Festival after the showing of the British films?' stormed the Austrian émigré Willy Meisl.

The media blackout meant that Winterbottom, back at home, had no way of keeping tabs on the second round of the tournament (which would be stolen from Brazil by unfancied Uruguay). His hasty exit proved to be as ill-judged as England's last-minute preparations. 'I should have stayed,' he would tell Ken Jones. 'There was no television coverage, and newspapers carried only the barest details. I'd passed up on the opportunity to be better informed about the game.'

There were plenty of 'experts' who had never left their living-rooms, yet were ready with instant opinions. Stan Cullis, now an influential manager of Wolverhampton Wanderers, reckoned it would be a mistake to get too carried away with the airs and graces of South American football. 'One style isn't necessarily superior to another,' he told Billy Wright and Jimmy Mullen when they returned to Molineux. 'We don't lack skill, far from it, but few can match us for spirit.'

As for the FA, they formed a sub-committee – that last resort of the boardroom scoundrel – and then promptly forgot about the whole thing. The administrators' response could have been summed up by Samuel Johnson's famous epigram: 'A fly, Sir, may sting a stately horse and make him wince; but one is but an insect, and the other is still a horse.'

If there was any change in attitude after 1950, it came from those other hovering parasites – the national football writers. Previously one-eyed cheerleaders for the England team, they now discovered a new sense of scepticism. 'When we didn't quite come up to scratch they wrote harder things,' said Eddie Baily. 'To my mind it was all to do with the World Cup. They'd given us this big build-up and when things went wrong they felt let down. After that it was never the same.'

Lofty scales the heights

In March 1941, a precocious, thick-set youth named Nat Lofthouse played his first match for Bolton Wanderers. His style could hardly have been more different from that of Roy Bentley, the man who would succeed him as England's No. 9. Bentley liked to lose his marker by dropping deep, but if Lofthouse ever tried anything that fancy, he risked a fearful earbashing from his boss.

> **'Let's hear no more of these Continental marvels, British is still best.'**
> Newspaper verdict on England's win in Austria, 1952.

'You couldn't trap a back of wet cement,' the Bolton manager roared at him one day. 'There are only three things you *can* do at this game. Run, shoot and head.' As Lofthouse would later admit, 'It's the best piece of advice I ever received. Yes I was a bit clumsy ... but put the ball between the centre-half and the full-back for me to run on to and I'd fancy my chances.'

The author David Winner portrays Lofthouse as a model suburbanite. 'His favourite food was Lancashire hot-pot … He liked rock gardening. He and his wife Alma's favourite hobby was making rugs.' When the Victorian schoolmasters dreamed up their sporting programme, this was the sort of paragon they were hoping to produce: a modest, home-loving sportsman whose idea of a big night out was a glass of beer. (Just one a week, mind you.)

In his private life, Lofthouse was as mild as a mouse. But once he crossed that white line, he became a fierce competitor who would earn national renown as 'The Lion of Vienna'. The nickname dates from May 1952, when England travelled to Austria to meet a side who were recovering some of their pre-war zest. The score was 2–2

with a few minutes to go, and the Austrians were pressing hard, when Finney sent Lofthouse bearing down on goal with a delicious through pass.

Lofthouse gives a vivid description in his autobiography. 'Just when I had decided to shoot, Musil, like a frightened stag, suddenly darted from his goal. At that precise moment I hit the ball hard to the right of the Austrian goal and then felt a searing pain in my right leg as the goalkeeper missed the ball and gave me a tremendous – but for all that accidental – kick on my shinbone. As I went sprawling on the dark turf I heard the crowd begin to roar. Then darkness came.'

This scrambled winner was entirely in character, as Lofthouse took an almost masochistic delight in launching himself at defenders. As he put it, 'I used to relish the 50–50 challenge, in the air or on the ground, with a big centre-half.' Amazingly, his opponents always seemed to accept their punishment in the same hearty spirit.

The citadel falls: England goalkeeper Gil Merrick attempts a save during an undistinguished personal performance against Hungary, 1953. It was the first time England had lost at home to 'foreign' opposition. England captain Billy Wright is on the left of the picture; Alf Ramsey can be seen through the net.

FERENC PUSKÁS
Caps 85 (for Hungary)   Goals 84

HUNGARY'S COACH ONCE shocked an English audience with the claim that, when Puskás was 15, four of his contemporaries were technically superior. 'We went with Puskás because of his temperament,' Sebes said. 'The play of the others could range between brilliant and mediocre. We knew that even on the worst day of his life Puskás's form would not drop below an acceptable level.' Puskás was certainly a battler rather than a bottler (though he was reported to have smashed a bottle on the forehead of Pinheiro, the Brazilian centre-half, after the notorious quarter-final of the 1954 World Cup). Yet he knew when to give up on Hungary. Come the Revolution – which briefly deposed Hungary's Communist government in October 1956 – he fled to Spain, along with team-mates Sandor Kocsis and Zoltan Czibor. Puskás joined Real Madrid, where he would remain for nine seasons, scoring a remarkable 180 goals. This marks the moment when Hungarian football fell off the edge of a cliff. They would never again produce a team to rival the *Aranycsapat* – or 'Golden Squad' – of the 1950s.

'THE TWILIGHT OF THE (SOCCER) GODS'

Daily Mirror headline, November 1953.

'He sort of made friends with them all,' said Lofthouse's Bolton team-mate Roy Hartle, 'and they stayed friends over the years. I think there was more friendship in the game in those days. You played against someone and it was tough, but at the end of the game everything was forgotten, and the next time you met, you'd shake hands and go out and play.'

Hungary like the wolf

In the summer of 1953, England was beginning to emerge from the rigours of austerity. Queen Elizabeth had been crowned, the Ashes had been recovered, and Mount Everest had been conquered by a British Commonwealth expedition. For the first time since VE-Day, the whole country was on a high.

The England football team, too, was beginning to enjoy itself. In the curious little interregnum between the 1950 World Cup and the Hungarian masterclass, England lost just two matches out of 25. When they belted Belgium 5–0 at Wembley in November 1952, the headline 'RECOVERY COMPLETE: ENGLAND ON TOP AGAIN', reflected the general self-satisfaction. Belo Horizonte was starting to fade from the memory like a bad dream.

The news-stands looked rather different on the morning of 26 November 1953. 'OUTCLASSED! – AND THESE ARE THE LESSONS' screamed one paper. 'WE ARE SOCCER PUPILS NOW' groaned another. The previous day, a European team had triumphed on English soil for the first time.

This was serious. England had been annihilated 6–3 by Hungary's 'Magnificent Magyars', who seemed to move the ball quicker than thought itself. There could be no talk of freaks, flukes and lax referees when each of the Hungarians so clearly had the beating of his opposite number. The truth was obvious to every spectator, journalist and administrator: the game had moved on, but England were not moving with it.

It was Hungary's sense of assurance that really rammed the message home. Almost half-an-hour into the match, Ferenc Puskás took the ball on the right side of the area. Aware that Billy Wright was closing fast, he used the sole of his favoured left boot to pull the ball back, rather than making the expected turn inside. As Geoffrey Green put it, in one of sports writing's immortal images, 'Wright went past him like a fire engine going to the wrong fire'. Forty years later, Wright and Puskás met for an anniversary celebration at Molineux, and a voice from the crowd called 'That's the nearest you ever got to him, Bill.'

Take a look at the match highlights (which are easily available on YouTube), and you will see a few contenders for any Goal of the Month competition. Nandor Hidegkuti's opener, buried after 90 seconds, was struck from the edge of the area after a dreamy dummy. As for Puskás's first goal, fired in at the near post after his exquisite drag-back, it remains one of the cheekiest in football history. The best players stand out because they have that bit of extra time. In this case, Puskás's deception gave him fully four seconds to measure his finish from the edge of the six-yard box.

> **'The game was so near to what I'd always had in mind that I almost purred.'**
>
> Ron Greenwood, the future England manager, was among those who put patriotism to one side while watching the 'Magnificent Magyars'.

The Hungarians clearly had a surfeit of skill, and a flair for movement off the ball. But what marked them out above previous European teams was the range and quality of their shooting. For once it was the Continentals who let fly from any distance, while the English forwards fussed and fretted in front of goal. 'We'd been fed the idea that foreign teams wanted to walk the ball into the net,' said the future Manchester United manager Dave Sexton, who watched the game from the stands. 'They [the Hungarians] clubbed the ball. People blamed Gil Merrick for not getting to shots struck from outside the penalty area ... but I wasn't so sure.'

Men against Martians

If watching the Brazilians had been an eye-opener in 1950, these Hungarians were something else again. Presented with such exotic skills, England's footballers must have felt like Christopher Columbus stumbling across his first Caribbean tribe. Only without the superior firepower.

Military conscription, which was compulsory in Hungary, was at the root of the Magyars' greatness. The team's meticulous coach, Gusztáv Sebes, arranged for the most promising youngsters to spend their national service in the village of Kispest, home of Budapest Honvéd FC. He then used the Hungarian league to experiment with new tactics and different combinations of players. The chosen ones would end up with sinecures in the army, which is how Puskás – who could barely handle a gun – came to be known as 'the Galloping Major'.

> **'Like playing people from outer space.'**
> Centre-half Syd Owen puts England's experience into words.

Sebes's hothousing techniques created football's answer to the Triffids. On their way to Wembley, Hungary amassed a run of 24 matches with only one defeat, which included gold medals at the Helsinki Olympiad of 1952. They arrived at Wembley on top of their game, highly motivated and exhaustively prepared. Warned about the consequences of failure by the Communist party bosses, Sebes had ordered one of Budapest's training pitches to be trimmed to the exact dimensions of Wembley.

Winterbottom could only envy Sebes's far-reaching authority and influence. The England manager did not even have a vote on the composition of his own team. Sebes, by contrast, could get a player released

> **'One of these days we shall wake up and find six goals in the back of our net.'**
> *Times* football correspondent Geoffrey Green in prescient mood, shortly before the Hungarians' visit to Wembley.

from gaol if he wanted to. Gyula Lorant, Hungary's central defender at Wembley, was a suspected dissident who was sprung from detention camp to fill that critical role.

'The difference between us and the Hungarians was simple,' Winterbottom said later. 'Their team had been together for years. Each week they used to assemble for three days to practise as an international team and went to play against the top clubs as such and went out on tours together. Not only were the players learning from each other, they were picking up the instinctive teamwork. We just met a couple of days before each game.'

> **'If a good player has the ball, he should have the vision to spot three options. Puskás always saw at least five.'**
>
> Jeno Buzanszky, Hungary's right-back, on the 'Galloping Major'.

What's in a number?

Hungary's shirt numbers provided the first hint of their progressive thinking. The England players, as paralysed by convention as ever, were still lining up in their old numbers – 2 and 3 for the full-backs, 4 to 6 for the halves and the rest for the forwards (see below). The advent of the WM formation was conveniently ignored.

```
    11      9      7
        10      8
        6      4
    3      5      2
        1
```

The Hungarians did things differently. In the early minutes of the Wembley clash – which was one of the first football matches to be broadcast on BBC television – commentator Kenneth Wolstenholme made a gently condescending aside. 'You might be mystified by some of the

Hungarian numbers,' he suggested quizzically. 'The reason is they number the players rather logically, with the centre-half as 3 and the backs as 2 and 4.' A few minutes later he remarked with amazement on how 'the outside-*left* Czibor came across to pick up the ball in the outside-right position'.

In fact, the Hungarians were so tightly drilled that they could shift their formation with breathtaking ease. Everyone knows about Puskás's Wembley masterstrike, but what is less often mentioned is that Puskás – theoretically an inside-left – picked up the ball mid-way inside his own half. After another six passes, involving six team-mates, it found its way

> **'The finest team ever to sort out successfully the intricacies of this wonderful game.'**
> Billy Wright on the 'Magnificent Magyars'.

back to him inside the area. Hungary's fluidity was reminiscent of Sindelar's great Austrian team. They were playing an updated version of the old 'Danubian Whirl'.

> **'The first half was a shambles. We never knew who to mark.'**
> Gil Merrick, England's hapless goalkeeper, on the Hungary débâcle.

'To the British fan,' wrote Willy Meisl, 'Hungary's game must have looked like soccer-telepathy. If one player had the ball, all his colleagues moved as if they saw a kind of "astral" ball which at any moment might materialize into the real leather globe at their feet.'

For all Puskás's gifts, Hungary's man of the match was Nandor Hidegkuti. Again, shirt numbers are relevant here. The English defenders treated Hidegkuti as a centre-forward because he wore 9, yet he had little in common with a bull-at-a-gate striker like Lofthouse. He preferred to hang-back as a deep-lying pivot, feeding passes up to 'inside-forwards' Puskás and Sandor 'Golden Head' Kocsis. As a result, the shape of Hungary's front five was closer to a 'U' than the

> # 'DISASTER ON THE DANUBE'
> *Daily Mirror* headline after England's 7–1 hiding in Budapest.

conventional 'W'. And the overall formation might best be described as a 4–2–4, comparable to the one Brazil would use to win the 1958 World Cup. For all Wolstenholme's enthusiasm, the numbers were all over the place.

```
11        10       8       7
               9
                        5
  4           6       2
           3
           1
```

Hungary's alignment might seem simple enough to modern fans, used as we are to Andy Gray doodling diagrams on the screen. But for Winterbottom's primitive England side, it was quite out of this world. Harry Johnston, the centre-half, didn't know where to put himself. If he followed Hidegkuti, 'it left a hole between the two full-backs,' wrote the tactical analyst Jonathan Wilson. 'If he sat off him, Hidegkuti was able to drift around unchallenged, dictating the play.'

> # 'On that performance, Hungary would have overrun any team in the world, but sitting there, watching goal after goal go in, I could only bury my head in my hands.'
> Walter Winterbottom on England's 7–1 defeat in Budapest.

'To me,' wrote Johnston in his autobiography, 'the tragedy was the utter helplessness ... being unable to do anything to alter the grim outlook.'

Another one in the eye

In some quarters, the 'Hungarian Conquest' of 1953 was humorously compared to 1066 and the Battle of Hastings. The last time England had lost at home, geddit? But not everyone could see the joke.

Within the ranks of professional football, a sense of panic spread. The match 'gave eyes to the blind', wrote Brian Glanville in the central chapter of his book *Football Nemesis*. 'All at once everyone was crying, "Wolf!" –

> **'Thoroughbreds against carthorses.'**
> Tom Finney's verdict on the Budapest defeat.

everyone was wise, everyone was casting around for scapegoats and explanations, everyone, in short, had discerned the crisis which had existed for over thirty years.'

The Football League clubs were finally spurred into action. Typically, though, they set out on completely the wrong course. The perception was that continental players 'lasted' better than their English counterparts, who thus needed extra conditioning. As fitness was promoted up the agenda, the fiendish pace set by Middlesbrough's trainer Charlie Cole had one player exclaiming 'What are we training for, Charlie? The ruddy Grand National?' Yet no-one seemed too worried about Puskás's casual facility with keepy-ups. The Hungarians' 'jugglery' would have graced the *Cirque du Soleil.*

The International Selection Committee reacted to disaster with their usual level of composure. That is, none at all. Six members of England's shamefaced XI would never represent their country again, including Ramsey (who always claimed that Merrick should have saved at least three of Hungary's goals) and the unfortunate Johnston. But if the selectors thought a change of personnel would bring a change of fortune, they were quickly disabused. In May 1954, England travelled to Budapest for a return fixture. This time, they lost 7–1 – a result that remains the heaviest defeat in England's history.

Winterbottom's only tactical adjustment was to instruct Syd Owen, England's new centre-half, to stick to Hidegkuti at all costs. But if Owen managed to keep his man relatively quiet (Hidegkuti scored just one goal this time, as opposed to the three he rifled home at Wembley), the absence of any dedicated central defender left a gaping hole in the middle. Like the commander of some apocalyptic cavalry, the Galloping Major led his cohorts through the gap.

Once again, English self-esteem took a terrible pummelling. It was almost as if the sun had gone down on the Empire. Alan Hoby, football correspondent of the *Sunday People*, struck an elegiac note. 'As I glanced up at the Magyar banners and rows of red flags waving side by side I saw, forlorn and faded, a lonely Union Jack flying above the radio stand. It … re-emphasised for me the difference in the football techniques of the two nations – one bright and shining, the other feeble and faltering.'

Switzerland '54: no saving grace

Like fried breakfasts and herbaceous borders, steady goalkeepers are one of the things we pride ourselves on in this country. Just think of Frank Swift, Gordon Banks or Peter Shilton, each of whom developed a worldwide reputation as a safe pair of hands. But turn the coin over, and there have been just as many bloopers as troupers. What about Peter Bonetti in the Mexico quarter-final of 1970? David Seaman and Ronaldinho's free kick? Scott Carson and … well, you know the rest.

The fact is that English keepers are just as prone to untimely brain-fades as their Continental cousins. Just ask Gil Merrick. It was always going to be difficult for Merrick to come back from the two Hungarian hidings, particularly after certain players – Ramsey chief among them – had tried to pin all the blame on him. But what made his job especially tricky was the timing of it all. Just three weeks after the Budapest trip, England were off to Switzerland for the 1950 World Cup.

Merrick's struggles began in the opening match against Belgium, opponents England had repeatedly savaged over the previous three decades. This time they went 3–1 up, largely through the inspiration of Matthews, who had a vintage game on the wing. But the defence was horribly porous. Even after extra-time, England had to settle for a 4–4 draw.

1954 WORLD CUP SWITZERLAND

Round One:
England 4 – 4 Belgium (a.e.t.)

Broadis 26, 63	*Anoul 5, 71*
Lofthouse 36, 91	*Coppens 67*
	Dickinson (o.g.) 94

England 2 – 0 Switzerland
Mullen 43
Wilshaw 69

Quarter-final:
England 2 – 4 Uruguay

Lofthouse 16	*Borges 5, Varela 39, Schiaffino 46*
Finney 67	*Ambrois 78*

After a high-scoring draw and getting the rub of the green in a closely contested round one, England were put to the sword by the cup-holders Uruguay.

Ralph Finn, a journalist travelling with the England side, identified the problems at the back. 'Merrick, who has served England well in his time, has become shaky,' Finn wrote, 'and cannot be depended upon to pull off the brilliant out-of-the-bag save which can save a team by giving it confidence in its last line of resistance.' His verdict was endorsed by Matthews, who pointed out that 'When your goalkeeper is not playing with confidence or dominating his penalty area, the whole team senses it.'

The peculiar format of the tournament meant that England could still qualify for the second round by beating Switzerland, the hosts. They did so with relative comfort, easing home 2–0 after a rare tactical masterstroke from Winterbottom, who moved Wright to centre-half. But that only sent them through to face Uruguay, the holders. And with

D O N   R E V I E
Caps 6   Goals 4

REVIE IS BEST REMEMBERED NOW as one of four managers to pass through England's revolving door during the 1970s. But in his playing days, he was the first Englishman to emulate Hidegkuti's floating role behind

the forwards. The idea was hatched by Manchester City manager Les McDowall ahead of the 1954–5 season, and became known as the 'R-plan'. Winterbottom tried to follow suit with England, but he would have needed the full co-operation of the other players, not to mention the selectors, to build a team around Revie's deftness and vision. And that was never going to be forthcoming. Stanley Matthews was one who objected, writing that 'Don played very close to me and rather than complementing each other, we got in each other's way'. Even so, the system had one fine hour, when England beat Scotland 7–2 at Wembley in 1955. The *Glasgow Herald* reported that Cumming, the Scottish right-half, was 'enticed out of position by the roving Revie [and] never seemed to be doing anything but chasing. The gap for [right-back] Haddock to try to cope with could have contained the Irish Guards'.

Merrick now a ghostly presence in goal, the task was too great. Within five minutes, Uruguay were ahead through what Matthews called 'a soft one which crept in past Gil at his near post'. Perhaps an in-form Swift could have kept the opposition at bay, but Merrick conceded three more goals to complete a 4–2 reverse.

For the second World Cup running, England had gone out after playing their best football of the tournament. 'Some of our moves were almost Hungarian in style,' wrote Finn. 'We went down, but how gallantly we went down. And we could easily have won.'

> **'On his day, Merrick was as good as any, but he was prone to errors we could not afford. He was one of my big mistakes.'**
> Walter Winterbottom on goalkeeper Gil Merrick, villain of the 1954 World Cup.

Note the adverb: gallantly. In later years, the same word would come to accompany every England exit from a major tournament. Talk of battling rearguards has become a defensive reflex, a desperate attempt to soften the blow. But failure is still failure, no matter how grandly you dress it up.

BROKEN DREAMS

On 6 February, 1958, the whole tenor of England's decade changed in an instant. The previous eight years had been a story of hapless pratfalls and pompous dignitaries – a sort of Ealing comedy with shinpads. But the mood switched to the most sombre of tragedies when the plane carrying Manchester United home from a European Cup tie crashed on its take-off from Munich.

Travel was a dangerous business in those innocent, low-tech times. Just think of Dixie Dean and his head-on collision on the road to north Wales. Or Johnny Haynes and Ted Dexter – respective England captains of football and cricket in the 1960s – who would each wreck a knee-joint in a car accident and never play for their country again.

Unpleasant as they were, such routine snarl-ups pale beside the horror of the Munich air disaster. It is hard to over-emphasise its impact on the English game. Twenty-three people lost their lives. Among them were Roger Byrne – the full-back who was expected to captain England at the upcoming World Cup – and Tommy Taylor, the best centre-forward in the country.

Above all, the disaster robbed England of a gilded youth named Duncan Edwards. Already an automatic choice at the age of 21, Edwards's nascent career was clearly destined for greatness. His debut had come at the tender age of 18 years and 183 days, but even at that stage he towered over most of his opponents, both physically and technically.

'From the moment I first saw Duncan as a boy of fourteen, he had the assurance of a man,' said Manchester United's assistant coach Jimmy Murphy, 'with legs like tree trunks, a deep and powerful chest and a matchless zest for the game. I must have seen thousands of players but there was only one Duncan Edwards. Wing-half, centre-half, inside-forward – he could fill all these positions with the composure of a great natural footballer.'

There is always a danger of exaggerating the qualities of those who die young. They are the 'late greats', always preserved in aspic, always remembered with the same rosy glow that pervades their obituaries. In the imagination they never fade or lose their way – as so many great sportsmen have done in the twilight of their careers. But Sir Bobby Charlton, one of the survivors of the Munich crash, has always firmly denied that this rule applied to Edwards.

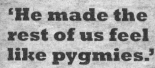

'He made the rest of us feel like pygmies.'
Bobby Charlton on Duncan Edwards.

'Sentiment can throw a man's judgement out of perspective,' Charlton said in 1999, at the unveiling ceremony of a statue in Edwards's native Dudley. 'Yet it is not the case with him . . . Duncan Edwards was the greatest. I see him in my mind's eye and I wonder that anyone should have so much talent.'

A pride of young lions

Edwards's finest England performance came in 1956 in Berlin – a few hours' drive from the Munich hospital where, just two years later, he would succumb to his injuries. Urging his team forward like a helmsman in heavy seas, Edwards surged past three West German defenders to open the scoring with a 30-yard humdinger. 'There have been few individual performances to match what he produced that day,' said Billy Wright. 'Duncan tackled like a lion, attacked at every opportunity and topped it off with that cracker of a goal.'

England won 3–1, and the next morning's German newspapers were full of militaristic imagery. Edwards was repeatedly compared to a tank. One writer nicknamed him 'Boom boom' on account of the 'Big Bertha shot in his boots'. Only two years earlier, the Germans had bumped and barged their way to the 1954 World Cup title. Now they clearly recognised something of themselves in this strapping Anglo-Saxon archetype.

For modern fans, descriptions of Edwards's barnstorming runs often evoke the image of Steven Gerrard in full flow, brushing opponents aside as he closes in on goal. There is even a facial resemblance between the two men, who were born within 20 miles of each other. But England's team for Berlin also included a player of contrasting delicacy, an aesthete of the greensward. Johnny Haynes, only two years older than Edwards, was emerging as a gifted inside-right at Fulham, where his trademark was the perfectly weighted through-ball. If Edwards bombarded defences, Haynes tied them up with a silken cord.

This was a moment full of promise for Winterbottom, whose under-23 team was beginning to bear fruit. Even after Edwards's tragic death, England's squad for the 1958 World Cup in Sweden would still contain 12 graduates from this finishing school. Strangely, though, the man who went on to become perhaps the greatest English midfielder of all – Bobby Charlton – would not feature in the World Cup finals at all. Caricatured by his critics as a player who could not last the full 90 minutes, Charlton did win a call-up to Sweden, but ended up watching the whole tournament from the stands.

Back down to earth

The Munich air disaster has since become one of the great 'what-if' stories of English sport – particularly where Edwards is concerned. Even at 21, the boy-genius was already installed as Billy Wright's natural successor, both as centre-half and captain. We think of Bobby Moore as the iconic captain of 1966, yet if that plane had taken off, Moore might never even have played for England.

In this parallel universe, it could have been Edwards leading England to World Cup glory. The only question is, which World Cup? But for the misery of Munich, they would have been strong contenders for the 1958 tournament. Even Winterbottom, usually so guarded about his team's prospects, had an inkling of greatness as the finals loomed. After a 4–0 victory over France in November 1957, he pulled Wright to one side and whispered 'Bill, I think we have a team that could make a really telling challenge for the world championship.'

The feeling was shared by Johnny Haynes, who had emerged as the string-puller of the team. 'The more experienced players began to think around this time that we really had a very fine chance to do something in the World Cup Finals,' Haynes wrote. 'We never discussed it, but I am sure we were all aware of it, and I am sure Walter Winterbottom was. He never made the point, but I think he spent that winter impatiently waiting for the summer to come, to prove finally that the combination he had found would succeed.'

With Edwards, Taylor and Byrne forming England's backbone, Winterbottom would have had a real beast of a squad. Instead, he was left with a mishmash, a side that was neither fish nor fowl. The tournament was only four months away when Manchester United's antiquated aircraft ploughed off the end of the Munich runway and hit an unoccupied house. According to Haynes, 'the England team was shattered. Each of these Manchester United boys was so much larger than life that I think everyone in the whole country was touched in some way, and we who had played with them in a score or more of games for England didn't merely lose team-mates – we lost friends. Psychologically, no one can stand up to that kind of thing without changing in some way.'

After such a traumatic lead-up, England were always likely to struggle in Sweden. In the event, they failed to win a single match, eking out three successive draws in the group phase, and then losing to the USSR in a play-off. The one moment of satisfaction was an attritional 0–0 against Brazil, the eventual champions. This was a rare, indeed unprecedented instance of England going into a match with a customised tactical plan. Bill Nicholson, Winterbottom's assistant, was sent away to scout out the opposition, and came up with a man-for-man marking system that brought in Don Howe as a second centre-half and sat Bill Slater, a cerebral midfielder, on Brazil's playmaker Didi. Perhaps the lessons of Wembley and Budapest were beginning to be absorbed after all.

> **'They are a team of hard fighters, and pure football teams do not win the World Cup.'**
>
> Sepp Herberger, West Germany's coach, tipped England to lift the Jules Rimet trophy in 1958. But that was before the Munich air disaster ...

Talking a good game: Walter Winterbottom, England's longest-serving and longest-winded manager, addresses his players during a practice match against Fulham at Craven Cottage, 1961.

'There are so many things wrong with British football and so few things right that I can quite honestly state that I have no desire to be capped again.'

Len Shackleton in his autobiography *The Clown Prince of Soccer* (1955).

'IT'S A GOLDEN DRAW: THOSE SUPERB SEÑORS HELD BY ENGLAND', crowed the *Daily Herald*. It might even have been a golden victory if England had been granted a penalty when their giant centre-forward Derek Kevan was upended in the penalty area. Kevan crashed to the ground like the original tree in the forest, but judging by the referee's nonchalant denials, nobody heard him fall.

1958 WORLD CUP SWEDEN

Round One:
England 2 – 2 USSR
Kevan 66 *Simonyan 13*
Finney 85 (pen.) *Ivanov 55*

England 0 – 0 Brazil

England 2 – 2 Austria
Haynes 56 *Koller 16*
Kevan 73 *Körner 70*

Play-off:
England 0 – 1 USSR
Ilyin 68

An England side tragically depleted by the death of key Manchester United players in the Munich air crash earlier that year performed creditably but failed to beat Russian goalkeeper Lev Yashin (right) in the first-round playoff match.

LEN SHACKLETON
Caps 5   Goals 1

SHACKLETON WAS ONE OF THE MOST skilful players England has produced. Tommy Lawton rated him as 'the only man to approach Matthews's ball control'. But he was also the most insubordinate bugger ever to pull on a pair of boots. In a line-up of all the great football mavericks who have clashed with their team-mates, managers and club chairmen, Shackleton must be top of the list. In his autobiography – which was entitled *The Clown Prince of Football* – he famously called one

Lev Yashin, the Eastern blocker

In 1945, when Moscow Dynamo came to England and demonstrated the short-passing style they called *passovotchka*, the Soviets had shown themselves to be artistic, acrobatic footballers. Yet their performance against England during the group stage of the 1958 World Cup was more Cold War than *glasnost*. Tom Finney, still the best player on the park at 36, had been kicked and raked until his legs were covered in bruises. The

of the chapters 'The Average Director's Knowledge of Foot-ball', then left the following page blank. He also suggested that referees would be better off if the players' numbers were written in Braille, among other remarks too humorous to mention. Shackleton spent more time in the awkward squad than the England squad, though he did win five inter-national caps, most notably when world champions West Germany came to Wembley in 1954. This game featured what Shackleton reckoned to be his finest goal, when he chipped goalkeeper Fritz Herkenrath – a tactic still virtually unknown in those days – with the most delicate of touches. 'Len Shackleton was the greatest personality I ever saw on a football field,' wrote Johnny Haynes. 'If every game had not been a personal exhibition match for Shack, if he had had a bit more devil in his play and a greater urge for goals and for victory for his team, I would say he could have been the greatest inside-forward of them all.'

next day, it took him 10 minutes to make it to the bathroom. His contribution to the tournament was over.

The rematch, played at the same stadium in Gothenburg, was even more frustrating. This was another of those England exits, familiar both to ancients and moderns, where some promising attacking play was foiled by the brilliance of the opposition keeper. In this case, the obstacle was Lev Yashin, a 6ft 3in giant whose all-black outfit had earned him the nickname of 'the Black Spider'. Recently voted the best keeper of the 20th century, Yashin was harder to pass than the Berlin Wall.

The best England could manage was to hit the post twice, through the Chelsea winger Peter Brabrook. This was another hard-luck story: when the Soviets also hit the post, capitalising on a poor clearance from English keeper Colin McDonald, the ball bounced sideways and trickled in. 'We were bitterly disappointed,' Don Howe would tell the journalist

Ken Jones. 'We played our best football in that game and deserved to win.'

Just to rub it in, England would be outlasted at the tournament by both Wales and Northern Ireland, each of whom won their play-off match to progress to the quarter-finals. Long-serving captain Billy Wright was left to mull over what might have been. 'In 1950 we knew nothing,' he said. 'In 1954 we had found out a bit more, by 1958 we would have caught up even more had we not lost the guts of the side at Munich. We didn't give so much away in defence now, we were just that shade short of ideas in attack.'

Sticks, stones and Sputniks

In 1958, the World Cup came of age. Once regarded as a footling sideshow, it was now gaining acceptance as the one true test of a nation's footballing prowess. A rival, even, to the all-round sporting fiesta of the Olympic Games.

This shift was reflected in some increasingly frenzied reporting. Back in 1954, England's quarter-final exit had been received more in sorrow than in anger. Four years later, the mood had changed. According to the author Niall Edworthy, post-imperial England was 'still coming to terms with its falling status in the new world order, [and] the failure of its national football team was interpreted as just one more example of the country's decline. The gentlemanly tone that characterised coverage of England in the immediate post-war years had given way to something altogether more vicious and vitriolic.'

> **'They lack class, but, as always, they have the hearts of lions.'**
>
> Vittorio Pozzo, the great Italian manager, salutes England's spirit after their opening match of the 1958 World Cup, a 2–2 draw with Russia.

The salvos began a month before the World Cup, when England lost 5–0 on a blazing hot day in Belgrade. 'For eleven staggered, crushed Englishmen – and a handful of their stunned countrymen in the stands – it was the funeral pyre of their World Cup dreams,' wrote Peter Lorenzo in the *Daily Herald* (later the *Sun*). 'On today's form our chances in Sweden have gone up in the smoke of those flaming torches that still smoulder around me

J O Y   B E V E R L E Y

'LORD HELP THE MISTER / who comes between me and my sisters' sang the Beverley Sisters, much to Billy Wright's alarm. The first celebrity to become a footballer's wife, Joy Beverley (above, centre) met Wright in April 1958. Her son Vincent was a football fan, and it had been arranged for the England captain to show him around Molineux. Three months later, the couple were married. Despite elaborate attempts at secrecy, the registry office was surrounded by at least 6000 well-wishers, including most of the national press. Mr and Mrs Wright have been described as 'Posh and Becks in black and white', but their characters could hardly have been more different from the camera junkies we know today. Wright was a self-effacing sort of chap, both on the field and off, and he found the extra attention excruciating.

as I write this, the saddest soccer dispatch I have ever had to send from foreign soil.'

The odd thing, to modern eyes at least, is that blame was rarely laid at the manager's door. The reporters all knew that Winterbottom didn't pick the team, and no-one was particularly interested in the nonentities who did. So they fixed their sights on the players instead. The first target was Derek Kevan, the blond Frankenstein who led the forward line. When Kevan was selected for the final World Cup warm-up against Russia, Lorenzo was appalled. 'Pass the vodka! Send me zooming in a Sputnik. I've just been told the England team are to meet Russia on Sunday and I just can't believe it.'

Even Kevan's biggest supporters admitted that he lacked subtlety. In fact, he made Nat Lofthouse look like Leonardo da Vinci. But he was also huge and uncompromising, the sort of striker defenders hate having to mark. And when he scored twice in the opening round, he was suddenly rehabilitated, becoming 'giant-hearted' and a 'never-say-die hero'.

Now the cross-hairs moved on to England's link-men: Haynes at inside-right, Bobby Robson at inside-left, and Bryan Douglas on the right wing. All three were said to be jaded after their clubs (Fulham, Fulham and Blackburn Rovers respectively) had spent the previous season battling for promotion from Division Two. 'I never felt stale or tired,' Haynes wrote bitterly. 'But then, perhaps I don't know if I play well. Perhaps only the experts in the stands and Press seats and TV booths know about that.'

> **'Not since Romulus and Remus has there been such a dist-inguished Wolf.'**
>
> Baron Brabazon of Tara, a Tory peer, salutes Billy Wright – of England and Wolverhampton Wanderers – on the occasion of his 100th international cap.

As so often, the journalists fixed on a player who was not getting a game – Bobby Charlton – and built him up as the solution to all England's problems. Still only 20, Charlton had made an instant impact on his debut two months earlier, scoring with a screaming 20-yard volley that had prompted the Scottish goalkeeper to rush out and shake his hand. His contributions were eye-catching, but they were also erratic, as Bob Ferrier – one of the more dispassionate reporters on the tour – has since made clear.

'[Charlton's] method of loitering with intent, of drifting around hoping for a scoring strike to turn up, made one wonder if that alone would be enough in a team which, because of its lack of general class, now demanded solid and continuous work from everyone,' wrote Ferrier in his book *Soccer Partnership: Walter Winterbottom and Billy Wright*. 'It seemed England would have to "carry" Bobby Charlton solely for his scoring potential, or discard him in favour of a better all-round and more workmanlike performer.'

> **'Everyone in England thinks we have a God-given right to win the World Cup.'**
> An exasperated Johnny Haynes, writing in 1962.

The same thinking had underpinned England's decision – hatched together by Winterbottom and chief selector Joe Mears – to leave Charlton among the reserves. But such rigorous arguments do not sit well on the back pages of a thrusting newspaper. Most of the pressmen remained convinced that Charlton should have been introduced, and wrote – somewhat inaccurately and irresponsibly – that the player himself was furious. When Winterbottom returned home, he found even his young son asking the same question. 'Dad, why didn't you pick Bobby Charlton?'

Bloodsuckers ahoy!

The summer of 1958 was a tough time to be an England footballer. The inkwells of Fleet Street had turned decidedly poisonous. But if the players thought the fuss would die down, they were wrong. When they toured South America the following year, and lost three consecutive matches, the critics pumped the volume up another notch. According to a gleeful Sam Leitch, another hatchet-man from the *Daily Herald*, England had been 'beaten in Brazil, pulverised in Peru and now mauled in Mexico'.

Leitch represented a new breed of football writer. He bashed his typewriter keys hard, and he bashed the players even harder. 'We are faced everywhere we go with guffaws, giggles and groans,' he wrote, as England flew on to Los Angeles. 'Even the Yanks are saying this team is a shambles.' The England captain Billy Wright was too charming to bite back, but the verdict on Leitch in his autobiography – 'a very sharp nose for the lively angle' – is as delicate a euphemism as you could hope to find.

The biggest trashing followed the match in Lima, where England went down 4–1. Losing to Brazil was one thing, but few back in England even knew Peru had a team. As Bob Ferrier put it, 'Peru meant Incas and llamas. Football? – never.'

Inevitably, Leitch took the lead, his prose phasing through purple and into some unseen spectrum as he strained to convey the full horror of the match. 'Struggling, pathetic shame oozed out of every England football boot here at the foot of the Andes mountains tonight as a lightweight, slap-happy side from the ten First Division teams of Peru thrashed us in a game which could so easily have ended 8–1. Beside me as I type, people jab at me through the twelve-foot high steel fence which protects us from the crowd. They beam and ask: Is this really the first national side from England?'

The most jarring note in the whole piece was Leitch's use of the word 'us'. Up until this moment, there had still been a feeling of 'We're all in this together' about England's newspaper coverage, encouraged by the fact that several correspondents were former players. But Leitch and his fellow leeches ended all that. Somewhere around the turn of the decade, the relationship polarised into two warring factions: scribblers v dribblers. And from there, it was just a short step to donkeys and turnips on the *Sun*'s back page.

Greaves finds his groove

England's lone goal against Peru may not have seemed too significant at the time, but it heralded the coming of another legendary striker. The ball was buried from the edge of the six-yard box by 19-year-old Jimmy Greaves, a cheeky Cockney with a celestial left foot. 'Jimmy Greaves was the greatest goal-scorer of all time,' wrote Tommy Lawton in 1973. 'People still discuss his work rate [but] I wouldn't care a lot about his work rate if he was scoring 30 goals a season. He could have pneumonia for the first 85 minutes as long as he scored two goals in the last five.'

For those who remember him from Saturday-morning TV, Greaves will always be a seedy-looking uncle in bad knitwear. But to defenders of the 1960s, he was no laughing matter. Greaves was the original fox in the box, using his fiendish acceleration to fasten onto the ball and zip it low into the far corner. Then he would change into his Carnaby Street threads and emerge from the dressing-room as a dashing Sixties hipster, bouncing from Annabel's to Soho like an English George Best.

Since the Second World War, England's centre-forwards had generally been hulking hit-men, selected for their aerial prowess. Greaves was a different sort of player, just 5ft 8in and happier with a weighted

> ## 'When Jimmy plays as he did that day I find myself wondering if there has ever been a player like him in the entire history of the game.'
>
> Johnny Haynes on Jimmy Greaves, who scored a hat-trick in England's 9–3 demolition of Scotland.

through-ball than a high cross from the corner flag. 'Greaves is tremendously fast but deceptively fast,' wrote Johnny Haynes, who specialised in delivering those passes. 'When he is moving with the ball defenders often look like reaching him but in fact they never get close, so smoothly does he accelerate. And when he is in shooting position, all this hectic speed seems to vanish and everything stops and he has all the time in the world to score.'

These uncanny gifts came to the fore in the Home Championship of 1960–1, which saw England romp to the title with a goal difference of plus 13. You have to go back to the late 19th century for the last time they managed that. Credit is due here to Winterbottom, who made a tactical shift to the 4–2–4 formation pioneered by Brazil at the last World Cup. The system lent itself to a measured approach through the middle, and suited the Haynes–Greaves axis perfectly. Both men enjoyed their best seasons with England, peaking in a 9–3 thrashing of Scotland that remains the heaviest defeat in Scottish history.

177

'There was no suggestion of a weak link anywhere in England's ranks,' wrote Ian Wooldridge in his *Sunday Dispatch* report. 'But if I had to choose two men to honour individually then it must be the two inside forwards provided by London clubs. Johnny Haynes, a magnificent general probing every weakness in Scotland's defence before deluging it with a stream of passes; Jimmy Greaves, a spritely genius who gave a Stefano-class[1] performance of ball control which made 100,000 fans gasp in disbelief.'

The fall guy that day was Frank Haffey, Scotland's third-choice goalkeeper, who became the punchline of a topical joke. 'What's the time?' ran the question. 'Nearly ten past Haffey.' In a foretaste of certain pizza advertisements, Haffey even posed for newspaper photographs in front of Big Ben, with his hands held at nine minutes past the hour. But the shame could not be laughed away so easily; within two years, Haffey had fled Scotland for Australia, where he became a cabaret singer. In 1999, he bumped into Denis Law at a function Down Under, and reportedly asked 'Is it safe to come back now, Denis?'

> **'ENGLAND DO THEIR WORST: ENERGY NIL, COURAGE NIL, PRIDE NIL.'**
> *Daily Mail* headline after England's 2–1 loss to Hungary in the 1962 World Cup.

Chile con Greavsie

In Billy Wright's autobiography, released early in 1962, the author suggested that the all-conquering England side of 1960–1 was the best he had seen since the war, a fraction ahead of the 1958 team that had been cut off in its prime by the Munich disaster.

Wright also gave his prediction for the 1962 World Cup. 'The side we send to Chile will be the strongest yet to have represented us at the World Cup,' he wrote. But that did not mean he was backing England for the title. 'When the World Cup is held in South America I would normally expect a South American side to win it.'

1: Alfredo di Stefano was Real Madrid's roaming centre-forward, generally considered one of the half-dozen greatest players of all.

'Number ten takes the corners, number ten takes the throw-ins, number ten does everything. So what do we do? We put a man on number ten. Goodbye England.'

Lajos Barotis, the Hungarian coach, reveals his tactics for Johnny Haynes ahead of the 1962 World Cup.

Wright's typically measured judgement would be borne out by events. There was nothing wrong with England's selection this time. They retained seven players from the glory year of 1960–1, and added the sterling defensive qualities of Ray Wilson and Bobby Moore. But it was that familiar story – brilliant on paper, flaky on grass. From the opening match, which they lost 2–1 to a limited Hungary side, England put themselves under serious pressure. Because they could only manage second place in their qualifying group, they had to play Brazil in the quarter-finals – and that was the one draw nobody wanted.

Looking back after the tournament, Haynes felt that England's build-up had been disrupted by Greaves's ground-breaking move from Chelsea to AC Milan in 1961. The transfer turned out to be a failure: Greaves hated the po-faced training regime instigated by Nereo Rocco, Milan's puritanical manager. (At one point, Rocco resorted to nailing Greaves's hotel door shut to keep him away from the nightlife, but he only climbed out of the window instead.) Four months later, Greaves returned to London to play for Spurs, but his dalliance with Italy had still cost him a full international season.

'This was the small tragedy which hit the team and which it may not have thrown off in time for the matches in Chile in the summer of 1962,' Haynes wrote. 'The rhythm was broken, the fast, open, direct forward work was gone.'

1962 WORLD CUP CHILE

Round One:
England 1 – 2 Hungary
Flowers 60   Tichy 17
                    Albert 61 (pen.)

England 3 – 1 Argentina
Flowers 17   Sanfilippo 81 (pen.)
Charlton 42
Greaves 67 (below)

England 0 – 0 Bulgaria

Quarter-final:
England 1 – 3 Brazil
Haynes 38   Garrincha 31, 59
                    Vavá 53

A solid first-round performance that left England in second qualifying spot in their group (behind Hungary) brought a quarter-final in which they were well beaten by the coming force in international football – and ultimate champions of this tournament – Brazil.

Dog days in Vina del Mar

England's best performance at the 1962 World Cup – indeed, their best in any World Cup to date – came in their second match against Argentina. The surprise promotion of Alan Peacock, a Middlesbrough striker with no international experience, paid off in a confident 3–1 win. In the *News of the World*, Frank Butler called it the finest showing he had seen from England overseas.

Yet Butler's enthusiasm was short-lived. England leaked momentum all the way through their 0–0 draw with Bulgaria – a sterile match which has been reckoned among the most boring in history. And then they had to meet Brazil – the reigning champions – in the coastal resort of Vina del Mar. With Pelé absent because of a groin injury, the game turned into a masterclass from Garrincha, Brazil's right-wing. Garrincha had been a

A pair of legends: Garrincha (left) and Bobby Charlton were the most valuable players of the 1962 and 1966 World Cups respectively. Charlton was knighted for services to football in 1994; Garrincha, who slept with hundreds of women and sired at least 14 children, is alleged to have lost his virginity to a goat.

childhood polio sufferer, and his brother gave him his nickname – which means 'little bird', or, more colloquially, 'cripple' – on account of his twisted legs. He limped when he walked, but with a football in front of him, he was miraculously transformed from a pigeon into a swift.

Garrincha had Stanley Matthews's ability to nonplus defenders, but allied that to greater pace and power, as well as a centre-forward's eye for goal. Against England, he must have had a dozen attempts. Two went in directly – a header and a ripping 30-yard shot – while a long-range free kick bounced off the goalkeeper's chest for Vavá to tap in.

'I was inclined to think that this was bad defensive play,' wrote Haynes of Garrincha's first goal. 'But Bobby Charlton insisted afterwards that it was a perfect goal, the corner-kick and the header both beautifully timed and executed. If anyone was to blame he said it was him for not keeping closely in touch with Garrincha.'

This time, there had been no hard-luck factor about England's exit. They had been beaten 3–1 by an immeasurably better team. The omens had been there since the first few minutes, when a stray dog found its way onto the pitch and ran rings around the English defenders. In the end, Greaves got down on his knees and snagged the invader, which responded by urinating all over his shirt. Some suggested it was the most valuable contribution Greaves would make all day.

'The man with two left feet.'

Journalist Norman Giller on Garrincha, whose legs both bowed to the left.

The best that can be said of England's campaign was that nobody died. (Although centre-half Peter Swan came horribly close when he contracted dysentery and received the wrong treatment from local doctors.) Morale in the camp was low. Greaves was disgusted with the team's lodgings at a high-altitude mining station. 'To have our meals,' he complained, 'we had to walk from our barrack-style quarters across a narrow, rickety wooden bridge with a 500-foot drop either side. It was great for building up an appetite.'

Even beyond the blinkered confines of the England camp, the 1962 World Cup was a disappointing competition. The country was in the grip of economic depression. Crowds were sparse. Tactics, from most teams, were stiflingly defensive. Brutal tackles accounted for three broken legs within the first two days. It all made for an even thinner atmosphere than the one England had grown used to in their mountain retreat.

On returning to England, the players bade farewell to Walter Winterbottom, who was stepping down to take up a post at the Central Council of Physical Recreation. Winterbottom had been England's professor, endearingly nutty but just a bit too nice. As Bobby Charlton put it, 'Walter had this impeccable accent, whereas football's a poor man's game, players expect to be sworn at.'

'WORLD WAR!'
Headline in Chilean newspaper after Chile's first-round punch-up with Italy, which produced two red cards and a broken nose.

Even so, every England fan owes a debt to this modest, persevering pilgrim. It is hard to imagine that anyone else could have achieved so much with so little power. Winterbottom had modernised the whole structure of the English game, introducing junior national teams and a culture of coaching that his acolytes – Bill Nicholson and Jimmy Adamson among them – would carry back into the Football League. He changed England's formation, and he changed their mindset too.

Yet more was still needed, as the travails of Chile had made abundantly clear. In the words of author David Downing, 'The way [England] played in the League didn't work at international level; they weren't at all sure why and they didn't know how to play it any other way. They went home as confused by their failure as they were chastened, and in dire need of someone to sort them out.' Fortunately, that someone was close at hand. The reign of the Blessed Alf was nigh.

A POISONED CHALICE

England 4, West Germany 2. The scoreline is engraved on the heart of every self-respecting football fan. Cups have been rarer than Top 40 singles for English sports teams, which may explain why the image of Bobby Moore holding up the Jules Rimet trophy in front of the Queen at Wembley still takes pride of place in our national photo album.

Moore, who died in 1993, has since been canonised as the patron saint of English football. And yet ... not everything about his golden summer is remembered with pride and joy. It all comes back to the deep-seated idea that winning is not good enough for England; they have to do it in a satisfying and morally superior way. Alf Ramsey may have been the most successful manager our national team has ever had, but he was also conservative and pragmatic; the embodiment of safety-first football.

> **'The 1966 World Cup was the worst thing ever to happen to our national game.'**
> Author and journalist Rob Steen.

For all the satisfaction we continue to derive from that fairytale of a final, there will always be a nagging feeling that England went about the tournament the wrong way. By omitting Jimmy Greaves, the single brightest talent in the country, Ramsey is perceived to have struck some sort of satanic bargain. Richard Wagner's opera *Das Rheingold* tells of a puny dwarf who renounced love in exchange for ultimate power. In 1966, Ramsey sacrificed artistry in his drive to win the Cup.

No-one who followed England's bumpy, up-tight progress through the tournament could have claimed that it was just like watching Brazil.

For the first match, against Uruguay, Ramsey started out with what was effectively five men in defence, and only one winger. By the time England had reached the knock-out stages, he had abandoned wingers altogether – a decision that Greaves himself lamented. 'The fact that England won the World Cup with these tactics inspired an army of imitators,' wrote Greaves, 'and I am convinced that football became less exciting and entertaining to watch once the flying flank players had been eliminated.'

In fact, Ramsey was only developing a trend that had existed in British football for more than half a century. Even in the early days of the

Alf-time team-talk: Ramsey dispenses some words of advice to his players after a practice game against Chelsea, September 1965. Jimmy Armfield is on the left.

Football League, brilliant individualists like Billy Meredith were already being described as 'stormy petrels'. Stanley Matthews was surely the greatest winger this country ever produced, yet he, too, was viewed with suspicion. It is still one of the great England scandals that Matthews won just 54 caps.

Even after steering England to their greatest sporting triumph, Ramsey remained a controversial figure, accused of every vice from arrogance to xenophobia. But perhaps his greatest strength as a manager was his refusal to compromise; his determination to go to hell in his own way. 'They may be moaning now,' Ramsey told the players, after a drab 1–0 win over West Germany in February 1966 had been greeted by boos and slow hand-claps from the Wembley crowd. 'But if we beat West Germany playing like that in the World Cup final they'll all be going mad.' He never spoke a truer word.

> **'To Alf's way of thinking, creative means lazy.'**
> Malcolm Allison, Manchester City's tactical mastermind.

The pepper and salt man

We have already met Ramsey once, as England's right-back in the early years of Winterbottom's regime. As a player, there had been something slightly bovine about his thick-set frame and placid demeanour. He was a lumberer, rather than a sprinter. 'I've seen milk turn faster,' the great Scottish manager Tommy Docherty used to say. But his team-mates valued his reading of the game and refusal to get drawn into hasty challenges – qualities that Ramsey himself would later admire in Bobby Moore, England's captain for most of his tenure.

> **'Hey, Alf, there's some of your relatives over there.'**
> Bobby Moore points out some Romany caravans on a coach ride through Czechoslovakia. Ramsey was widely rumoured to be descended from gypsy stock.

Even as a young man, Ramsey was obsessed with tactics – a characteristic that earned him the nickname 'The General'. If Alexander Pope 'never drank tea without a strategem', as Samuel Johnson put it, then Ramsey never had dinner without some sort of match analysis. 'Football was his one subject of conversation,' said Jackie Milburn, who roomed with him in the early 1950s. 'He was always a pepper and salt man, working out moves and analysing formations with the cruet on the table.'

It was this dedication that helped make Ramsey, in his seven years with Ipswich, the most influential English manager since Herbert Chapman. Derided by the press as 'Ramsey's Rustics', Ipswich had a cobbled-together squad whose total value was reckoned at some £30,000. But the conversion of the wingers into wide midfielders, who hung back and lobbed passes up to the front-runners, bamboozled most opponents; it left the opposing full-backs unsure whether to push up, and leave a gap behind, or hold their ground and let Ipswich dominate possession.

When Ipswich were promoted from the Second Division, in 1961, Ramsey was lauded. But when they won the League, the following year, there was an air of shock, outrage almost, that such a small and unfashionable club should have outshone the glitterati of the First Division.

A small and unfashionable figure himself, Ramsey was thrilled to have overturned the odds with Ipswich. Yet in his own quiet way, he spent his life trying to gravitate towards the establishment, and escape his humble origins in Essex. One of the defining moments of his reign came when an interviewer asked him where his parents lived. The reply, delivered in Ramsey's stilted attempt at BBC English, was both arch and awkward: 'In Dagenham, I believe.'

> **'Do we always play like that?' 'No.' 'That's the first bit of good news I've had all evening.'**
>
> Exchange between Alf Ramsey and Jimmy Armfield, then the England captain, after a 5–2 defeat against France in Ramsey's first game in charge.

Father of the side

When Ramsey became England manager, he changed the whole landscape of the national game. No longer would the football manager be a facilitator, a backroom boffin. Instead he would step into the foreground, becoming the single most powerful man in English sport – and the single biggest target too.

JIMMY HILL
Caps 0   Chins 1

JIMMY 'THE BEARD' HILL NEVER PLAYED for England, but his go-getting work as chairman of the Professional Footballers' Association meant a great deal to those who did. In 1960, the PFA held a ballot on strike action against the minimum wage (which then stood at £20 a week). It was won by 694 votes to 18, and a month later the Football League caved in. Hill's Fulham team-mate Johnny Haynes immediately became the best-paid player in the English game, on £100 a week. 'There has never been any doubt in my mind that the huge improvement in working conditions helped enormously in producing that [1966] England team,' said Hill. 'Players grew in self-confidence, worked harder at the game. They felt better about themselves. And it showed.'

The FA expressed their interest to Ipswich in October 1962. They found Ramsey keen, but insistent that he would not put up with the same interference as his predecessor. The manager 'must be allowed to pick his team alone and to decide how players will play,' he had told Brian James in a *Daily Mail* interview the previous month. His bosses agreed, and 8 May 1963 represents a major landmark in English football: the day the International Selection Committee was finally put out of its muppetry.

Ramsey ran the England team as if it were just another Football League club, albeit one with an unusually large playing staff. This made him a very different proposition to Winterbottom, who – as Brian Glanville put it – 'was never a players' man, could never bridge the gap left by his complete lack of experience of club management'. Where Winterbottom had been a respected but remote schoolmaster, Ramsey was a father figure: loyal, supportive and protective, yet still capable of instilling fear. A quarter-master sergeant during the war, he backed his players to the hilt, yet demanded total discipline in return.

One of the formative moments in the build-up to the World Cup occurred when six players – including Moore, Bobby Charlton and Gordon Banks – left the team hotel without telling him, the night before England were due to fly to Portugal. When they returned, they found their passports on their beds – Ramsey's way of telling them that he knew. At breakfast in Lisbon, two days later, he announced 'There are some people who I need to see. They know who they are.' The six followed him out and got a 'right bollocking', in the words of reserve striker Johnny Byrne. As Charlton remembered it, '[Ramsey] said that had there been time to organise replacements we would have been left at home. I don't know whether Alf would have taken things that far. But he had made his point.'

> **'A crisis at Ipswich, dear boy, is when the white wine served in the boardroom is not sufficiently chilled.'**
> John Cobbold, Ramsey's aristocratic chairman at Ipswich, responds to press criticism.

The most important thing, from the players' perspective, was that everything was always kept in-house. 'Of course, he would criticise us to our faces,' said Martin Peters, who would become one of Ramsey's most valued midfielders. 'But it was always behind closed doors and when he went out to speak to the media he would never repeat to them what he had said to us. He gave us everything and we gave him everything back.'

The wingless wonders take flight

Ramsey set out his stall as early as June 1963. 'We *will* win the World Cup,' he told reporters after an 8–1 thrashing of Switzerland in Basle. The prediction, which Ramsey later admitted was 'just a case of saying the first

> ## 'George, if I had another fucking full-back you wouldn't be playing tomorrow.'
> Ramsey to George Cohen after the defender had upended him during a training session in Madrid.

thing that came into my mind', would give the pressmen a cheap excuse to bash him after every England defeat for the next three years. But it also helped convince the players that they had a genuine chance.

'I remember hearing him on the radio when he said, in that voice of his, "We will win the World Cup",' recalled Ray Wilson. 'And like most of the lads I thought, "For Christ's sake." It was a hell of a pressure, that was. But Alf was great at passing on self-belief. I think we needed that at the time.'

Now all Ramsey had to do was deliver on his promise. And that meant identifying the right players, and the right formation to deploy them in. If we take Greaves out of the equation – as Ramsey was always so keen to do – England had three great talents to work with: Gordon Banks in goal, Moore at the centre of defence, and Bobby Charlton surging forward from midfield. Anyone would have picked them. But Ramsey's real triumph lay in assembling an eclectic supporting cast which gelled like Brylcreem.

Like all great managers, Ramsey was also a great selector. Who else would have brought in Jack Charlton

> ## 'The winger was dead once you played four defenders. Alf saw that and it just took the rest of us a little longer to understand.'
> Dave Bowen, whose reign as Wales coach was almost concurrent with Ramsey's.

and Nobby Stiles, neither the most gifted of ball-players, for their extra bite in defence? Who else would have spotted the potential of Alan Ball and Martin Peters, both still unproven at club level, as tireless linkmen in the middle? And who would have found such an efficient way to deploy them? 'Almost everybody played with wingers,' said Franz Beckenbauer, 'so our

---

GEORGE EASTHAM
Caps 19   Goals 2

A SKILFUL YET FRAIL-LOOKING inside-forward, Eastham was unlucky not to appear in the 1966 World Cup. After scoring in the penultimate warm-up match, against Denmark in Copenhagen, he was pushed down the pecking order by Martin Peters, and never played for England again. Still, Eastham had already won a victory that would transform English football. In 1963, he took his first club – Newcastle United – to court for restraint of trade. When Mr Justice Wilberforce ruled in Eastham's favour, he brought down the whole feudal system of 'retain-and-transfer' (in which a club could hold on to a player's registration after his contract had expired, so preventing him from moving elsewhere). Along with the abolition of the maximum wage in 1961, this breakthrough opened the way for modern players to earn the astronomical sums we are used to today. If Eastham had a penny for every footballer who has become a millionaire on the back of his efforts ... well, he'd be almost as rich as them.

---

team and others found it hard to do anything against this, because the system was strange for them. I think it was this system that won the World Cup for England.'

Ramsey's critics used the phrase 'wingless wonders' to decry his lack of adventure. There was, of course, a romantic thrill to the idea of a true winger – a Matthews or a Finney – jinking around defenders and

> **'Unfortunately, you people see everything in black and white. I stand by my belief that England will win the World Cup, but I didn't say that I expect to win every match in the meantime.'**
>
> Alf Ramsey to reporters after a home defeat to Austria in 1965.

delighting the crowd. But the real courage lay in defying convention. Ramsey realised sooner than anyone that the now-standard 4-2-4 formation had made it far harder for a team to go rampaging down the flanks. He had seen Peter Thompson, the Liverpool outside-left, perform so dynamically on the 1964 tour of South America that the Brazilians called him 'the White Pelé'. And yet there was rarely any end product; as soon as Thompson had beaten one man, another came across to block him off.

Ramsey kept faith with one winger during the group stage of the World Cup, on the grounds that he expected Uruguay, Mexico and France to be shaky in defence. John Connelly played the first game, Terry Paine the second, and Ian Callaghan the third – but none of them made any great impact. So, for the knock-out stages, Ramsey reverted to his first instinct – a trio of hard-working midfielders, with Ball and Peters fetching and carrying and Bobby Charlton as chief playmaker. The shape is generally described as a 4-3-3, though in reality it looked more like this:

Hunt   **Hurst**

Peters   **B. Charlton**   **Ball**

Stiles

Wilson   **Moore**   **J. Charlton**   **Cohen**

Banks

Detained at their manager's pleasure

England made their final preparations for the World Cup at Lilleshall, a training facility deep in the Shropshire countryside. The players were to be interned for 18 days, with no breaks for good behaviour, and not a drop of alcohol allowed (except for one visit to a neighbouring golf club, when Ramsey bought the beers in half-pint measures).

The routine was simple and unvarying: football and physical training in the morning, then non-contact sports, such as tennis or basketball, in the afternoon, and a film – almost always a Western – in the evening. Bedtime was 9 p.m. sharp, no matter what. In his autobiography *1966 And All That*, Geoff Hurst explained that the projector had been shut down just before the end of *Butch Cassidy and the Sundance Kid* on three separate occasions. 'It wasn't until 1990 that I realised he got shot!'

The attention to detail was minute. Players were moved around in different rooming combinations to prevent cliques developing. The team doctor, Alan Bass, gave a demonstration in the proper technique for clipping toenails. Meanwhile the sadistic training regime tested even the lungs of George Cohen, Alan Ball and Martin Peters, three of the finest athletes who had ever represented England. (After his extraordinary efforts in the World Cup final, Brian Glanville would compare Ball to Emil Zatopek, the great distance runner of the 1950s.) 'Alf wanted to push us to the utmost limit of human endurance,' Jack Charlton said later. 'It was a test of character as much as a physical training programme.'

It was also a chance for Ramsey to assert his authority over the drinking clique, which was led by his captain Bobby Moore. A smooth but strangely elusive character, Moore bore a faint resemblance to a young Steve McQueen, and was renowned for his ability to sink vatfuls of booze with no ill-effects. As the West Ham defender John Charles admitted, 'Mooro was as good as gold on and off the field, but he was a piss-head. He liked a gin and tonic. He liked a lager too. You couldn't get him drunk. He was on a par with Oliver Reed!'

Hanging out with Moore did for the England career of Johnny Byrne, another West Ham man who shared his captain's thirst but not his uncanny powers of recuperation. It may even have done for Jimmy Greaves. The pair of them, both East-Enders by birth, used to sit at the back of the bus and snigger at Ramsey. On one drive in 1963, the journalist

> ## 'From that day on I never expected to be in the England squad until the letter from the FA dropped through my letter box.'
> Bobby Moore after briefly losing his place to Norman 'Bites Yer Legs' Hunter two months before the World Cup.

Ken Jones overheard the manager hiss under his breath 'If needs be, I'll win the World Cup without either of those two.'

Ramsey fired a number of warning shots across Moore's bows, once leaving him out for the trip to Yugoslavia in May 1966 to make room for Leeds hardman Norman Hunter. Ultimately, though, he knew that Moore was the rock at the heart of his defence – and defence was what Ramsey cared about most. As a forward, Greaves was far more expendable. As the Chelsea and England forward Barry Bridges put it, 'If you crossed [Ramsey], he would not get you straight away but he would get you in the end. You would get your comeuppance. I sometimes wonder if that's what did for Greavsie.'

Escape to victory

After all the controlled fury of England's build-up, their first match of the tournament – a 0–0 draw against Uruguay – was a huge anticlimax. The most exciting part of the whole day came when trainer Harold Shepherdson forgot to check that the players had their identity cards with them; a police motorcyclist had to charge back to the team hotel in Hendon to save seven of the first eleven from disqualification.

Once the game had started, Uruguay sat back in their own half, soaked up pressure, and hardly staged an attack of their own. 'Up front, we were three against eight some of the time,' recalled winger John Connelly, who would not appear again during the tournament. The final whistle brought a cacophony of boos.

Creeping anxiously into the dressing-room, the players were surprised to find Ramsey in good spirits – delighted, in fact, by the efficiency of his back six. 'You may not have won, but you didn't lose, and you didn't give away a goal either,' he told them. 'Whatever anyone says, remember you can still qualify, provided you keep a clean sheet and don't lose a game.'

For all his emphasis on fitness and athleticism, Ramsey understood the need for a few beers after a match. The day after the Uruguay game, he took the squad on a boozy, stress-busting trip to Pinewood Studios to watch the filming of the new James

> ## 'Alf, you give me the World Cup Willies.'
> Desmond Hackett in the *Daily Express*, making caustic reference to the tournament mascot.

The lion in summer: England football team mascot World Cup Willie arrives at the Football Association. Inside the suit is George Claydon, a dwarf actor who later played one of the Oompa-Loompas in *Charlie and the Chocolate Factory*.

Bond movie *You Only Live Twice*. After Sean Connery had given the players a short pep-talk, Ramsey responded with one of his infamous malapropisms: 'Thank you, Seen.' Greaves turned to his back-seat buddy Moore and quipped 'That's the funniest thing I've ever shorn.'

Against Mexico, a week later, England found themselves confronted with another human wall – although you might not have known it from footage of Bobby Charlton's memorable opening goal. Picking up the ball inside the England half, Charlton took advantage of a retreating defence to carry the ball unchallenged towards the edge of the Mexican penalty area. He then turned onto his right foot and fired into the top corner with astonishing sweetness. When you consider the tension that had been building up over England's low strike-rate, Charlton's prodigious piledriver was perfectly timed. It should be right up there in any list of goals of the century – the greatest Bobby dazzler of them all.

> **'There were one or two people tonight who thought they were good players. And you were one of them.'**
>
> Alf Ramsey delivers the biggest insult he can think of to Ray Wilson after an 'undisciplined' 2–0 win over France.

Trials and confrontations

'ENGLAND'S SPARK IS MISSING' announced the *Daily Mirror*'s back page after the final group match against France, which produced a ponderous 2–0 win. More to the point, so was Jimmy Greaves. Brutally challenged by Jean Bonnel, Greaves had suffered a deep cut to his shin which needed 14 stitches, and which would give Ramsey the perfect excuse to leave him out.

But the tackle everyone was talking about was the one Nobby Stiles had unleashed on Jacques Simon, France's skilful midfielder. A toothless, short-sighted imp, Stiles seemed about as dangerous as Popeye without his spinach – and yet his studs were feared across the Football League. 'If I wasn't jeered at and booed, I considered I wasn't doing my job,' he once said.

Administrators from both FIFA and the FA joined the campaign to have Stiles banished from the tournament. But while his foul on Simon was certainly unpleasant, there was no logical reason why he should have been singled out ahead of, say, Portugal's João Morais, who had cynically hacked down Pelé to send Brazil packing. When Ramsey met his bosses to discuss the issue, his message was simple. 'If he goes, so do I. You will be looking for a new manager.'

Ramsey's display of loyalty only amplified the spirit in an already tight-knit squad. They would need it in their quarter-final, against an Argentinian side who were not only masters of the dark arts, but dangerously skilful on the ball. 'There was no doubt in my mind that they were the most serious threat to our chances,' wrote Bobby Charlton later. 'They were always together and they always got the job done. No fair races were allowed. Try to go past them and they would upend you. They spat. They were probably the meanest, roughest team I ever played against.'

With Greaves out of the picture, England finally fixed on the XI that would take them all the way: Peters on the left, Ball on the right, and Hurst leading the line. They made a lively start – four corners in the first four minutes – and that may have been crucial, because it put the Argentinians into disruptive mode when they could so easily have been

---

PETER SWAN
Caps 19   Goals 0

A RELIABLE CENTRE-HALF through England's great season of 1960–1, Swan was dismayingly accident-prone off the field. He came close to death in Chile in 1962, after contracting dysentery. Then, in 1965, he was gaoled for his part in a betting ring set up by the former Everton midfielder Jimmy Gauld. Swan was accused of accepting a £100 bribe, and ended up serving a four-month sentence alongside fellow England international Tony Kay. A hard-working midfielder who won his only cap against Switzerland in 1963, Kay was probably the bigger loss to England. He could easily have had Nobby Stiles's World Cup place – were it not for his life ban.

> **'Not so much a football match as an international incident.'**
>
> Hugh McIlvanney on England v Argentina.

creating. Tensions were soon rising between Herr Kreitlein, the tiny German referee, and the towering Argentine captain Antonio Rattín, who insisted on contesting every decision. Booked on 32 minutes, for a trip on Bobby Charlton, Rattín was sensationally sent off just four minutes later, having abused the officious Kreitlein one time too often.

'I do not speak Spanish, but the look on his face told me everything,' said Kreitlein afterwards, which must make Rattín the first professional footballer to be sent off for wearing a moody expression. On that reasoning, Roy Keane would barely have lasted a match. Still, after fully eight minutes of pushing, shoving and arguing, Rattín finally dragged himself off the field, and staged a slow, provocative walk around to the tunnel. He then sat down on the red carpet that had been laid out for the Queen. Some reports even claim that he stuck his middle finger up in her general direction. This was *lèse majesté* of the first water.

With 12 minutes to play, Peters supplied the cross for Hurst to head the only goal. But the Argentinians were never going to go quietly. Once the final whistle had blown, one of them urinated on the wall of the tunnel, another spat at a FIFA official, and the whole team hammered on the locked door

of the England dressing-room. 'Send them in!' yelled Jack Charlton. 'I'll fight them all!'

Even more damaging, from the perspective of future Anglo-Argentinian relations, was Ramsey's interview with Kenneth Wolstenholme after the match. 'We still have to produce our best football,' he said. 'It is not possible until we meet the right type of opposition, a team which come out to play football, not as *animals*, as we have seen in the World Cup.'

Ramsey's blunt remarks caused a furore in the media, and a bomb threat to the English embassy in Mexico City. Yet that was nothing compared to the trouble he was storing up for the future. Never comfortable on their visits to South America, England were now destined to become hunted men.

> ## 'Most teams have one hardman, perhaps two, but this Argentinian team had about eight or nine.'
>
> Geoff Hurst.

Getting shirty: Alf Ramsey prevents George Cohen from swapping shirts after England's bad-tempered win over Argentina in the 1966 World Cup quarter-final. 'I played under Alf for eight years,' said Martin Peters, 'and that was the only time I ever saw him lose his rag'.

> **'After Alf Ramsey's description of the Argentinian team as animals, may I, on behalf of the Dog Owners' Association, immediately dissociate the dog world from this description, as being most unfair to our many members and their pets who insist on control at all times.'**
>
> Alan Scott, honorary secretary of the DOA.

The panther in (golden) boots

Ramsey's defensive gameplan was as effective as it was unpopular. It took England seven-and-a-half hours of World Cup football to concede their first goal. Talk about Greenwich Mean Time.

The goal was scored from the penalty spot by Eusébio of Portugal, with nine minutes to go in the semi-final. Nicknamed the Black Panther, Eusébio won the Golden Boot in 1966, and a less well-organised England team would probably have succumbed to him, just as they had succumbed to the Black Spider in 1958. But Stiles shepherded him cleverly onto his weaker left side, and England ran out 2–1 winners.

'Gentleman, you know I don't normally talk about individual players,' said Ramsey in the dressing-room after the game. 'But I think you will agree that Nobby has produced a truly professional performance.'

After the unpleasant scenes that had marred the quarter-final, the semi-final was a genuinely beautiful game. Both sides were capable of fighting like alleycats, but on this occasion they preferred to pass the ball like Corinthians, leaving open space all over the field. As Pelé pointed out, in a critical assessment of the tournament as a whole, 'Only by allowing the other team to attack can you do so yourselves.'

Freed up to use his vision and touch, Bobby Charlton had perhaps his finest game for England. He passed the ball beautifully and scored both goals – the first neatly side-footed through a goal-mouth melee, the second another rip-snorter from the edge of the area. England were through to the final, and through in some style. According to Tass, the Soviet news agency, their victory had been 'like a spring of clear water breaking through the murky sea of dirty football which has covered recent matches in the championships'.

They think it's all over

Whole books have been written on the 120-odd minutes of the 1966 World Cup final. The photographs and footage, particularly of Geoff Hurst's final goal, have become so familiar that it takes an effort of will to see them afresh.

'When I saw Nobby coming away with the ball from players twice his size, I thought, well, if he can do it so can the rest of us.'
Bobby Moore on Nobby Stiles.

The game got off to the most unlikely start: a multiple defensive cock-up from England, who conceded a soft goal for the first time in the tournament. Ray Wilson inexplicably headed a high ball straight to the feet of Helmut Haller, who sent in a low shot to the far post. Either Jack Charlton or Gordon Banks could have stopped it, but they both hesitated for an instant, waiting for the other to act, and the ball was in.

Six minutes later, the Germans reciprocated with a defensive howler of their own. Moore was fouled some 40 yards out, and as he hopped up again, he saw Hurst running sideways towards an untenanted six-yard box. The delivery was perfect, the downward header sure.

> ## 'Bobby Charlton thought that "tackle" was what you go fishing with.'
> The terrier-like Alan Ball on the contrasting approaches of England's midfielders.

Play ebbed and flowed, in roughly equal measure, for the next 60 minutes. Appropriately enough, for a contest between two such mechanical teams, there was little input from each side's most gifted player; Bobby Charlton and Franz Beckenbauer had settled for marking each other out of the match. But then, with 12 minutes to go, England took the lead for the first time through a crisp Peters volley after a goal-mouth scramble. Known to his team-mates as the Duke of Kent, on account of his patrician profile, Peters was England's stealth bomber: he ghosted into the penalty box so subtly that no-one saw him coming.

The shot that launched a thousand arguments: Geoff Hurst's piledriver came back off the underside of the crossbar. The Russian linesman Tofik Bakhramov awarded the goal, and was later accused of bearing a grudge from Stalingrad.

As the clock ticked down, it seemed as though Peters's dramatic intervention might have won the game. But then, disaster: another bout of penalty-box pinball broke out at England's end, and this time the ball broke for Wolfgang Weber, just a couple of yards out. He simply couldn't miss. The Germans had pulled back to 2–2. And within four seconds of the restart, normal time was over.

Ramsey's response to this catastrophe was critical. 'In the lives of most successful leaders, there is a single moment which can define the essence of their heroic stature,' wrote his biographer Leo McKinstry. 'For Alf Ramsey, that moment occurred at 4.50 p.m. on 30 July 1966.' He could so easily have come out ranting, but instead he got his exhausted players on their feet and told them 'All right. You've won the World Cup once. Now go and win it again.

> ## 'Sit down, Harold.'
> Alf Ramsey to Harold Shepherdson, the England trainer, in a very British response to Hurst's hat-trick.

Look at the Germans. They're flat out. Down on the grass. Having massages. They can't live with you. Not for another half-hour. Not through extra-time.'

So it proved, as Ball in particular kept bouncing down the right like some perpetual motion machine. Ten minutes into the first period, he found the energy to reach a long ball in the right-hand corner, and pulled it back to the near post. Hurst controlled the ball, swivelled, and hit it onto the crossbar, from where it bounced down onto the goal-line. England claimed the goal, and their celebrations were upheld by Tofik Bakhramov, the Russian linesman. The arguments are still going on.

One immortal moment still remained. As the clock wound down, for the final time, Moore ignored his team-mates' cries to hack the ball into the crowd, and found Hurst with another pinpoint pass. Hurst took it on, to within 25 yards of goal, and let fly with his left foot. He claimed he was just trying to hit it into the stands, but it flew into the top corner instead.

The BBC commentary, by Kenneth Wolstenholme, is now held up as the ultimate example of the art. 'Some of the crowd are on the pitch,' Wolstenholme roared. 'They think it's all over. [PAUSE] It is now!' Over on ITV, Hugh Johns's effort was perhaps even more effusive. 'Here's Hurst. He might make it three. He has! He has! So that's it! That's it!' Unfortunately, *Here's Hurst* never quite made it as a topical quiz show on primetime TV.

The truth is out there ... somewhere

So how about England's third goal, then? Did the ball cross the line? In a word, no. Scientists at Oxford University made their own contribution to the debate in 1995, announcing that computer analysis of the available footage had come out on the German side. But you shouldn't really need gadgetry to see that: the naked eye is good enough.

All sorts of myths and legends have grown up around the incident. Some have pointed to Roger Hunt's reaction, which was to throw up his hands and turn away. If it hadn't been a *bona fide* goal, the argument goes, Hunt would have followed up with a tap-in. But this is nonsense: Weber was always going to reach the rebound before him.

Other commentators have questioned Bakhramov's integrity. In a

PICKLES THE DOG
(England)
Caps 0   Cups 1

FOUR MONTHS BEFORE the start of the tournament, the World Cup disappeared from its stand at the Stampex Exhibition in Westminster. It was a huge embarrassment for the country. 'An atomic explosion could scarcely have been given more coverage,' commented the official FA report. There followed a farcical sequence of events in which FA chairman Joe Mears received phone calls, ransom demands for £15,000, and eventually a parcel containing the trophy's removable top. (The equivalent, presumably, of a hostage's ear.) An unemployed former soldier named Edward Bletchley was arrested within a few days, and later sentenced to two years in gaol, but the location of the trophy remained a mystery. Then, after a week of search-

ing, it was discovered by Pickles, a small black-and-white mongrel who sniffed it out from the bottom of a garden hedge in Beulah Hill, South London. Pickles became a celebrity, going on to star with Eric Sykes and June Whitfield in the film *The Spy With the Cold Nose*, and had the same agent as Spike Milligan. But he suffered a premature death by choking when he snagged his lead on a tree while in pursuit of a cat.

1966 WORLD CUP ENGLAND

Round One:
England 0 – 0 Uruguay

England 2 – 0 Mexico
B. Charlton 37
Hunt 75

England 2 – 0 France
Hunt 38, 75

Quarter-final:
England 1 – 0 Argentina
Hurst 78

Semi-final:
England 2 – 1 Portugal
B. Charlton 30, 80   Eusébio 82 (pen.)

Final:
England 4 – 2 West Germany (a.e.t.)
Hurst 18, 101, 120   Haller 12
Peters 78   Weber 89

England's finest hour, sadly unmatched to the present day. In his first World Cup as manager, Alf Ramsey took his team all the way to the final, where they defeated West Germany in one of the most controversial games ever played.

Toothless tiger: Nobby Stiles about to embark on his notorious victory jig, Wembley 1966. Three-year-olds have had a better sense of rhythm.

2006 edition of *Referee* magazine, it was reported that 'When asked on his deathbed how he knew the ball was over the line [Bakhramov] is alleged to have uttered only one word – "Stalingrad".'

When it comes to conspiracy theories, no-one can match João Havelange, the then president of the Brazilian Football Confederation. Having seen two Brazilian goals disallowed during their first-round match against Hungary, Havelange complained that his team had been handicapped by having to play their biggest matches under referees from England and West Germany.

Havelange was not alone in this opinion, but where he broke new ground was in his suggestion that political motives were involved. In fact, he had a pat explanation for each of the four quarter-finalists.

'The conspiracy went like this,' writes James Corbett in his book *England Expects*. 'Portugal would be allowed through so that the British government could regain a foothold in black Africa; the USSR to promote trade interests; and West Germany ... so that Britain could enter the EEC and gain a political counterweight to Charles de Gaulle's France. England's interests were, of course, paramount.'

In 1974, Havelange would succeed Stanley Rous as FIFA president – a job he held on to for 24 years. Not bad for a bloke with a screw missing. Now, did I ever tell you about the time I was abducted by aliens?

The real World Cup final

Another man who was less than enchanted by England's triumph was Denis Law, the Scotland and Manchester United centre-forward. Law arranged a golf game to avoid having to watch the final, but as he came up the 17th fairway, already three holes down, a passer-by yelled 'Have you heard? England won?' Law flung his club into the nearest bush and exclaimed 'That just about completes my bloody day!'

Nine months later, Law would have his say in a curious postscript to England's World Cup glory. England had gone 19 matches unbeaten by this stage, and fancied themselves to roll Scotland at Wembley, despite the undoubted talents of Law, Billy Bremner and Jim Baxter. But it didn't quite turn out that way. Jack Charlton and Ray Wilson both suffered injuries

Bravehearts: Bobby Lennox is congratulated by team mates Willie Wallace (yes, really) and Jim Baxter (right) after scoring Scotland's second goal against England at Wembley, April 1967.

during the match, and the Scots squeezed home 3–2 against nine fit men.

'They went absolutely mad over it,' said Moore. 'The eyes of some of the players were wild. Their supporters came pouring off the terraces to cut up the pitch, waving lumps of earth at us and saying this was the turf on which they destroyed the world champions. Some of them were seriously suggesting we ought to hand over the World Cup.'

It was a classic Scottish reaction. The Jocks might have missed out on the main event of the international football calendar, but one victory over England was enough to make them kings of the world. This attitude – in which every other match was just a warm-up for their big tilt at the Sassenachs – had always infuriated Ramsey, and he wasn't afraid to show it. In April 1964, a Glaswegian reporter was unwise enough to offer an effusive greeting – 'Welcome back to Scotland, Mr Ramsey' – as the players stepped off the plane. 'You must be fucking joking,' he replied.

> **'They splashed in the fountains of Trafalgar Square, and marched round the capital demanding "Who won eh?" "Whaurs yer World Cup noo?"'**
>
> James Corbett on the Scottish invasion of 1967.

FORTY
YEARS OF
HURT
1966–2008

METHOD TURNS TO MADNESS

Just what is it that makes 1970s football so different, so appealing? Could it be the long hair and bushy sideburns, which made it hard to tell the difference between Spurs and Slade? Could it be the figure-hugging shorts, that seemed to have been spray-painted on? Or could it be the number of colourful characters who suddenly emerged from the monochrome wasteland of the Football League?

Alan Hudson, Frank Worthington, Rodney Marsh, Tony Currie, Charlie George, Stan Bowles – these players were the toast of the fanzines, and why not? They had mullets to die for and talent to burn. Take a look at Worthington's immortal goal against Ipswich in 1979 if you need convincing. Three keepy-ups, followed by a delicious flick back over his own head, and then a deadly volley. It makes Gazza's famous Euro '96 strike against Scotland look pedestrian.

> **'I spent all my money on booze, gambling and women – but at least I didn't waste any of it.'**
> Stan Bowles.

As Rob Steen put it, in his book *The Mavericks* (1994), this was the decade 'when flair wore flares'. Yet Steen does not pretend that 1970s football was all dummies, back-heels and bicycle kicks. Far from it. The whole *point* of the mavericks is that they were determined to be different, to beat the system. For the most part, English football remained 'a grey game played by grey people on grey days,' as Marsh told an American audience in 1979.

Marsh and his fellow showmen were determined to play the game on their own terms, or they wouldn't play it at all. And that was never going to endear them to Ramsey or his successor, Don Revie. 'All the rebels had a very fixed idea of how the game should be played,' said Frank McLintock, the Arsenal captain. 'They took liberties. It was all "bollocks to that" and "who's he to tell me what to do".' When Charlie George made his one and only England appearance, in 1976, Revie asked him to switch to the wing at half-time. George refused, was substituted 15 minutes later, and stormed past the manager with a defiant 'Fuck you!'

Like revolutionaries in a totalitarian state, these players were driven into extremism by a sport that did its best to reject them. Wherever they went, they were harried by hit men like Norman 'Bites Yer Legs' Hunter or Ron 'Chopper' Harris. And then there were the crowd chants. 'Wanky-wanky-wanky-wanky-Worthington'. 'Where's your handbag, Charlie George?' Perhaps it wasn't so surprising that George, like Gascoigne after

The mane man: playboy footballer Frank Worthington, who called his racy autobiography *One Hump or Two?* Asked in 1993 who he had played for, Worthington responded 'I had 11 clubs – 12 if you count Stringfellows.'

> **'Why should I have to prove what I can do? It's just not on when I know within my heart that I should be the man leading the full England side against the World Champs.'**
>
> Charlie George explains why he rejected an England B call-up in 1978.

him, went a bit doolally. He was fined £400 for punching a photographer and once broke his own elbow in a determined attempt to commit GBH on a Stoke City defender.

There was little opportunity to see the likes of George, Worthington or the rest in England colours. They all played, at one point or another, but the only one of Steen's mavericks who reached 10 international caps was Tony Currie, a silky midfielder whose trademark was blowing kisses at the crowd. 'Why didn't they pick Worthington, Hudson, Bowles and Currie in the same team?' Currie asked, with typical modesty. 'I'd love to have seen somebody brave enough to do that.'

The answer is simple: since the shining example of the 1966 World Cup, England's managers had put their faith in method. The success of the national team was far too important to be risked on the performance of one or two creative midfielders. What if Messrs Bowles or Hudson happened to get out of bed the wrong side that day? Far better to invest in 10 super-fit athletes who could rush around the park; that way it was harder to assign blame if things went wrong.

All this might have been defensible if England had been winning. But after going out of the 1970 World Cup at the quarter-final stage, they failed to qualify for another major competition until the European Championships of 1980. *Ten whole years*! It was like the 1920s all over again, only this time the humiliation was televised.

'Cautious, joyless football was scarcely bearable even when it was bringing victories,' wrote *The Observer*'s Hugh McIlvanney, in one of the decade's defining commentaries. 'Ramsey's method was, to be fair, justifiable in 1966, when it was important that England should make a powerful show in the World Cup, but since then it has become an embarrassment.'

None of this stops the 1970s from exerting their own special charm. But it is the dramatic highlights we love: Alan Hudson's one great game against West Germany, Jeff Astle firing wide in Guadalajara with Brazil at his mercy, or Kevin Keegan being named European Footballer of the Year. The everyday tedium of stereotyped, thud-and-blunder football has mercifully faded from the memory.

> ## 'Marsh, if you don't work hard, I'm going to pull you off at half-time.' 'Blimey, boss! At Manchester City all we get is a cup of tea and an orange!'
> Exchange between Alf Ramsey and the scampish Rodney Marsh.

Ramsey talks a bad game

Ramsey's relationship with the media was never exactly fraternal. 'At best Alf could tolerate journalists, at worst he would cut them off at the knees,' wrote the BBC's Bryon Butler.

Surprisingly, the success of 1966 seemed to make relations even chillier. Perhaps this was because it raised expectations, or more likely because Ramsey became still more introverted and difficult to deal with. 'I can live without them [reporters] because I am judged by the results that the England team gets,' he once said. 'I doubt very much whether they can live without me.'

There was an element of naivety in this argument. Sooner or later, Ramsey's results were going to turn against him. And when they did, there was a whole phalanx of pundits waiting to pull him down. Hell hath no fury like a football correspondent scorned.

If journalists ranked at the top of Ramsey's personal hate list, foreigners were not far behind. His denunciation of Argentina in 1966

> **'There was a general, utter contempt from him. I don't think anyone could make you feel more like a turd under his boot than Ramsey. It is amazing how he did it.'**
> Peter Batt of *The Sun*.

was a low point, equivalent to sending his players to Mexico four years later with 'Kick Me' written across the back of their shirts. Yet it was far from being a one-off. After a European Championship semi-final in 1968, Ramsey managed to accuse Yugoslavia of being cheats and cowards in a single breath.

Held in Florence, the game had been a rough one from the very beginning, when Norman Hunter effectively crippled Ivan Osim with a horrible studs-up challenge. After that, things degenerated to the point where Alan Mullery, Nobby Stiles's successor in the holding role, was sent off, having retaliated to persistent Yugoslavian fouling by kicking Dobrivoje Trivić in the balls.

At the press conference after the game, Ramsey scoffed at questions about Hunter's tackle, pointing out that Osim had fouled Ball a couple of minutes earlier. 'I am sure that Alan Ball was at least as badly hurt as Osim,' he said. 'The difference is that Alan Ball has more courage.'

This was the sort of attitude that prompted one of Moore's great one-liners. 'As a public relations man,' he quipped, '[Ramsey] would have made a splendid concentration camp commandant.'

> **'If you hadn't done it, I would have.'**
> Ramsey to Alan Mullery after his sending-off in Florence.

You're nicked, skipper!

There are few stranger stories in English football history than that of Bobby Moore and the Bogotá bracelet. This bizarre incident erupted less than a fortnight before the start of the 1970 World Cup, and came mighty close to depriving England of their captain and talisman for the early stages of the tournament.

Always adept at divesting forwards of the ball, Moore was now accused of stealing an emerald and diamond bracelet from its case. He and Bobby Charlton had wandered into the *Fuego Verde* (Green Fire) jewellery shop, looking (unsuccessfully) to pick up presents for their wives. Then, as they lounged on a sofa in the lobby of the Hotel Tequendama, a few yards away from the store, the assistant came rushing out and started rummaging around the cushions. She claimed that a bracelet had disappeared.

'It all happened very quickly,' Clara Padilla told reporters. 'Bobby Moore and two of his team-mates came to the counter and started talking to me. Then I saw Mr Moore open a glass case, take out the bracelet and put it in his pocket.'

It has often been suggested that this fit-up was part of a dirty tricks campaign against England, who – in Charlton's words – 'were about as popular with the locals as an outbreak of plague'. But all the evidence suggests that it was a regular scam, used by unscrupulous salesmen to extort money from tourists. When Moore was placed under house arrest, a week later, the former Brazilian coach Joao Saldanha came to his defence, revealing that similar accusations had been directed at the Botafogo team a couple of years earlier.

'The allegations against Bobby Moore are disgraceful,' Saldanha said. 'This is slander. It is against nature, against football. Moore is an honourable man.'

On 27 May, a reconstruction was held at *Fuego Verde*. The little shop was packed with lawyers, policemen, witnesses and reporters. This could almost have been one of Agatha Christie's drawing-room dénouements – and it did produce a moment of Poirot-style revelation. Faltering under cross-examination, Padilla claimed that Moore had placed the bracelet in the left pocket of his England jacket. Moore then raised his arm to show that there was no left pocket in his England jacket. 'He was led away to

Flight to freedom: England captain Bobby Moore on a plane en route to Mexico following his release from police custody in Bogotá, where he had been held on suspicion of stealing a bracelet.

cheers of "Viva Bobby",' as the historian James Corbett writes, 'and Padilla fell into floods of tears.'

Moore was released the next day (after some heavy diplomatic pressure from Harold Wilson had oiled the creaking wheels of the Colombian justice system). He had sailed through the whole sordid affair with characteristic grace and stoicism. But he never quite forgave Ramsey for taking the rest of the squad back to Mexico while he was banged up in Bogotá.

England get their Findus burnt

If that flight to Mexico City was among the low points of Ramsey's time in charge, it was even more miserable for the pressmen, who had just discovered that the biggest story of the year had broken, and they were flying in the wrong direction.

Just to add further spice to the brew, the plane hit an electrical storm somewhere over Panama. Jeff Astle, always a shaky traveller, tried to calm his nerves with a stiff drink or seven. By the time the plane landed he was virtually insensible, and had to be half carried through the airport with a cape over his head. A piece in *El Heraldo* described England as 'a team of thieves and drunks'.

The whole campaign seemed to be dogged by a PR jinx. England were not the only team to import food and water to Mexico, but surely no other country produced an advertising campaign quite as insensitive as that run by Findus, the team's main sponsors. 'What happens if foreign food gives our boys a bellyache?' 'Don't worry, it's no risk a team manager will take in a foreign country.'

The Mexican authorities responded by banning all English meat or dairy products, on the grounds that England had recently been affected by foot and mouth disease. Most of the Findus food parcels had to be piled up and burned on the quayside of Mexico City, leaving the players to survive on fish-fingers for the rest of the tour. 'I have not had a fish-finger in my life since then,' said Alan Mullery.

> **'Bobby Charlton had earned himself the nickname "*Il Calvino Divino*" – The Divine Baldy.'**
> Author James Corbett on one of the few Englishmen to win plaudits in Mexico.

When the tournament started, England failed to win over the sceptics with a workmanlike 1–0 win over Romania. It was a typical Ramsey victory, based on a commanding defensive performance by Moore. But there was no mistaking the ill-feeling from the stands. Each time an English player was fouled – which was roughly every four minutes – the crowd would let out a deafening cheer.

Save of the century

The omens for the next game were not encouraging. The night before the match, hundreds of hostile fans gathered outside England's team hotel with drums and whistles. Passing motorists honked their horns from dusk till dawn. As Emlyn Hughes said, 'It sounded like a thousand West Indian cricket supporters in full cry.'

With or without the noise, the English players might have found it hard to sleep. They were about to come up against Brazil, the tournament favourites, and arguably the greatest team in World Cup history. Even Ramsey had been alarmed by Brazil's 4–1 demolition of Czechoslovakia in their opening match. 'By Christ, these people can play,' he told the journalist Ken Jones.

Brazil were slightly hampered by the absence of Gerson, their

midfield general. But they still had Jairzinho and Rivelino – surely the finest wing combination ever seen – playing on either side of the divine Pelé. In the thin air, under the blazing sun, in front of a hostile crowd, this was football's Mission Impossible. Remarkably, though, England started the stronger, with Manchester City's golden boy Francis Lee causing problems down the right. The game was still goalless when the players

'How long can England persist with tactics essentially negative in theory and largely negative in practice? How long can they eschew wingers when wingers are doing so much for other sides?'

Brian Glanville in garment-rending mode, as England prepared for their quarter-final.

Safe as the Banks of England: Gordon Banks hits the ground after making one of the most famous saves in football history during England's 1970 group-phase game against Brazil in Guadalajara.

'O BALL! O ASTLE! O ENGLAND!'

Daily Express headline on England's 1–0 loss to Brazil.

went in at half-time – although Brazil should really have been one ahead via Pelé's downward header. It had taken the most famous save in the history of the game to deny him.

Gordon Banks was a renowned perfectionist, and this stop remains as near as any goalkeeper has ever come to perfection. Pelé was already shouting 'Goal' when Banks threw himself backwards, downwards and to his right, somehow deflecting the ball over the bar. As far as the England team was concerned, it was probably the finest moment of the 1970s (which says something about their attacking impotence over the course of the decade).

'At that moment I hated Gordon Banks more than any man in soccer,' Pelé said afterwards. 'But when I cooled down I had to applaud him with my heart for the greatest save I had ever seen.' Moore resorted to English irony. 'You're getting old Banksy, you used to hold on to those.'

That save may have kept England in touch, but Banks could do nothing about the intricate attack that set up Jairzinho on 59 minutes. Nicknamed *Furacao* – or 'the Hurricane' – the right-winger scored in every match Brazil played throughout the tournament. Banks came out quickly to narrow the angle, but the finish was special: Jairzinho's crunching shot flew in off the underside of the bar.

England had chances too. With 25 minutes to go, Brazil's left-half Everaldo miskicked to an unmarked Jeff Astle, only 10 yards out. The goal gaped as wide before him as Cherie Blair's smile. But the ball fell to his weaker left foot, and he dragged his snap-shot wide. 'How could Jeff miss that chance?' mused a devastated Alan Ball the next day, as he sat by the pool.

England's players each lost a minimum of ten pounds in weight, on a day when the mercury touched 98 degrees. Yet their unflinching efforts had helped win back the crowd's respect. After the final whistle, Pelé embraced Moore – whose tackle on a speeding Jairzinho is almost as venerated as Banks's save – and swapped shirts. 'You no thief, Bobby,' he said.

1970 WORLD CUP MEXICO

Round One:
England 1 – 0 Romania
Hurst 65

England 0 – 1 Brazil
Jairzinho 59

England 1 – 0 Czechoslovakia
Clarke 50 (pen.)

Quarter-final:
England 2 – 3 West Germany (a.e.t.)

Mullery 31	*Beckenbauer 68*
Peters 49	*Seeler 76*
	Müller 108

A thrilling clash against Brazil in Round One sets
England up for a needle quarter-final against West
Germany, who exact sweet revenge for their defeat in
the '66 finals through Gerd Müller's extra-time
winner (below).

223

BACK HOME
Sales 500,000   Highest chart position 1

THE FIRST SINGLE to be recorded by a sports team, 'Back Home' has a lot to answer for. But England's anthem for the 1970 World Cup remains a decent record, the standard by which every one of its (mostly execrable) imitators must be judged. Written by Bill Martin and Phil Coulter – who had also been responsible for Sandie Shaw's 'Puppet on a String', and, less happily, Cliff Richard's 'Congratulations' – it climbed to No. 1 within three weeks of its release, dislodging Norman Greenbaum's 'Spirit In The Sky'. The players appeared on *Top of the Pops*, dressed in dinner jackets and black ties. When they returned home from Mexico, Gordon Banks was met at the airport and handed a silver disc marking 250,000 copies sold.

The Cat flaps, the Kaiser rules

How remarkable that the greatest save and the worst howler in English goalkeeping history should have taken place within a week of each other. Unfortunately for Ramsey, it would be the error – committed by Banks's hapless stand-in Peter Bonetti – that defined England's tournament.

Bonetti's moment of badness came, ironically, in the middle of one of England's finest performances overseas. It was just after half-time in Leon, where England were leading West Germany 2–0 in the quarter-final. Charlton, Mullery and Peters had dominated possession with the kind of low-tempo, fast-breaking football that English teams have traditionally found so hard to master. Ramsey always claimed that his squad for the 1970 World Cup was stronger than the 1966 model, and at this point it would have been hard to disagree.

Both goals were made and scored in typical Ramsey fashion, with the ball being played out from the middle to Keith Newton, the overlapping full-back, as he bombed down the right wing. These were routine moves, stereotyped even, yet there was no mistaking the precision of Newton's crosses, nor the efficiency of the finishes – the first by Mullery, and the second by Peters, who removed his invisibility cloak to poke home on the far post.

Ramsey was so confident of victory by now that he made moves to bring off Bobby Charlton. The semi-final was only three days away, after all. And then, in one moment of hesitation, the bottom dropped out of England's world.

The danger stemmed from Beckenbauer, the man who would be Kaiser. He went past Mullery near the right-hand corner of the penalty box, and sent in a low cross shot. It was a speculative effort that Banks would have snaffled with one hand tied behind his back. Unfortunately, Banks was in bed with acute food poisoning. Bonetti may have been a star at Chelsea, but he had never played in a match of this magnitude before. He simply froze under pressure, performing a decent impression of London Bridge as the ball squirmed under his body.

> **'I have never seen England give away two such goals.'**
> Ramsey comes as close as he ever would to criticising his players.

225

According to Bonetti's room-mate, Dave Sadler, 'You could just feel the tension coming into Peter when he realised he might have to perform. He'd had the odd game, but by and large, he was happy to be the second string to the best keeper in the world. When he was told he might have to go in, the nerves started immediately.'

Ramsey's biographer, Leo McKinstry, has another explanation for the goalkeeper's air of unease. Bonetti was one of four players whose wives had come out to Mexico, and were staying in a hotel across town. Stories of parties and high living had been filtering through to the squad. As the *Daily Mail*'s Jeff Powell told McKinstry, 'Bonetti was distracted because he had heard rumours that something might be going on. Frances [Bonetti] lost the plot. The other footballers' wives, like Tina [Moore], were used to travelling, they kept their head, but Frances lost control of her emotions.' The point is backed up by Geoff Hurst, who said 'My own feeling at the time was that Peter's mind was not wholly on the job. It was across the city, with his wife Frances.'

Known as 'The Cat' in his South London manor, Bonetti continued to have a dog of a day. Eight minutes from time, he stood motionless as Uwe Seeler sent a freakish back-header arcing across the goal and in at the far post. Germany had taken the game to extra-time, just as they had at Wembley four years earlier. In Leon, though, there was to be no happy ending. When Ramsey tried to rouse his troops, saying 'You did it in 1966, you can do it again,' his words rang hollow. 'Yeah,' scoffed Mullery, 'but it wasn't 100 degrees in the shade at Wembley'. With chilling inevitability, Gerd Müller fastened onto another looping ball in the six-yard box and slammed it into the net. Bonetti, once again, was a spectator.

> **'Welcome back, lads. Better luck in '74.'**
>
> A consolatory banner is held up at Heathrow Airport.

In his book *Jules Rimet Still Dreaming*? Ken Jones describes tracking Ramsey down to England's team hotel two hours after the game. 'I still can't believe it,' the manager said, in reference to Banks's inexplicable gut-rot. 'Of all the players to lose, it had to be him.' Four days later, Harold Wilson's narrow defeat in the general election was widely attributed to post-World Cup gloom. Montezuma was taking his revenge.

A sub divides

The substitution of Bobby Charlton in Leon is generally regarded as a humungous tactical blunder. In the popular imagination, Ramsey went into that match as England's Churchill, and emerged as Douglas Haig. Yet many people forget that West Germany had already scored their first goal by the time that England made the switch.

Over the past four decades, Beckenbauer has made repeated assertions along the lines of 'Charlton was at the heart of the game', or 'How glad I was to see the back of Bobby Charlton!' Yet the fact is that West Germany had been on the point of collapse, only receiving the kiss of life when Beckenbauer's scuffed shot bobbled under Bonetti's helpless body. There was only one villain in this story, and he was wearing gloves.

'Sir Alf Ramsey's team are out because the best goalkeeper most people have ever seen turned sick,' wrote the ever-insightful Hugh McIlvanney in the *Observer*, 'and one who is only slightly less gifted was overwhelmed by the suddenness of his promotion. Those who ranted smugly in distant television studios about the tactical blunders of Ramsey were toying with the edges of the issue. Errors there were and Ramsey in private has acknowledged one or two but the England manager is entitled to claim that his side were felled by something close to an act of God.'

> **'He is a great manager of bad teams, but when he has a good team he does not know what to do.'**
> Malcolm Allison, a long-time critic of Ramsey.

None of these arguments prevented Ramsey from accepting personal responsibility, as he always tried to do. On the flight home he apologised to Charlton. 'I was thinking about the next match,' he said. 'That was a mistake I will always regret. Now I'd like to thank you for all you have done for me and England.' It was the sporting equivalent of a 'Dear John' letter. Charlton knew at once that he would not be adding to his record tally of 106 caps. The bald bomber was pushing 33 now, and there was no chance of him being around for the next World Cup.

Had Ramsey applied the same ruthless logic to the rest of his squad,

> **'The magnitude of our performance was really just like a dream.'**
> Franz Beckenbauer on Germany's 3–1 win at Wembley.

the story of England's decade might have been a happier one. But instinctive loyalty was at the heart of everything he did as a manager. Having worked so hard to build a powerful team, Ramsey found it twice as difficult to pull his masterpiece apart. Over the next three years, some of his favourite players would be allowed to limp on well past their expiration date.

'After 1970, he should have started to rebuild right away,' said Chelsea striker Peter Osgood, 'because if we qualified for 1974, it was obvious that Bobby Moore would be too old, and Mullery, Hurst and Lee weren't going to be around. He left it too late. Mooro played until 1973, which was too long.'

Gunther Netzer: the Germanator

The alarm bells began ringing when West Germany beat England again, this time in the first leg of a European Championship quarter-final in 1972. Leon might have been a lucky break, but when the Germans came to Wembley for the first leg, their tactical and technical supremacy was unmistakeable.

The England team for that match had a familiar spine: Banks in goal, Moore at left-back, with Ball and Peters running the midfield. Strangely, though, Ramsey sent them out without the usual ball-winning terrier in front of the back four. Here was another decision he must have regretted, since it left space for Gunther Netzer, one of the great unfulfilled talents of German football, to produce the finest 90 minutes of his career.

> **'LEAVE NETZER TO ME.'**
> *Daily Mail* headline, quoting Peter Storey, on the morning of England's match in Berlin.

Netzer wore his hair long, like Charlie George, and ran with the ball as fluently as Bobby Charlton. West Germany scored their first goal from a corner after Netzer had charged 50 yards up the centre of the field. A clumsy tackle by Moore then allowed Netzer to add the second himself via a penalty.

Netzer was rarely a first choice for the German coach, Helmut Schoen, who always said 'Overath is more reliable.' In fact, he had more in common with the English mavericks, the Hudsons and the Worthingtons, than he did with the steady Siegfrieds who made up the rest of the German side. But on this occasion he was allowed to dictate the game, bringing a touch of jazzy improvisation to his team-mates' 4/4 beat.

Ramsey, it seemed, was losing his touch. For the second leg, in Berlin, he lurched in the opposite direction, calling up Arsenal's uncompromising anchor-man Peter Storey to stiffen the sinews in midfield. A first-rate bad boy, Storey was once quoted as saying 'If it wasn't for people like me, the Sugar Plum Fairy could play centre-forward.' After retirement, he would be gaoled twice for a series of lurid offences, including running a brothel in East London, counterfeiting gold coins, and importing pornographic videos.

The task in Berlin was to overturn a 3–1 deficit from the first leg. In the event, England hardly tried. With Storey and Hunter to the fore, they attacked the Germans in the wrong sort of way. 'Every one of their players has left his autograph on my legs,' Netzer complained afterwards. Given that Netzer and Co. had just put on the most devastating show at Wembley since the Magyars, it is feasible that Ramsey feared a reprise of the 7–1 defeat in Budapest. What he got instead was a dishonourable 0–0 draw, in a match that represents the high-water mark of English negativity.

As David Downing writes in his book *England v Germany*, 'the *Welt Am Sonntag* correspondent spoke for many when he lamented the English players' betrayal of their own country's reputation for fair play, a reputation for which the Germans had once had so much respect.'

Clown and out

England's two biggest footballing catastrophes are easy to identify. The battle of Belo Horizonte leads the field, closely followed by the Hungarian conquest of 1953. Beyond that, it gets a little hazy. But Poland's visit to

The greatest manager England never had: Brian Clough (centre) with his Derby County internationals Colin Todd and Roy McFarland before England's 1973 World Cup qualifier against Poland.

Wembley in 1973 must surely be a strong contender for the bronze.

This was the match that saw England fail to qualify for the World Cup for the first time. It was also the match that brought Alf Ramsey's 11-year reign to a close. Two decades earlier, Ferenc Puskás and Nándor Hidegkuti had effectively ended his career as an international right-back. Now it was the eccentric Polish goalkeeper Jan Tomaszewski who did for him as a manager.

Better known today for supplying London with plumbers, Poland threw a gigantic spanner in the works. When England had been drawn alongside them in a three-team qualifying group, with Wales making up the numbers, it was thought to be a decent result. But the Poles were no pushovers: they were the reigning Olympic champions, and would go on to finish third in the 1974 World Cup itself.

The gun at Ramsey's head was cocked when England went to Katowice, in June 1973, and came away with a 2–0 defeat. Again, there was evidence of declining standards in the English defence. They conceded a sloppy early goal from a free kick – an area where they had once been so reliable – and another through an error from Bobby Moore, who tried to dribble out of defence and was dispossessed with embarrassing ease. England's once-regal captain had become a liability.

As England prepared for the return match against Poland – surely the most important game in this country since the World Cup final – Ramsey asked the Football League to postpone the fixtures from the previous Saturday. Alan Hardaker, the League secretary, responded as only an English football administrator could. 'If England do lose

> **'He could have thrown his hanky at the ball and made a better job of it.'**
>
> An unnamed reporter remarks on Peter Shilton's gaffe against Poland, 1973.

against Poland, the game is not going to die,' Hardaker said. 'It will be a terrible thing for six weeks, and then everybody will forget about it.'

The match itself was decided by a magnificent goalkeeping performance from Tomaszewski – the man famously derided by Brian Clough on television as 'a clown' – and another series of fatal errors from England. As Grzegorz Lato broke down Poland's left, it looked as if he would lose the ball to Norman Hunter, who had replaced the struggling Moore. But Hunter tried to turn back inside, rather than clogging the ball deep into the stands. Lato nicked it back off him, and passed it to Jan Domarski, bearing down on goal.

It was not too late for England. Domarski's shot was low and only mildly threatening. But Peter Shilton, Banks's successor, got caught in two minds. 'What I should have done was make a blocking save, or parry the shot away for a corner. But I tried to get hold of the ball by scooping it into my body and retaining possession.' He let the shot squirt under his body, just as Bonetti had in Leon.

Ironically, the error had been caused by England's attempts to play positive football, keeping the ball in play because they had to win the game. The hard men were trying – and failing – to turn over a new leaf. Though Allan Clarke equalised with a penalty, England were frustrated by the protean form of Tomaszewski. As Ken Jones writes, 'he thwarted

MARTIN CHIVERS
Caps 24 Goals 13

'CHEE-VERS, CHEE-VERS', the Tottenham faithful would sing. At his best, Chivers was the biggest and most feared striker in the country. At his worst, he would play like a big girl's blouse. Hunter Davies's *The Glory Game*, which tells the story of Spurs' 1971–2 season from the inside, is full of tales of Chivers's run-ins with his coaches, Bill Nicholson and Eddie Baily, who were convinced that he should have scored twice as many goals if only he had made more of an effort. With England too, Chivers was something of a loner. Kevin Keegan has described how 'he would report, nod to the card-players, then go to his room'. Chivers was England's centre-forward on the fateful day of their 1–1 draw with Poland in 1973, but did one of his patented disappearing acts and was substituted late on by Kevin Hector. He never played for England again.

England with practically every part of his body: hands, feet, legs, torso, even his backside. One shot struck the back of his head.' The final score, a 1–1 draw, condemned England's footballers to watching the 1974 World Cup from their own front rooms.

The Valentine's Day massacre

'What upset me more than anything,' said Hunter of his infamous missed challenge on Lato, 'was that Alf lost his job.' Emlyn Hughes, who would inherit the captaincy under the new regime, remained insistent that 'It should never have been allowed to happen, because Alf Ramsey was the greatest England manager of all time.'

Hughes was only half-right. Yes, Alf Ramsey *was* the greatest England manager of all time. But by 1973, he was beginning to lose his mojo. Towards the end of the Wembley disaster, Bobby Moore, watching from the sidelines, urged him to bring on a left-sided player for extra width. Ramsey seemed paralysed by doubt, and it was only in the last five minutes that he shouted, 'Kevin, get stripped.'

Harold Shepherdson, the trainer, leapt up and yanked at Kevin Keegan's clothing with such agitated enthusiasm that he removed tracksuit, shorts and underpants in one go. If the player was shocked, so too was his manager, who had actually been calling for Kevin Hector, the Derby County striker. Once the confusion had been cleared up, Hector came on with around two minutes left, and promptly had a header cleared off the line. It later emerged that Ramsey's watch had stopped during the final stages of the match. Such inefficiency would have been unimaginable just a couple of years earlier.

Ramsey's fate was decided on 14 February, when the FA formed a committee to investigate his conduct. The vote was close, but Sir Harold Thompson, a pompous chemistry don who had always found Ramsey insufferable, insisted that he should go. In April, FA chairman Sir Andrew Stephen delivered the news. Ramsey was sacked, with a feeble pay-off of £8,000.

It was a shabby way to treat one of the great figures of English football. 'Before I wrote my book on tactics, I thought Ramsey had been lucky in 1966,' says Jonathan Wilson. 'Now I realise he was a genius.'

BORN TO RUN

Seventies football was about one thing above all else: £££. It was money that drove defenders to increasingly grisly lengths, looking to protect their £50 win bonuses. And it was money that underpinned the devil-may-care lifestyles of the mavericks. If we're rich enough to pull birds, drive fast cars and wear designer clothes, they asked, why do we need England? After all, George Best had never bothered too much about international football.

On Ramsey's departure, England found the perfect manager for these mercenary times. His name was Don Revie, though he would come to be known as Don Readies. Over 14 seasons at Leeds United, Revie had become an almost messianic figure, a boss to rival Bruce Springsteen. But as an England manager, he was barely up to Eurovision standard.

Notoriety seemed to follow Revie about. His Leeds teams earned a reputation for violence and viciousness. But his defining moment arrived in the summer of 1977. England had already missed out on Euro 1976, and when they went down 2–0 to Italy in Rome, it seemed that they would be skipping the 1978 World Cup as well. The knives – or should we say the nibs – were out. And then Revie committed the ultimate sin. He walked out on his team and his country. As Springsteen sang, 'Tramps like us, baby we were born to run.'

On 12 July, the news broke in the *Daily Mail.* Jeff Powell, Revie's long-time friend and supporter, had landed perhaps the greatest scoop in the history of English football journalism. Rarely has that hackneyed phrase 'I can reveal …' seemed more appropriate. Revie was leaving to take up a £340,000 offer from the United Arab Emirates. In a desperate attempt to justify his actions, he explained that 'The past three years have been very rough for me and my family … the job was bringing too much heartache to those nearest to us. It was rough on my son and daughter and it's not very nice to hear your father constantly attacked.'

Revie has been perceived as a grasping grifter ever since. His name, it was discovered, was an anagram of *envie d'or*, or 'Love of gold'. Yet there was another side to his character too. Curiously, Don the Deserter was also Revie the Romantic. He would tell the

> **'He should have been castrated for the way he left England.'**
> Bury manager Bob Stokoe administers the unkindest cut.

players, 'Breathe fire! Pull on that shirt and show the people what you can do! Put England right up there for them! Make them proud to sing!' Revie was a great one for singing. The first move he made on his managerial debut, against Czechoslovakia in October 1974, was not to change the formation, but to get the crowd roaring 'Land of Hope And Glory' as the teams came out.

Desperate Don: a wild-eyed Don Revie instructs his captain Alan Ball, who later became one of his most vocal critics.

'People say he wanted the best for himself but I honestly believe his main concern was the best for the players,' said Kevin Keegan, one of Revie's few supporters in the England dressing-room. 'His team-talks were sensational. Most people thought of him as a tactician – perhaps he saw himself that way – but I saw him as a motivator. Sometimes he, and we, would be almost crying.'

As the cynics might add, crying all the way to the bank.

A Mighty Mouse-trap

While the FA were searching for Ramsey's full-time replacement, England played seven games under a caretaker manager. Joe Mercer's first words to his players were 'I didn't want this bloody job in the first place.' But he said them with a smile on his face. Mercer said everything with a smile on his face.

One of the great England midfielders of the war years, Mercer took a free-wheeling, fun-loving approach to football. His single summer in charge provided some light-hearted relief in the middle of an otherwise dismal decade. 'I call 'em footballers,' Mercer once said. 'If they're good enough, I pick 'em. If not, I don't.' There were reprieves, during his brief tenure, for two members of the rebel brigade: Frank Worthington and Stan Bowles. 'For the first time,' wrote Keegan, 'I felt we had an England team able to play from the back to the front. Joe picked entertaining players, the kind that fans might have selected.'

Keegan was another player who enjoyed a resurgence under Mercer. It is surprising, in retrospect, that he had never gelled with Ramsey, because they were both self-made men. 'Practically everything Kevin achieved as a player came from exceptional determination,' said Ron Ashman, who managed Keegan in his early days at Scunthorpe United. 'It never came easy for him. But he worked and worked to make himself a great player.'

A natural extrovert, who became known as 'Mighty Mouse' in his time with Hamburg, Keegan had a knack for attracting attention. This was useful when it came to winning endorsements (notably from Brut, who ran a hilariously camp TV campaign featuring Keegan and Henry Cooper throwing towels at each other in a steamy locker-room), or appearing on *Superstars* with Brian Jacks. But it could also cause him problems, as when England were killing time during an hour-long stopover in Belgrade airport in 1975.

Special KK: Kevin Keegan, the crown-prince of English football, came to the fore during Joe Mercer's brief spell as caretaker manager.

Bored with the waiting, the team started to get a little frisky. Alec Lindsay, another Liverpool player, hopped onto a luggage carousel and capered about. At which point 'a huge, grey-uniformed, jackbooted policeman strode on to the scene,' Brian Glanville reported. '[He] picked up poor Keegan at one end while a brown suited man took the other and carried him bodily out of the entrance hall. When eventually he returned, he was in tears. He had been beaten up.'

The guards assembled a lengthy charge-sheet against Keegan, who was accused of sexually assaulting an air-hostess and disturbing the peace, among other things. The whole affair was reminiscent of Bobby Moore's perverted persecution in Bogotá, although there was no suggestion this time that England had been deliberately targeted. The storm had only blown up in the first place because kindly Uncle Joe had dropped the official dress code, leaving the team looking like a bunch of scruffy tourists.

Mercer insisted that the whole party should stay at the airport. 'We can all go home, no problem,' he told the players, 'but Kevin won't be able to come with us. He'll have to stay and answer any charges. The only way we'll get him out is by sticking together and answering them back on the field. It's their country off the field, but they can't stop us on it.'

Henry V could hardly have put it better. After a few hours' wrangling, Keegan was cleared. And when England met Yugoslavia at the Red Star Stadium, two days later, he popped up to score the second goal in a 2–2 draw.

Raving Revie and his racy revels

Known as 'Mr Handsome' in his playing days, Revie was a charismatic man and a legendary manager of Leeds United. During his time at Elland Road, he often seemed to be running a cult rather than a football club. The great Leeds teams of the 1960s inspired utter devotion among insiders, fear and loathing in everyone else.

Revie had some quirky methods. The players would assemble for parlour games before every match, whether it be bingo, carpet bowls or indoor putting competitions. They would then be given lovingly compiled dossiers, assessing each opponent in intimate detail. On a Thursday night, Revie would personally administer soapy massages. And when Leeds went out on the field, their teamwork was as tight-knit as a Roman legion. The suffix 'United' has never seemed more appropriate.

Yet, for all his emphasis on bonding rituals, Revie never managed to relax and enjoy the game like Mercer did. His skin was thinner than rice paper – hardly an ideal attribute for any football manager. 'There was too much worry, too much acrimony, too many things lost that should have been won,' wrote his biographer, Andrew Mourant.

'Revie's waking hours were riddled with phobias and rituals,' Mourant added. 'Taking the same route to his dugout before a match, a fear of ornamental elephants, a readiness to believe that a gypsy curse on Elland Road was preventing his side from winning, even a distaste for birds in pictures or as motifs.'

It seems likely that Revie suffered from what we would now call obsessive compulsive disorder. His hang-ups even drove him to remove the peacock from Leeds United's club badge. According to Gary Sprake, Leeds's accident-prone goalkeeper, Revie spent his life 'knotted with fear'.

Always on the fiddle

The portents, on Revie's promotion to the national team, seemed encouraging enough. He opened his account with a memorable 3–0 win over Czechoslovakia in a European Championship qualifier, and had soon added a 2-0 demolition of West Germany, in a match that featured a splendid debut from Alan Hudson.

But the trouble with Revie was that he was never satisfied. Already, he was falling into the oldest trap in the book, fussing and fiddling with the team until no-one knew where they stood. His first action as England manager had been to take 85 players – that's almost eight full teams – to Manchester for a get-together. It was a good indication of things to come: more than 50 different men would be called on during his 29 matches in charge.

'He was changing his mind all the time,' said Ted Croker, the FA secretary. 'Because he had had the tremendous success [at Leeds] of playing one or two people in different roles … [Revie] got the impression he could do it at England level, that he could take the eleven best players in the country and make a team of them. But the time you have with players is so short that you can't vary much what they're doing at club level.'

Revie showed further naivety in trying to enforce the same team-building exercises he had used at Leeds. The England players were never going to settle for evenings around the fireside, especially when they were combined with an early curfew. 'He would go, "Come on, lads, we're having bowls tonight," on a Friday night,' said Mick Channon, the Southampton striker. 'Of course we used to sneak out. I used to rebel against being told what do. You treat people like children and they behave like them.'

After his first year in the job, Revie's England were unbeaten on the field, but increasingly fragmented off it. He seemed incapable of getting through a month without controversy. Keegan walked out on the squad in May 1975, having been dropped with no explanation. Alan Ball would suffer the same fate in September, after a six-match run as captain. 'Some of the players are donkeys,' a furious Ball retorted. 'Give them a sugar lump and they will run all day and play bingo and carpet bowls all night.'

Ball's fall had less to do with footballing reasons than the fact that he enjoyed a quiet drink (or sometimes a noisy one). His exit drained any remaining colour from a grey team known as 'Revie's Robots'. 'I'm a fan of Ball only as a player,' said Keegan, 'for there are aspects of his character that don't appeal to me, yet there is no denying that he is a character, and once he had gone England began recruiting a rather characterless team. Not unexpectedly, they returned some nondescript results.'

Roman horror day

One of the many downsides of non-qualification from the previous World Cup was that England were now unseeded for the 1978 tournament. When the draw was held, and his team landed in the same group as Italy, Revie must have hurled his horoscope down in disgust.

The pressure seemed to get to him when England travelled to Rome in November 1976. He picked a bizarre, misshapen team in which two ball-winning terriers – Trevor Cherry and Brian Greenhoff – were supposed to run the midfield. The emphasis, as in so many cowardly England selections over the years, was on nullifying the opposition. But with no wingers in Revie's side, it was unclear how they were supposed to mount any attacks of their own.

Keegan suggested afterwards that the Italians had deliberately let Greenhoff have plenty of the ball, realising that he would not be able to hurt them.[1] Meanwhile, Stan Bowles – the one concession to creativity in the team – tried to make the most of limited service. 'I thought Bowles played better in Italy than anyone,' said Mick Channon. 'But for Revie, picking him was against the grain. It wasn't Don Revie. He seemed to be doing things he wasn't sure about … doing what the press wanted and hoping it would come right.'

It was clear what England's best midfield would have been: Alan Ball, Gerry Francis and Colin Bell. But Ball had been banished, and the other two were injured. Italy won 2–0, and should have scored plenty more. The way the Italians tore England apart, they could have been playing at the Colosseum.

1: Many of Italy's attacks were launched by a creative inside-forward named Fabio Capello, of whom more later.

> **'Kevvy, this is the worst England side I have ever seen. You have problems here.'**
>
> Dutch striker Johnny Rep to Keegan during Holland's 2–0 win at Wembley in 1977.

JOHAN CRUYFF
Caps 48 (for Holland)   Goals 33

BY THE TIME of Holland's 1977 appearance at Wembley, 'Total Football' was at its height. Cruyff and Co. won 2–0, through a pair of goals from Jan Peters, and could have had plenty more. They were almost as far out of England's league as Hungary had been in 1953. The Dutch manager Jan Zwartkruis suggested afterwards that Cruyff had played like the Scarlet Pimpernel, though perhaps the Orange Pimpernel might have been more appropriate. 'The Dutch game is different,' said Zvartkruis. 'It is a fantasy. We use our imagination. We take risks.' At the height of Revie's hag-ridden regime (tough on flair, tough on the causes of flair), their performance provoked sighs of envy. 'Isn't it staggering that a little country of 10 million people fields the best tactical side in the world?' asked Kevin Keegan.

> **'[Revie] presented to the public a sensational and notorious example of disloyalty, breach of duty, discourtesy and selfishness.'**
>
> Mr Justice Cantley sums up before his appeal verdict.

Revie now became convinced that the FA were about to sack him. He turned up late for England's tour of South America the following summer, claiming that he had been on a scouting mission to watch Italy train. He had been scouting alright, but for gold rather than insights. Travelling to a clandestine meeting in the Middle East, he donned a bulky overcoat and dark glasses. It is never a good sign when the England manager starts behaving like Inspector Clouseau.

> **'If Stan Bowles could pass a betting shop like he could pass a football, he wouldn't have a problem.'**
>
> Ernie Tagg, manager of Crewe Alexandria.

Two weeks later, the *Daily Mail* delivered its bombshell – Jeff Powell's news story, accompanied by an interview which netted Revie a tidy £20,000 in itself. 'For years everyone seems to have believed I've just been feathering my nest,' said Revie, reading the public right for once. 'So perhaps the time has come to put myself first.'

A furious FA hit back, charging Revie with bringing the game into disrepute. The case dragged on for over a year, as Revie challenged their attempt to ban him from any involvement in English football for the next decade. In the end, he won the appeal, leaving the administrators facing a £150,000 bill for costs. But he also had to listen to the judge's withering assessment of his character, which was described as 'deceitful, greedy and selfish'. In the eyes of the public, Mr Handsome had become Mr Loathsome.

'They looted the goal posts
and the cross bars, the nets
and the corner flags. They
whipped out dirks from
their kilts and cut out the
penalty spots for souvenirs,
then they began carving up
keepsake patches of turf.
Almost the only things left
were the twin towers.'

Kevin Keegan on the Scottish fans' kleptomania in
response to their 2–1 win at Wembley in Revie's final
match in charge.

The rise of Reverend Ron

One of the most powerful figures in 1970s football, Sir Harold Thompson was an irascible chemistry professor known to his enemies as 'the Atom Bomb'. The FA's new chairman wore his learning heavily, and was definitely not a man you wanted standing behind you with a cheese-knife.

By 1977, Thompson was building up a fine collection of managerial scalps. Having already played Brutus to Ramsey's Caesar, he now led the campaign to destroy Revie's reputation. But there was no danger of any nuclear fall-outs between Thompson and Ron Greenwood, the charming, utterly upright gentleman who followed Revie into the hot seat. The two men were old allies from Oxford University, where Greenwood had coached the Blues in the late 1950s.

If Greenwood is now the least remembered of England's 12 full-time managers, it is probably because he was just so nice. If England were ever going to take a gamble on the mercurial, charismatic, harebrained genius of Brian Clough, this, surely, would have been the moment to do so. But Thompson was not a man who approved of insolence or flippancy – two qualities for which Clough was famed. Greenwood was far more his glass of port, being the nearest thing to a don that English football had yet produced.

> **'It was like inviting a village vicar to take over from a foot-in-door salesman.'**
>
> Jimmy Greaves on the contrast between 'Reverend Ron' Greenwood and 'Don the Deserter' Revie.

'Emlyn Hughes was to tell me they half-expected me to walk through the door with a mortar-board on my head and a gown over my shoulders,' wrote Greenwood, as he described an early visit to Anfield. 'They had heard those old and ludicrous rumours that I was a footballing egghead.' It was almost as if Walter Winterbottom had returned to the England team.

A great idealist, Greenwood was not interested in clanking, mechanical teams that could churn out results by the dozen. He wanted

Let us play: 'Reverend Ron' Greenwood during a training session at the 1982 World Cup. Jimmy Greaves suggested that Greenwood – who became England manager at 55 – was the right man for the job at the wrong time.

to nourish the soul. 'Spectators have got fed up with seeing a bunch of fit people run around,' he said. 'They want to see skill with it.'

He was lucky enough to have a decent crop of ball-players to choose from. These men were genuinely gifted, yet mercifully free of the self-destructive tendencies that had afflicted Bowles and Co. Take Trevor Brooking, a Grenadier-backed midfielder who had learned the ropes under Greenwood himself at West Ham, and who shared his dignified, decorous demeanour. 'The worst expression likely to cross Brooking's lips is "Oh, scum!"' wrote Kevin Keegan. 'This will be said in a suburban drawl that sends the lads into hysterics.'

Brooking had been floating around the side since the last days of Ramsey, but it was only now that he developed into England's playmaker-general. His symbiotic relationship with Keegan gave the side its heartbeat. As Greenwood himself put it, 'They cooked up goals for England that suggested telepathy. There was a special relationship between them on the field that springs from familiarity, confidence – and something beyond my ken.'

Brooking's promotion to first violin meant that Glenn Hoddle would have to play second fiddle – never a comfortable position for a man who felt he should be conducting the whole damn orchestra. Handed his first international cap at the age of 22, Hoddle was the coming man of

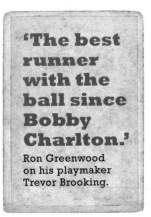

'The best runner with the ball since Bobby Charlton.'

Ron Greenwood on his playmaker Trevor Brooking.

English football, a languid virtuoso whose extraordinary talents prompted a graffiti campaign proclaiming 'Hoddle is God'. It was said of him that Brazil would have picked him in a flash. But it was also said of him (as it has been said of every creative English footballer since time immemorial) that he was never there when the going got tough.

It soon became clear that Brooking and Hoddle could not play in the same team. They were just too similar, both delightful distributors of the ball, neither able to dispossess a five-year-old child.

And England's anchorman, Ray Wilkins, was not exactly a hard case either.

Never one to go forward when a lateral pass presented itself, Wilkins was widely known as 'The Crab'. It was rumoured that a team-mate once peered down his shorts to see if he had square balls. 'He should have been a Socrates,' said Rodney Marsh of Wilkins, 'but he ended up playing these little passes, like Nobby Stiles. He became a continuity player.'

Wilkins might have passed the ball like Stiles, but he didn't tackle like him. And therein lay Greenwood's problem. His early England teams were easy on the eye, but they also lacked a hard edge, a ball-winner in front of the back four. Like West Ham, they were prone to playing pretty patterns and finishing halfway up the table.

A Europhile at large

Greenwood's transformation of the England team drew a wave of plaudits from across the Continent. 'He thinks European,' said Germany's manager Helmet Schoen. 'Unlike a lot of people in English football, he can see beyond Dover.'

> ### 'Disappointment is part of football.'
> **Ron Greenwood justifies dropping Glenn Hoddle after he scored a spectacular goal on his England debut.**

The victories, such as England's masterful 2–0 spanking of Spain in March 1980, were wildly celebrated. 'Every player in this side is phenomenal,' gushed Italy's manager Enzo Bearzot. Even when they lost, as in Munich two years earlier, Schoen's assistant Jupp Derwall still commented that Greenwood was 'on the way to creating not just a good England side, but a very very good one'.

Do we detect a touch of self-interest in these approving notices? Greenwood may have been expanding England's range, but he was also in danger of dragging them away from what they did best: direct, robust, up-and-at-'em football, preferably leavened by a touch of inspiration from a Charlton or a Mannion in midfield. That, after all, had been England's blueprint when they won the World Cup.

'Reinvent thyselves,' was the lesson from Reverend Ron. Unfortunately, sport is not as simple as that. Any psychologist will tell you that when the heat is on, people revert to what they know best. England proved the point at the 1980 European Championships.

Greenwood's men went to Italy with the best qualifying record of any team, but their first match, against Belgium, turned into a familiar slugfest. The Belgians sat back, with nine men behind the ball, and England responded by hoofing the ball upfield and sending high crosses into the box.

'I'm not particularly strong in the air,' lamented Tony Woodcock, a clever, Sheringham-esque striker with a perm to rival Keegan's. 'They were throwing balls in, there was a Belgian there twice as big as I am. I might as well not have been there.' A 1–1 draw proved to be a decent result for Belgium, who went on to finish as runners-up to West Germany. England went out in the first round.

The English disease

Throughout the 1970s, hooliganism[1] had been the cancer in football's heart. The authorities did their best to ignore it, yet by 1980 the symptoms were all too obvious. England's game against Belgium was the first in a major championships to be interrupted by riots.

Fighting started around the half-hour mark, when the boneheads in the union jack underpants took exception to the Italians cheering Belgium's equaliser. The police soon stopped them in their tracks, with a baton charge and tear gas canisters. But they also stopped the game for five minutes, as England's goalkeeper Ray Clemence was overcome by the fumes.

> **'Put them all on a boat back to England – and then pull out the plug.'**
>
> Ron Greenwood's solution to the hooligan problem, 1980.

'The game never took off once it restarted,' Greenwood recalled. 'Stoppages always tend to unsettle because they break everybody's concentration. But I think we were bothered most of all because we were very conscious that it was our supporters who had stepped out of line.'

Prime Minister Margaret Thatcher described the thuggery as 'a disgraceful embarrassment'. Sir Harold Thompson referred to the offenders as 'sewer rats'. Such soundbites would recur with depressing regularity over the next two decades, for the problem was destined to get worse before it got better. This was one area in which Britannia ruled the waves.

From Turin 1980 to Dublin 1995, England teams were doomed to be pursued around the world by these half-witted furies, the dregs of the human race. This so-called 'English disease' reached a feverish peak during Italia '90, when Greenwood's successor Bobby Robson developed what amounted to a persecution complex.

'It just creates around us a feeling of … oh bloody hell, they don't belong to us, do they?' he told the author Pete Davies. 'It just creates a feeling around us of being unclean – because we know that they are England, and they're our supporters, and it's something we don't represent – yet we do, because they follow us. And we hate them. We just hate them.'

1: The term apparently derives from one Patrick Hooligan, a small-time criminal who terrorised Southwark, South London, in the late 19th century.

You only rant when you're winning

The year 1981 was not a good vintage for the England team. They lost five games – a record for any calendar year in their long and painful history. Greenwood also turned 60 in November, making him the first man to manage England in his seventh decade. These facts may not have been unrelated.

> **'If they are not seen here again for 50 years, it will be too soon.'**
>
> Swiss police chief after English fans run riot in Basle, May 1981.

'I thought Ron was the right man for the England job, but at the wrong time,' wrote Jimmy Greaves. 'To the players he was selecting he was not far off a grandfatherly figure.'

Everyone hoped that England had bottomed out in Basle, where the team lost 2–1 to Switzerland and the supporters ran riot in the streets. On the plane home, Greenwood made up his mind to resign. He was only talked out of it by the players, with Keegan, inevitably, to the fore. Greenwood recalls that he was 'unbelievably touched that they cared this way'.

Then, in September 1981, England travelled to Oslo. The Norwegians, at this stage, were still outright minnows; England had played them five times before, running up 24 goals in the process. And the match stuck to the script for the first half-hour, as Robson poached an early goal from a Keegan flick-on.

The atmosphere in the stadium changed dramatically on 34 minutes, when a cross from Tom Lund looped over Ray Clemence, and dropped in at the far post. Six minutes later, Hallvar Thoresen doubled Norway's tally – and the ecstasy of the home fans – when he pounced on a loose ball from just ten yards out.

No element of the match, or indeed Greenwood's whole term in office, is as well remembered now as Bjørge Lillelien's slow-motion rant for state broadcaster NRK. 'Yurrrggggh! Der stod Ingelland!' he bellowed, puffing out each word so breathlessly you might have thought he had just staggered off the pitch himself. 'Lord Nelson! Lord Beaverbrook! Winston Churchill! Henry Cooper! Clement Attlee! Anthony Eden! Lady Diana!

'FOR GOD'S SAKE GO.'
An exasperated *Sun* headline takes aim at Ron
Greenwood, June 1980.

Der stod dem all! Der stod dem all! Maggie Thatcher, can you hear me?
Can you hear me, Maggie? Your boys took one hell of a beating tonight!'

It may sound like a 78 rpm record played at 45, but Lillelien's tirade
was voted the greatest bit of commentary ever by *Observer Sport Monthly*
magazine in 2002. 'Passionate, uninhibited and a bit weird,' wrote Lee
Honeyball, 'football fans everywhere from Scotland to Argentina knew
exactly what he was saying: that there is no pleasure as sweet as beating
England at their own game.'

Keegan's midnight dash

In the lead-up to the 1982 World Cup, England's fortunes swung around
like a hammock in a hurricane. By rights, they should never have made it
to the finals at all. They won just four of their eight qualifiers, only
squeezing through because their rivals were equally inconsistent.

Mixed in among the dross was one storming performance in
Budapest, where the old firm of Keegan and Brooking scored all three
goals. Brooking's second was an absolute belter, a rising drive from the
right-hand side of the penalty area that lodged in the stanchion between
post and crossbar. 'It was the best shot of my career,' Brooking says.

To Greenwood's eternal frustration, both men were *hors de combat*
by the time the team had assembled in Spain. Brooking was carrying a
groin problem, while Keegan's back had locked up again. Greenwood put
them in a room together, commenting wryly that 'misery loves company'.

The best run Keegan made in the whole tournament was his secret
dash to Hamburg to see a back specialist. The whole escapade was cooked
up so late one night that there were no taxis available from Bilbao – where
the team was stationed – to the airport in Madrid, and Keegan ended up
borrowing the hotel receptionist's tiny two-seater car.

'I did not sleep,' wrote Greenwood. 'I just lay there thinking of
England's most celebrated footballer pushing on through the darkness
towards the Spanish capital. I would not have let anyone else make the

1982 WORLD CUP SPAIN

Round One:
England 3 – 1 France
Robson 1, 67 *Soler 24*
Mariner 83 (below, to left of Keegan)

England 2 – 0 Czechoslovakia
Francis 62
Barmos (o.g.) 66

England 1 – 0 Kuwait
Francis 27

Round Two:
England 0 – 0 West Germany

England 0 – 0 Spain

Under the new management of Ron Greenwood, and after two World Cups in the wilderness, England return, play superbly in the opening round, but exit in the second qualifying round, having not lost a single match.

journey but Kevin was such a man of the world that I knew he would be all right. I imagined how other players might react if I told them: "Drive yourself down to Madrid in the middle of the night, jump onto a plane for Hamburg and handle everything by yourself." They would have thought me stark, raving mad. But not Kevin Keegan. He was different.'

Greenwood makes like a tree

It was a shame that England did not show such a sense of adventure in the tournament itself. At least, not at the business end. They did get off to a bit of a flier, setting a new World Cup record when Bryan Robson scored after just 27 seconds against France. By the end of the opening stage, they had become the only England side to win its first three games at a major tournament. But any neutral observer would have had to admit that they were gifted two goals by the Czechs, and laboured to despatch the unfancied Kuwaitis.

The standard of opposition climbed dramatically in the second round. On 29 June 1982, England faced West Germany. The *Sun* greeted the morning of the match with a headline – 'ACHTUNG STATIONS' – that would be echoed in the *Daily Mirror* 14 years later. In the event, England were held to a bloodless 0–0 draw by the Germans, whose play throughout this tournament was mean-spirited and cynical.

The draw left England dangling above the abyss. Just as in the European Championships two years earlier, they needed a convincing victory over Spain if they were to make further progress. It was England's crunchiest crisis in 12 years. And, as usual, all the pre-match debate surrounded Brooking and Keegan, who had returned after a couple of days in Hamburg saying 'I feel a lot better, boss.'

With just under half-an-hour to go, and the game still scoreless, Greenwood sent on the players he considered 'my two trumps'. Brooking was immediately at the heart of things, left unmarked by the Spanish to run the game with his usual élan. But Keegan was a shadow of his former self. When Robson floated in a perfect cross, finding him unmarked some six yards out, the Mighty Mouse made a horrible hash of his free header. 'A sickener,' he said afterwards. 'I'd scored from 50 worse positions.'

It was the end for Reverend Ron, but at least it was a humane end. Greenwood was able to retire to his seaside retreat in Brighton with dignity intact. His influence over English football had been beneficial, in style if not necessarily results. And it was not over yet. Bobby Robson and Terry Venables, who had gone to Spain as assistant coaches, would both end up managing the England team in their own right.

When Alf Ramsey used the word 'animals' to describe the Argentine football team of 1966, he was tapping into a long tradition of mistrust. The English have always been 'las piratas' (the pirates) to the Argentines, just as we are 'les rosbifs' to the French and 'those bloody whingeing Poms' to the Aussies.

The name originated with England's original occupation of the Falkland Islands, all the way back in 1833, plus any number of feisty encounters on the Spanish Main. Yet if you want a moment of real sporting piracy, a hijack that would have done credit to the dastardly Blackbeard, look no further than Diego Maradona's 'Hand of God' goal two decades later.

For those who do not already have the image burned into their retinas, the goal was scored when Maradona went up for a high ball with Peter Shilton – a goalkeeper who stood some eight inches taller than him – and casually punched the ball into the net. When Gary Lineker said that Maradona's left foot was like a hand, this was not quite what he had in mind.

Maradona's deception must rank as one of the greatest hoaxes in the history of sport, on a par with Ben Johnson's drug-assisted 100-metre dash or Hansie Cronje's fishy declaration in Cape Town. Shilton and his team-mates never really got over their sense of injustice. Yet the incident is still celebrated and enjoyed across the world as the moment when England were duped by a cheeky scamp from the backstreets of Buenos Aires.

English moralists may find it bizarre that a blatant handball should be remembered with more excitement and affection than the genuinely brilliant run that Maradona pulled off five minutes later, carrying the ball past a quintet of defenders and into the net. It is certainly true that if an Englishman had scored with a deliberate handball in a World Cup quarter-final, we would still be beating ourselves up about it.

But this is missing the point: what makes Maradona's finger-poke so resonant is the sense of the traditional power structure being challenged. It was a David and Goliath situation in every sense: Shilton towered over Maradona just as England, in the view of most Argentines, had patronised and abused their country for years. As rock star Fito Paez declared, 'The first goal was the greatest in Argentina's history – even more so than the second because Diego hoodwinked the pirates.'

There were more than just footballing scores to settle. By the mid-1980s, Ramsey's gaffe had been overshadowed by the far greater grievance of the Falklands War. This bloody and quite disproportionate conflict had accounted for over 900 lives – an extraordinary figure for a barren group of islands described by President Reagan as 'that little ice-cold bunch of land'.

As England and Argentina prepared for their 1986 quarter-final – the second of three great World Cup encounters – the Argentines made no apology for bringing politics into sport. 'To beat the English would represent a double satisfaction for everything that happened in the *Malvinas*,' said Nery Pumpido, their goalkeeper. Pumpido got his wish, as the pirates were made to walk the plank.

Uncle Bobby against the world

Today, Bobby Robson is English football's favourite uncle. So it takes an effort of will to imagine just what a controversial, unpopular and vilified figure he was during his eight years as coach of the national team. Within a couple of years of taking on the job from Greenwood, Robson was the subject of some of the most vicious headlines ever seen in the popular press.

'Other [managers], like Terry Venables, have found that affability and good humour can be handy weapons in fending off the critics,' wrote Niall Edworthy in his book *The Second Most Important Job in the Country*. 'But with Robson ... well, he might as well have told them to stick their typewriters in a dark place for all it was worth. They could not have been more abusive if they tried.'

The storm of scorn began with Robson's very first match in Copenhagen. England managed to nick a 2–2 draw, a decent result against a fast and mobile Danish side. But Robson took a hammering anyway. It wasn't so much the result (although a jingoistic press corps seemed to imagine that Denmark had stood still since Vivian Woodward's day). The big issue was the absence of Keegan, who had been overlooked for the first time since 1975.

> **'England's performance created the biggest stink since the sewermen went on strike.'**
>
> Terry McNeill in the *News of the World* after England's 1–0 defeat to Denmark in 1983.

Accustomed to being treated like sporting royalty, Keegan mounted his high horse. 'I was upset because [Robson] didn't tell me before he told the press,' he said. 'After 63 caps and ten years' experience I thought I was worth a 10p phone call.' On Robson's next visit to Keegan's heartland of St James' Park, he was showered with more expectorate than a punk at the 100 Club. It was an experience he would have to get used to.

As the match in Copenhagen had shown, there was nothing rotten in the state of Denmark's football. Leagues all over Europe were waving deals at silky players like Jesper Olsen and Michael Laudrup. As the English defender Kenny Sansom put it, 'They'd come on a bundle. It was no freak result. You could see how much some of their players had improved from going abroad.'

This meant trouble for England, for the return fixture at Wembley proved to be a head-to-head eliminator. The winner would go to the 1984 finals of the European Championships. The loser would face the consequences. As Robson put it, 'We must get to France for the European Championship finals next year to sustain public interest in a product that is being hit by the recession.'

Perhaps it was this doomsday thinking that prompted Robson to leave Glenn Hoddle on the bench and pick three defensively minded midfielders instead. He said he wanted something 'a bit spiky' from his team, but it was the Danes who showed more penetration and earned the vital penalty when Phil Neal handled a Laudrup cross. Barcelona's Allan Simonsen stepped up and scored the only goal of the game, condemning Robson to what he described as 'the blackest day of my career'.

The pain of defeat was only increased by the recalled Hoddle's masterclass in the dead rubber which followed against Hungary. His stunning free-kick was one of three unanswered efforts in Budapest. 'From the start, he was performing small feats of virtuosity, chest traps, side steps and the like, which put the traditionally gifted Hungarians to shame on their own ground,' wrote Brian Glanville. Even so, it would be another two years before Robson trusted Hoddle enough to make him a regular.

The numbers don't add up

If this was a grim era for lovers of possession football, Robson cannot take all the blame. Long-ball tactics had infiltrated the FA's culture through the work of Graham Taylor, who had been supervising the England youth team, and the national director of coaching Charles Hughes.

> **'He poisoned the wells of English football.'**
> Brian Glanville on Charles Hughes, the FA's national director of coaching.

Taylor's theories – later to be exposed at the top level – were based on match analysis, an outdated system that had emerged some 40 years earlier. Pioneered by wing-commander Charles Reep, an analytically-minded Arsenal fan, these primitive ideas annulled creativity and relied on outrunning the opposition rather than outwitting them. Hughes, meanwhile, used similar calculations to prove that the 'position of maximum opportunity' – or 'POMO' for short – was somewhere in line with the back post. Hardly a revelation to shake football to its foundations.

During the 1950s and 60s, Reep had carried out a study of almost 600 matches, gathered from three World Cups as well as the English leagues. The results showed that 91.5 per cent of all moves consisted of three received passes or fewer, and he used this statistic to argue that fancy football is a waste of time; you would be better off hoofing the ball long and hoping someone would get on the end of it.

This is a bizarre line of reasoning, akin to saying that because English people spend 90 per cent of their evenings watching television, there is no point going out. All Reep's findings really showed is that 'kick-and-rush' is far easier to play than 'pass-and-move'. Which is quite different to proving it superior. As the tactical analyst Jonathan Wilson wrote, 'It is, frankly, horrifying, that a philosophy founded on such a basic misinterpretation of figures could have been allowed to become a cornerstone of English coaching.'

For Robson's men, the battering-ram approach was particularly ineffective because they lacked a top-class target-man to aim for. Even if you accepted the logic of punting the ball forward at every opportunity, who was going to put it in the net? Until the emergence of Gary Lineker in 1985, Robson was forced to experiment with players like Peter Withe, Paul Walsh, Brian Stein and Luther Blissett. All with international strike rates to justify selection in a Cow's Arse And Banjo XI.

Barnes breaks the colour bar

Time for another quiz question. Who was the first black footballer to score for England? After 110 years of internationals, two men broke the mould in the same match, the 9-0 win over Luxembourg in November 1982, which featured a hat-trick from Luther Blissett and a lone strike from Mark Chamberlain. It was Blissett who netted first, scuffing a miscued volley into an open goal from about six yards out.

For the first black player to appear in an England team, you need to go back another four years. Viv Anderson, who made his debut in a friendly against Czechoslovakia in November 1978, was an attacking right-back who had 'the knack of getting one of his long spindly legs wrapped around the ball at the most opportune moment,' as the author James Corbett writes. Trivia buffs might also note that his strike against Yugoslavia in 1986 remains the last England goal to be scored by a player sporting a moustache. (Goatees and half-sets need not apply.)

But the man who really smashed the colour bar was John Barnes, a bewilderingly gifted midfielder who would win 79 caps over 12 years in

LUTHER BLISSETT
Caps 14   Goals 3

A BARREL-CHESTED powerhouse at Graham Taylor's Watford, Blissett was signed by AC Milan for £1 million in 1983. He went on to become one of the most celebrated names in Italian football, but for all the wrong reasons. 'Blissett played only for one season twenty years ago, but you still say his name and everybody laughs,' said the football writer Tommaso Pellizzarri. 'He just looked physically ridiculous, this big man running in his strange way with his long legs, and he failed to score goals in the most incredible way. The worst player we have ever seen!' Bizarrely, Luther Blissett was then adopted as a pseudonym for a secretive group of Italian anarchists. As the author David Winner reported, 'Q, written by four Genoans under the name Luther Blissett, was an anticlerical thriller set during the bloody repression of the sixteenth century, and was nominated for a literary prize by the *Guardian*.' The whole phenomenon was explored by an episode of *Fantasy Football* in 2004, which can be viewed on YouTube.

and around the England team. (This is another record for a black footballer, which will probably be overtaken by Rio Ferdinand some time in 2010.) Barnes was born in Jamaica and arrived in England at the age of 11, when his father – a military attaché – was posted to London. Discovered playing park football, he went on to become the one concession to creativity in Graham Taylor's Watford side.

The sadness with Barnes, as with so many meteoric England stars, was that he never quite lived up to the richness of his early promise. The seminal Barnes moment came in his tenth game, against Brazil at the once-magnificent Maracanã Stadium. It was a nothing tour in some ways, organised to fill the gap left by England's non-qualification for Euro 1984. But Robson needed some succour after his miserable start in the job, and he got it in the final minute of the first half. Collecting a crossfield pass from centre-forward Mark Hateley on his chest, Barnes swerved infield off the left flank, leaving his marker Leandro standing and scything through the heart of the defence.

Brazil had not lost at their dilapidated headquarters for 27 years, but now they were being beaten at their own game. Barnes belied the cratered surface – moonwalkers have had smoother strolls – to strut his way past four defenders and virtually dribble the ball into the net. 'I don't remember much about my goal,' Barnes, then a precocious 20-year-old, later reflected. 'I always liken it to an out-of-body experience. I look at it on TV now and I can't remember doing any of it.'

But for Tony Woodcock's dash across his eyeline, Barnes would have shot as he encroached on the penalty area and English football would have been denied a rare jewel. Instead, generous applause cascaded around the stands. The goal was later described by one Rio newspaper as the finest ever scored at the Maracanã, and has also been compared to Maradona's 60-yard run-and-strike against England two years later. The difference is that Barnes scored in a midsummer preamble to the World Cup qualifying campaign, rather than the 1986 finals themselves. That crucial context separates the good from the great.

Beach boy: England's left-wing John Barnes relaxes on the Copacabana, 9 June 1984. The following day he would score one of the most breathtaking individual goals ever seen at Rio de Janeiro's Maracanã Stadium.

A giant of the six-yard box

For all the brilliance of Barnes's goal, England 2–0 victory over Brazil was perhaps not quite as earth-shattering as it seemed. 'Have you ever seen such a poor Brazilian team?' whispered England's assistant coach Don Howe afterwards. Yet the symbolism of success in Brazil's backyard remained powerful, and it earned Robson a much-needed reprieve. 'The effect was tremendous,' said Ray Wilkins. 'It improved our spirit no end and we all felt that the gaffer had turned a corner.'

So it proved as England came through their World Cup qualifiers undefeated. They weren't quite flying – a 1–0 win in Northern Ireland was universally derided – but neither were they drowning. And the spine of a pretty handy team was beginning to develop. In midfield, Bryan Robson was at the peak of his powers, driving play forward in the all-action fashion that earned him the nickname Captain Marvel. In attack, Gary Lineker was dipping a stylish toe into the international pool, scoring a hat-trick in his ninth match against Turkey. And in defence, Engand could lean on the mighty Peter Shilton, unrivalled at this moment as the best goalkeeper in the world.

> **'A million quid for Mark Hateley? But he can't even trap a dead rat.'**
>
> Stan Bowles on the England striker of the early 1980s.

Like all great keepers, Shilton ruled the penalty area as much by sheer presence as shot-stopping ability. 'I get the feeling that they're conscious of my reputation and determination when hitting shots at me,' he once said, in explaining his Jedi-style mind control over strikers. 'They try and hit the perfect ball all the time and don't give themselves any margin for error.' Shilton may have had the luxury of a watertight back four in front of him, marshalled by the Ipswich centre-half Terry Butcher. But to concede just two goals in the eight qualifying matches was still an extraordinary feat.

The last big question for Robson, as far as the World Cup was concerned, was what to do with Hoddle. The French could never understand why Hoddle was treated so shabbily, especially after his achievements at Monaco at the end of the decade. As his club captain Jean-

Luc Ettori put it, 'For us, Glenn was *le bon dieu* – he was a god. There is nothing else to say.' But actually there was. Hoddle may have been magnificent with the ball at his feet, but he was notoriously bad at finding space, which explains why his team-mates often struggled to get it to him in the first place. Still, his time was coming. Always perceived as a floaty fancy-dan, Hoddle would show a different side of himself in Mexico.

Hoddle and a Mexican stand-off

Bobby Robson's world collapsed when his namesake Bryan dislocated a shoulder in a warm-up match against Mexico. The management tried to keep the problem quiet, and sent Robson out wearing a protective harness, which demonstrates just how critical he was felt to be to England's prospects. But in the second group game, against Morocco, a defender pulled him back and it popped straight out again.

Already wilting, England were virtually prostrate when Ray Wilkins lost his temper with an offside decision and hurled the ball at the referee – so earning one of the daftest red cards in English history. In the heat of a lunchtime kick-off in Monterrey, it really was a case of mad dogs and Englishmen. At this desperate moment, they found an unexpected hero in Hoddle. As Bobby Robson explained: 'Glenn ran his heart out to get us a goalless draw. It was a performance that inspired everyone. We went on to have a decent World Cup and I have never forgotten how Glenn fought like a tiger when we were up against it.'

The newspapers were also inspired by England's draw, but not quite in the same way. The front page of the *Sun* called it a 'NIGHT OF SHAME', while on the back John Sadler wrote that 'England are the big name jokes of the World Cup – the mugs of Monterrey. They still have a chance – as slim as a wafer – of qualifying from this group. But that will

> **'I couldn't see myself playing for England again after that World Cup.'**
> Terry Fenwick, who helped turn the team's fortunes around in Mexico with a revolt against Robson's tactics. He didn't.

not wipe out the humiliation of this result against a team with no pedigree and no tradition from the Third World.'

As forecasts go, this was up there with Michael Fish's 'Don't worry about the hurricane!' moment the following year. England were about to put together two of their best World Cup performances, so wiping their early struggles from the record. The turnaround began with a reshuffle from 3-5-2 to 4-4-2, proposed by full-back Terry Fenwick at an emergency team meeting. It may be an indication of Bobby Robson's limitations that player power forced rethinks during both his World Cup campaigns. But at least he was flexible.

The new-look England entered their must-win match against Poland with two conventional wide-men in Trevor Steven and Steve Hodge, plus Liverpool's Peter Beardsley – an old-fashioned inside-forward – to man the supply lines for Lineker. The formation worked a treat, and the first goal was a cracker: from England's goal-line to the Polish goal in 18 seconds and six passes. This was English football at its best: fast, direct, yet skilful with it. Lineker was on the end of the move, delivering what can only be described as a poacher's finish. By half-time, he had a hat-trick. And in the last-16 match against Paraguay, he was on the scoresheet twice more

Happiness is a 3–0 victory over Paraguay: England's goalscorers Peter Beardsley (left) and Gary Lineker celebrate at the Azteca Stadium, 18 June 1986.

from close range. The inconvenience of a blatant elbow in the throat from Rogelio Delgado hardly seemed to bother him.

'I score goals by losing defenders, first and foremost … by taking a chance and running into space,' Lineker would tell the author Pete Davies four years later. 'If I make twenty runs to the near post and each time I lose my defender, and nineteen times the ball goes over my head or behind me – then one time I'm three yards out, the ball comes to the right place, and I tap it in – then people say, right place, right time.'

Maradona punches England's lights out

While England's tournament was gathering pace, it was the footspeed of one outstanding individual that was worrying Robson. 'I've got 24 hours to devise a way of stopping Maradona,' he said ahead of the quarter-final. 'It won't be easy. Without Maradona, Argentina would have no chance of winning the World Cup. That's how great he is.'

The sapping sun of Mexico City – so oppressive in the middle of the day – brought extra heat to a match already carrying the incendiary baggage of the Falklands War. Argentina's *Barras bravas*, their self-styled hard-core ultras, burned British flags before boarding flights to Mexico, the Mexican army was put on standby and the *Sun* declared 'IT'S WAR, SENOR!' Its Argentinian equivalent *Cronica* retaliated with 'WE'RE COMING TO GET YOU, PIRATES'.

The flawed genius that was Maradona could not have produced two goals of greater contrast than his pair in the Azteca Stadium. The first was a duplicitous dodge, the second a masterpiece. Together they left bile in the stomach of Englishmen and brought unadulterated bliss to the Argentines. Across South America, there was a perverse admiration for what he had done. The Latins have a word for it: *viveza*, meaning jauntiness, cheekiness, or – in this case – craftiness.

The match was finely balanced when England, who had opted not to man-mark Maradona, lost his run in the 52nd minute. Maradona interchanged with striker Jorge Valdano but the move broke down. In his autobiography, Kenny Sansom explained that England had prepared an offside trap for this kind of attack, but that 'forgetful Steve Hodge' had failed to push out with the rest of the team. Instead Hodge hooked the ball back towards Shilton in a high, looping parabola.

The fist and the fury: Maradona's notorious first goal of the 1986 World Cup quarter-final sent England into paroxysms of rage; his second, scored just five minutes later, sent them packing.

Maradona had continued his surge regardless, and he leapt with the goalkeeper. Commentating on the game for BBC radio, Bryon Butler described the events poignantly: 'He got his left hand to the ball, he stretched, he turned it past Shilton. Shilton could not believe it. And the ball, with a little sigh of apology, just bounces into the English net.'

The match was refereed by a greenhorn – Ali Bennaceur of Tunisia – who stood firm against all objections. 'It was a sickly feeling,' said Shilton, after

> **'I was having a laugh. I had good fortune that God allowed the goal to stand.'**
> Diego Maradona on his infamous punched goal against England.

realising that his words were worthless. The other Argentines were genuinely baffled by England's reactions. 'We had no idea he guided the ball in with his hand,' said midfielder Sergio Batista. 'It never occurred to us until after the game. Shilton and Fenwick began arguing with the referee but we couldn't understand why – not until we saw the replay.'

'A lot of people said to me "Why didn't you go and crunch him?",' Shilton admitted afterwards. 'But it wasn't like that. He actually played the ball into the box and started running for a one-two. He was running into the box at full pelt. I suddenly realised what was happening and I felt that I could go and get it. And I think I would have got a fist to it. And that's why he handled it. He knew I was going to beat him to it.'

> **'I've seen that done in Sunday morning matches on the local park and they don't get away with it there.'**
> Glenn Hoddle on the Hand of God goal.

While England were still reeling, Maradona took advantage of their confusion by slaloming through the white shirts in a majestic burst of acceleration. He beat at least four defenders, ran half the length of the field, and dummied Shilton brilliantly at the end to double Argentina's advantage. Now Robson sent on John Barnes and Chris Waddle to run at the Argentine defenders, and there was a glimpse of what might have been as the pair of them created a sense of panic. With 10 minutes to go, Barnes got free down the left and sent in a perfect cross to set up Lineker's sixth goal of the tournament (and with it the Golden Boot). Just before the end the same combination might have constructed a dramatic equaliser, but while Lineker ended up in the net, the ball flew over the bar.

England had been beaten by one man. Such was his importance to Argentina, in fact, that Maradona was treated differently within his own squad: a Lord Snooty with special privileges. He employed his own personal trainer and masseur, and kept late hours, often retiring after 2 a.m. Carlos Bilardo, his manager, said 'I realised from an early stage that he had to have a different regime from the others. I said to myself "There is Maradona and there is the rest of the team".'

While the appeal of many great sportsmen transcends national borders, Maradona has rarely been lionised beyond Argentina and Naples, his adopted home in Italy. As Joe Lovejoy pointed out in the *Sunday Times*, so much of what we have learned of him has been a sad disappointment. 'Even the famous euphemism used to describe the infamous goal he punched in – the Hand of God – was not his,' Lovejoy said. 'It was spoon-fed to him by an Argentinian journalist after the game.'

1986 WORLD CUP MEXICO

Round One:

England 0 – 1 Portugal

Carlos Manuel 76

England 0 – 0 Morocco

England 3 – 0 Poland

Lineker 9
14, 34

Round Two:

England 3 – 0 Paraguay

Lineker 31, 73
Beardsley 56

Quarter-final:

England 1 – 2 Argentina

Lineker 81   Maradona 51, 54

After a very shaky start, England grew in confidence and reached the quarter-finals, a grudge encounter with erstwhile Falklands War adversaries Argentina. Argentina prevailed, courtesy of a little cheating assistance from the 'Hand of God'.

Baby hit me one more time

In the early 1980s, there was a sense of uncertainty about the whole direction of English society. Margaret Thatcher was battling the unions. The New Romantics and the Two-Tone crew were creating their own young urban tribes. The spectre of racism was spilling over into inner-city violence in London and Liverpool. It was a turbulent age, summed up by the fact that the prime minister was a woman who seemed determined to be a man, while the nation's most influential pop star, Boy George, was heading in the opposite direction.

All the paranoia and tension of the 1980s was reflected in the growth of hooliganism. This was *the* decade for footballing thuggery – a phenomenon which reached a hellish peak with the Heysel disaster of May 1985. The final of the European Cup brought Liverpool up against Juventus in a crumbling stadium that had not been overhauled for more than half a century. And when the Liverpool fans charged their rivals, a wall collapsed, killing 39 and injuring hundreds. English clubs were indefinitely suspended from European competitions – a ban that was only lifted six years later. For a while, Bobby Robson feared the same fate might befall the national team.

As the purchasing power of the pound rose, the hooligans could travel ever further in search of their sado-masochistic thrills. One small but shameful incident took place on the plane from Rio to Santiago just after Barnes's wondergoal against Brazil. According to the journalist Ken Jones, a group of England 'supporters' were on the plane and spent the journey singing 'Blacks out, send them back', and berating FA secretary Ted Croker. 'He prefers Sambos to us.'

Hooliganism was one explanation for declining Football League audiences through the 1980s. As in all times of conflict, women and children were the first to depart. 'The game drifts slowly into the possession of what we are now supposed to call the underclass,' wrote the journalist Russell Davies, 'and a whole middle-class public grows without ever dreaming of visiting a Football League ground.'

Thatcher viewed football fans as scum and wanted a zero-tolerance approach. Her preferred solution, compulsory ID cards for every fan, was considered to be unworkable and probably counter-productive. Of course, most supporters remained well-behaved – even at Millwall – but no-one ever noticed the moral majority. The media hyped every punch into a riot, and every broken glass into a rampage. Which, in turn, encouraged the Neanderthals to play to the cameras. This really was a vicious cycle.

A similar phenomenon applied to the law-enforcement agencies during Italia '90, who seemed to look upon a visit from the England fans as a challenge to battle. In his account of the tournament, the author Pete Davies described the way the *carabinieri* virtually incited violence, massing in riot gear and thwacking their truncheons on their thighs. 'In Stockholm when they'd chucked a glass, the Swedish police looked disgusted, and tidied up. In Cagliari, they charged.'

Davies also described a reporter arriving at Naples airport with his radio gear, and 'a taxi driver spotting him and saying, as he offered his open car door, "Hooligan camp?" ' The so-called 'English disease' was aptly named; like any sickness, it had the knack of perpetuating itself.

'You're a bloody marvel, skipper'

If one image sums up England's fortunes in the years between Mexico '86 and Italia '90, it is that of Terry Butcher, his white shirt drenched to the waist in blood, and a mad gleam in his eyes. These were grim times for Bobby Robson and his team, whose performance at the 1988 European Championships – three straight losses and a humiliating exit – remains England's worst in any major tournament. A few days afterwards, a below-par Lineker was diagnosed with jaundice.

Everyone seemed to be debating Robson's failings, even MPs in the House of Commons. It wasn't just the results, though the 1–1 draw against Saudi Arabia in November 1988 drew such ferocious headlines as 'IN THE NAME OF ALLAH GO!' His private life was also being investigated by a new breed of sporting news reporters known in the business as the 'rotters'. (According to Brian Glanville, the nickname was inadvertently coined by FA secretary Ted Croker, who once interrupted a diatribe about irresponsible reporting to explain that 'We're not talking about you sports people, we're talking about the rotters.')

These muck-rakers had already tarnished the reputation of superstar cricketer Ian Botham with a series of sex and drugs allegations, and now the *News of the World* linked Robson with as many as five mistresses. The women were listed like a roster of substitutes (which, in effect, the paper was claiming they were): 'No. 3 Blonde Bosom Buddy – No. 4 Dishy

Gore blimey: Terry Butcher shrugs off the minor inconvenience of a copiously bleeding head wound during England's World Cup qualifying game with Sweden, 1989.

Dutch Treat – No. 5 Soccer Star's Missus'.

If this represented gratuitous scandal-mongering, the newspaper surely crossed any line of decency with the line on its news pages where it described Robson as 'the most vilified Englishman since Lord Haw Haw – and they hanged him as a wartime traitor'. As Niall Edworthy put it, 'murderers and child molesters have suffered less abuse'.

Robson could have thrown it all in. Back in 1984, he had been wooed by Barcelona, and his stock had surely risen since then. But like his captain Butcher, he fought on, emerging bloodied yet unbowed from the struggle. After the European shambles in West Germany, England put together a run of 17 games unbeaten – only three short of the record, and two behind Alf Ramsey's best effort in and around the 1966 World Cup. At the heart of this sequence was the 0–0 draw in Sweden where Butcher suffered his head wound through an aerial collision with centre-forward Johnny Ekstrom just before half-time. Seven stitches were applied at the interval, and as Robson sent his men out for the second period, he told them: 'Have a look at your skipper. Let none of you let him down.'

Qualification for Italia '90 was finally secured with another 0–0 draw, this time against Poland in Katowice. England's outfielders were miserably inert in this match, prompting the *Daily Star*'s Bryan Cooney to remark afterwards that 'There are so many donkeys in his side that Robson should open an animal sanctuary and dispense carrot juice.' But the goalkeeper was monumental. Sixteen years earlier, Shilton's Wembley howler had allowed Poland to eliminate England from the 1974 World Cup. This time, at the age of 40, he finally achieved redemption.

Gascoigne and Platt: the hare and the tortoise

England's squad for Italy contained two midfielders who would go on to perform great deeds for their country. Dismissed by one journalist as 'an Aston Villa humper', David Platt had won five caps without anyone really noticing. Paul Gascoigne, by contrast, was the darling of the press. Twenty-three years old going on 14, 'Gazza' had already played 11 times, scored a couple of goals, and wowed the fans with his vision and creative instinct.

The one man unconvinced by Gascoigne was Robson, who famously called him 'daft as a brush' after his first England appearance against Albania. Given strict instructions to stay on the right-hand side, Gascoigne immediately rushed over to the left to play alongside his old Geordie mate Chris Waddle. Still, underneath it all, Robson knew that he had a player of limitless potential as long as a couple of quirks could be ironed out. 'With his genius, he's capable of doing things that make you think, *bloody hell* … his free kicks, his dribbling, he's something special.'

In the end, Gascoigne won his chance in England's first World Cup game, and would more than justify his place. He finished the tournament as the only Englishman in FIFA's all-star team of the tournament. From the first match there were signs of what Brian Glanville called 'a flair, a superlative technique, a tactical sophistication, seldom matched by an English player since the war'.

There was no-one else to match him that wet and stormy night. England's opening opponents were the Republic of Ireland, a team revitalised, yet certainly not refined, by the long-ball tactics of manager Jack Charlton. The ball kept hurtling down through the sheeting rain,

Eyes down: Bobby Robson and his chief coach Don Howe (left), 1986. Treasured in hindsight as England's most successful manager since Ramsey, Robson suffered as many media attacks as his hapless successor Graham Taylor during his eight years in charge.

only to be dispatched back up into the saturated atmosphere. Robson's men came away with a 1–1 draw, which was at least one goal better than they had managed against the same opponents at Euro '88. But that was not enough to prevent the Sun from calling it 'the most appalling performance by an England team in living memory'. The front-page headline was 'BRING 'EM HOME'.

'PSV OFF BUNGLER BOBBY'

Headline following Robson's revelation that he was taking a job with PSV Eindhoven.

Wright sweeps the critics off their feet

By this stage, Robson had already admitted that he would be leaving the England job for PSV Eindhoven at the end of the tournament. 'He has taken his thirty pieces of silver before a ball is even kicked,' wrote James Lawton in the *Express*. 'What is really monstrous is the level of FA loyalty Robson has spurned.'

In fact, the lack of loyalty had been the other way around. Robson had already been warned that his contract would not be renewed at the end of the World Cup. Defeats, the FA could handle. But not sleazy *News of the World* exposés. They were like daggers to the heart of Bert Millichip, who was not only the FA chairman but also the solicitor who had done the conveyancing on Robson's first house with his wife Elsie.

Robson, then, would be a dead man walking if England lost their second match to Holland (another team that had beaten them during the European Championships). Perhaps this emboldened the players to mount another successful challenge to their boss's tactics. At least they knew they wouldn't have to worry about being cast out, Fenwick-style, at the end of the month.

This time, the reshuffle brought in Mark Wright as a sweeper. The idea had been to strengthen the defence against the raids of Marco van Basten, who had scored a hat-trick in the match in Dusseldorf. Paradoxically, it improved England's attacking options, allowing Barnes and Waddle to fly up the flanks while wing-backs Stuart Pearce and Paul Parker pushed forward in support. England did not score, but they made plenty of chances and were plainly superior to a sulky Dutch side.

The only downside for England was the latest injury to Bryan Robson, who would not play again in a major tournament. Accounts differ as to the explanation. In his book *Gazza: My Story* Paul Gascoigne writes that he and Robson – a drinker of Bobby Moore-ish proportions – spent the evening celebrating the team's improved performance. At the end of it Robson picked up Gascoigne's bed during some laddish horseplay and accidentally dropped it on his own big toe.

'Gazza's always telling people that story but he's got a hopeless memory,' Robson responded in the *Sun*. 'There was a bit of mucking about in his room and I did suffer a bruised toenail but that was all. The real reason I flew home was because I had a persistent Achilles injury and I had an operation within a couple of days of returning.'

Either way, it was a hammer blow for Robson, who had had problems with his groin during the 1982 World Cup and a dislocated shoulder in 1986. In 1990, he had even flown in a faith-healer, one Olga Stringfellow, to try to fix his Achilles, but to no avail. 'Somebody up there doesn't like me,' he complained.

1990 WORLD CUP ITALY

Round One:
England 1 – 1 Rep. of Ireland
Lineker 8   Sheedy 73

England 0 – 0 Netherlands

England 1 – 0 Egypt
Wright 64

Round Two:
England 1 – 0 Belgium (a.e.t.)
Platt 119

Quarter-final:
England 3 – 2 Cameroon (a.e.t.)
Platt 25   Kundé 61 (pen.)
Lineker 83 (pen.), 105 (pen.)   Ekéké 65

Semi-final:
England 1 – 1 West Germany (a.e.t.)
Lineker 80   Brehme 60
(West Germany win 4–3 on penalties)

In their best showing to date since 1966, England, managed by Bobby Robson, scraped through the first three rounds, only to come up against the dreaded old adversary West Germany in the semis. Heartbreaking England penalty misses saw the Germans advance to the finals and their third World Cup.

Crying shame: his World Cup over, Gazza sheds the most famous public tears since Alexander the Great. No one knew it at the time, but the world had already seen the best of the prodigiously gifted Geordie.

> **'Football is a very simple game. For 90 minutes 22 men go running after the ball – and at the end the Germans win.'**
> Gary Lineker.

It's not over till Pavarotti sings

When England beat Egypt in their final group game, the *Sun* had a sudden change of heart. 'Our soccer heroes shook off the Sphinx jinx and anNILEated the Egyptians,' screamed the front page. Then, in the round of 16, England sneaked past Belgium, who had the better of a fluent but low-scoring game in Bologna. Penalties were only averted by a magical goal in the penultimate minute of extra-time, when Platt hooked a volley over his shoulder with devastating precision.

Cameroon, without four suspended players, looked like a terrific quarter-final draw. In fact, they played fearless, febrile football in a game of three penalties. England's sweeper system had coped well with conventional attackers, but it was all at sea against a side which flowed forward in waves. Robson responded by removing Butcher midway through the second half, and sending on Trevor Steven to work the right flank. 'A flat back four saved us,' he said, after his side had turned a 2–1 deficit into a nervy 3–2 win. The only trouble was that Robson – a man of whom it was often said 'His indecision is final' – was left with no idea what formation to play against West Germany in the semis.

As it happened, no defence in the world could have stopped Andreas Brehme's freakish 60th-minute goal – a free-kick that struck Paul Parker's knee, ballooned up and looped into the back of the net. Shilton had been on such majestic form that it seemed only a deflection or a one-on-one would be able to beat him. And that was exactly what the Germans got: a lucky break of the ball.

England's spirits were not broken, though. Robson performed the same switch as in the quarter-final: Steven for Butcher, sweeper to flat four. And then a high, hopeful ball fell to Lineker. Buffeted by three defenders, he still controlled it masterfully on his thigh to score one of the finest goals of his career.

It was extra-time again; the third in a row for England. They didn't look tired, though; if anything, they seemed to have the edge on energy. Then Gascoigne over-ran the ball and caught Thomas Berthold's ankle in a clumsy attempt to win it back. The yellow card put him out of England's next match, and brought those famous tears to his eyes. Lineker walked over to check on him, then turned to the bench and made a series of gestures that could have been interpreted as a referral to the funny farm.

'The question I get asked more than anything else is "Who was I talking to and what was I saying,"' Lineker admitted recently. 'I just turned to Bobby Robson and said "Keep an eye on him. Have a word with him." He had basically lost the plot.' In fact Gascoigne pulled himself together and kept forging on to the end of extra-time, his commitment to his team-mates undimmed.

No more goals meant that England faced what Pete Davies called the 'ersatz excitement of the penalty shout-out' for the first time in a major tournament (but sadly not the last). The Germans were majestic. 'Perfect technique, ice cool,' recalled Butcher. But Stuart Pearce shot too close to Bodo Ilgner, and an exhausted Waddle blazed several feet over the crossbar. England's dream was over, again.

As 'Nessun Dorma' played on the BBC's credits – a tune described by one wag as 'Verdi's "You can't win 'em all"' – a pattern was emerging. Since 1982, England had shown the ability to qualify for major tournaments, and the spirit to fight back from their traditional slow start, only to go out in increasingly frustrating ways. All of which begs the question, is it better to have gone to the World Cup and lost? Or would it be less painful, as in the 1970s, to have missed the whole shebang in the first place?

Paul Gascoigne's Turin breakdown has generated more think-pieces, sociology lectures and doctoral theses than any other moment in English football. David Beckham may have worn a sarong. David Ginola may have had better hair. But it was Gazza – a man who looked like a chip-shop proprietor – who did most to spread the word of football. Some of his fans were intellectuals. Some, amazingly, were female. After the dark days of the 1980s, Gascoigne emerged as an unlikely saviour, a man-child whose tears washed away the sins of the game.

'I knew the second he cried that it was going to be huge,' said the writer and comedienne Rhona Cameron. 'That it was going to be a massive image and that we would see it forever. He wasn't just a bit tearful; he was sobbing, and his face was so red. He was like a little boy and it was so moving.'

The irony of it all is that Gascoigne could hardly have been less middle-class if he tried. He was a chav before the term had even been invented, the leader of the shell-suit brigade. But when he pulled on his boots, he became a prince. Running with the ball, the young Gascoigne had the thundering vigour of the best English midfielders, his elbows pumping out like

> ### 'Who is Gazza?'
> Mr Justice Harman, while hearing Gascoigne's case for an injunction against an unauthorised biography.

pistons. He could dribble too, as befits a latter-day 'tanner-ball player', and his range and delicacy of passing would have shamed many a Continental playmaker.

'A priapic monolith in the Mediterranean sun.'

Karl Miller, editor of the *London Review of Books*, waxes lyrical on the Gascoigne of Italia '90.

Gascoigne's reckless verve made him an aspirational figure. He played football the way we all imagine ourselves playing, if only we had the skill. After his feats at Italia '90, the poet and author Ian Hamilton wrote that 'Gascoigne had altered our expectations; he had even put a strain on our vocabulary ... We, as fans, moved up a league. At last and maybe just for once we had a player of world class, who could treat the Gullitts and Van Bastens, the Baggios and Viallis, as if they were just another mob of big lads in some Gateshead school yard.'

Everyone knows what happened next, even if Gazzaphiles prefer not to talk about it. In May 1991, Gascoigne ruptured his anterior cruciate ligament with a wild-eyed challenge on Gary Charles of Nottingham Forest. As the *Daily Telegraph* remarked, this was 'Gazzamania' of a different kind. It took him 16 months just to get back on the pitch, after a horrendous operation involving bone grafts from his kneecap. From that moment on, he rarely strung more than a few decent matches together. It was not just his knee that held him back, though the range of movement was permanently affected. He was also battling with what Jane Nottage, his PR attaché, called a 'dark, self-destructive side'.

Despite spending most of the 1990s in either Rome or Glasgow, Gascoigne remained the biggest news story in English football. He got into scraps at nightclubs. He hit his wife Sheryl, then offered tearful apologies. He went on depression-fuelled binges (though Gazza being Gazza, these were more likely to involve kebabs than cocaine).

But the Gascoigne we prefer to remember is the Gascoigne of Italia '90. Outside England, this tournament has gone down as the biggest World Cup flop in history, full of cynical defending and stultifying matches. In England, though, we were all too thrilled by the emergence of a genuinely exciting talent to care. Suddenly everyone was talking about the latest match, whether at school, in the office, or the pub. Football was becoming the beautiful game once again.

Root one football

Some images lodge themselves so deeply in the national imagination that they cannot be prised out. Neil Kinnock's unscheduled dip in the Brighton surf was one such indelible moment. Another was the *Sun* back page which turned Graham Taylor, Robson's successor as England manager, into a turnip.

'SWEDES 2 TURNIPS 1' roared the headline after England had lost a crucial World Cup qualifier in Stockholm. The choice of a root vegetable was cruel, vindictive and brilliantly memorable. It was also appropriate, in a funny kind of way, because Taylor was nothing if not grounded.

The son of a sports journalist from Scunthorpe, Taylor made few waves as a lower-league full-back. Yet he pulled himself up by his bootstraps until he had reached the highest sporting office in the land. Like a cut-price Ramsey, he came to identify with players like himself, workaday footballers who had to sweat and strive to make the grade.

Take Geoff Thomas of Crystal Palace, a former electrician who worked his way up from non-League football to win an international debut in 1991. Or Carlton Palmer, a man now considered to be the archetypal English clogger. You have to wonder whether either of them would have got a look-in under any other manager. Heroes to their own club supporters, they became villains as soon as they pulled on the white of England.

Taylor apologists – a rare and hardy breed – will tell you that England's options were badly restricted by injury. Yet there was nothing wrong with Peter Beardsley, one of the stars of Italia '90. And how about Chris Waddle, now at the peak of his career, who felt so underappreciated in England that he went to play for Olympic Marseille? The one time Taylor did speak to him, it was to give him a headmasterly scolding for coming off his wing too often: 'I expect to see white paint on the soles of your boots at the end of a match.'

Waddle was far too much the individual to get on with Taylor, a man who saw football as a game of geometry and percentages. From Lincoln City to Watford and Aston Villa, his managerial career had been built on the success of the 'pressing game': a barnstorming, take-no-prisoners approach that mostly bypassed the midfield. 'When the score's

0–0 and there are three or four minutes to go, what do players do? They get the ball forward,' Taylor once said. 'But if they can do that in the last few minutes, why can't they do that from the start?'

The pressing game had turned Watford from fourth-division nonentities into FA Cup finalists and League runners-up. It had also turned off many of the floating fans who were thinking of drifting back to football. It was horrible to watch, unsatisfying to play, and hugely unpopular with the media. Offering Taylor the England job, many people felt, was like asking an orang-utan to play the violin.

Pun in a million

Taylor's preference for graft over glamour was all too evident during the critical match of Euro '92. England were facing the hosts, Sweden, in what was effectively a play-off to reach the semi-finals. Watching his side flounder through the second-half, Taylor withdrew Lineker after 64 minutes, replacing him with Arsenal's tall target-man Alan Smith.

Here was a classic clash of cultures. Lineker's method was all about snaky, cleverly timed forward runs. He was deadly with a Beardsley figure to feed off, but there was little point lobbing long balls up to him and expecting him to hold off the defenders. The way Taylor's game-plan worked, England would have been better off with Giant Haystacks.

'Taylor was cursing every time the ball went up to Gary and he lost it,' says Smith now. 'He told me and Alan Shearer to warm up and I assumed one of

> **'Some lists are finite, but others are endless: such as the list of reasons why Graham Taylor should never have been appointed England manager.'**
> *The Rough Guide to Cult Football* (2003).

> **'Carlton Palmer can trap the ball further than I can kick it.'**
>
> Ron Atkinson.

us would be going in to partner Gary. So it was a bit of a shock when I realised that Gary was coming off.

'A lot was made of it after the game, because it was the last time Lineker played for England, and there had always been friction between him and Taylor. It was a bit awkward for my wife, too, because our families had become friends at Leicester and she was up in the stand with Michelle Lineker, who was in tears.'

With eight minutes left, Tomas Brolin played a one-two on the edge of England's area and poked an unstoppable shot into the top corner. Taylor's goose was cooked – or, at least, his vegetables were roasted. The turnip headline has since been attributed to Dave Clement, a sub-editor on the *Sun*. Like all the best jokes, it inspired a series of pale imitations, including the rather less memorable 'SPANISH 1 ONIONS 0' after a friendly in Santander three months later.

If England had slipped up against Turkey, their rivals for World Cup qualification, Taylor could have expected another sprinkling of culinary puns. As it was, they beat the Turks home and away, with Gascoigne scoring three times. But when they suffered a disastrous 2–0 defeat to Norway in Oslo, Taylor lurched out of the frying pan and into the fire. This time, his head was superimposed on a pile of horse dung under the screaming headline 'NORSE MANURE'.

That game revealed Taylor's tactical limitations. At Aston Villa, he had been fond of deploying giant centre-forwards on the wings, reasoning that the opposition full-backs were usually shorter men who could be beaten in the air. Now he

> **'They gave up in the last 15 minutes. I've never seen an England team do that before.'**
>
> Norwegian coach Egil Olsen after England's 2–0 defeat in Oslo.

THE Sun

20p

WHO'S THIS?
FIND OUT IN
SUN WOMAN

...erday, November 24, 1993   **20p**   Audited daily sale for October 3,778,312

THAT'S YER
ALLOTMENT

At last Turnip Taylor turns up his to...

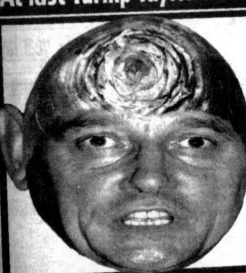

**Jackson
ordered
to face
court on
child sex
claims**

...charge ... given court date

By PETER SEABROOK
our Gardening Correspon...

ENGLAND soccer ma...
Graham "The Turnip"
lor hurled himself on t...
compost heap yester...

Taylor — England...
for three years — ...
admitted he had lo...
vegetable plot and re...

The 49-year-old Turni...
just six days after ...
failed to reach next ...
World Cup finals.

He said: "No one can...
the depths of my persor...
appointment at not rea...

"I do, however, w...
wish my successor ...
good fortune in E...
endeavours to win th...
European Championship...

WINTER

The Sun awarded Ta...
nickname after ev...
Sweden gave us a 2-1...
in last year's Eur...
championships.

Yesterday former...
coach Don Howe, ...
named caretaker manag...

We were so concerne...
Turnip's future after he...
out to grass that we c...
our gardening exper...
Seabrook.

Peter said: "The lif...
ex-turnip will be th...
miserable.

"There are few more...
ing sights for a garde...
a vegetable which is ro...
to rot.

"My advice is to ke...
a cool place during the...
then plant him out in...

Sun Says: Page 6; Turnip ...

Continued on Page Four

THE OFFICIAL A-LEVEL REPORT See pages 23, 24, 25   **£26,000 SUN BINGO** p...

282

looked at Jostein Flo, Norway's towering right-wing, and figured that the same trick was about to be played on him. So in went Gary Pallister, normally a pillar of central defence, at left-back.

All logical enough, you might think, except that Flo immediately started roaming around the field, from the right wing to the left and then back into midfield. Pallister was forced to follow him, which left England horribly unbalanced. 'The rest of the Norwegian forwards were little Yorkshire terrier-type players,' recalls Colin Gibson, the *Daily Telegraph* football correspondent at the time. 'They carved us up. And the worst thing about it is that we had all predicted that Flo would drag Pallister out of position as soon as Taylor named his team.'

Taylor stars in a video nasty

The legacy of the Taylor years was defined, above all, by a Channel Four documentary. The title, *Do I Not Like That*, was a reference to one of many unforgettable Taylorisms captured by the fly in the dugout. Other gems included 'Can you not knock it, Carlton?' (Translation: please kick the ball upfield, Mr Palmer.) And, in the final reel, Taylor's despairing message to the linesman in Rotterdam: 'Will you say to the fella, the referee has got me the sack ... Thank him ever so much for that, won't you?'

During certain parts of the film, you have to wonder whether Taylor is actively performing for the cameras. One of the most memorable set-pieces is a grandstanding press conference in which he rounds on Rob Shepherd, the football correspondent for *Today*, and tells him 'If you were one of my players, with a face like that, you would never have a chance! Put a smile on your face, man!'

Shepherd himself has said that 'There was an element of [Taylor] knowing he was being filmed for that documentary. I always felt that he agreed to do that programme because he felt it would be a eulogy to his time in charge … [But] it ended up being an epitaph to the bad side of his management.'

'Do I not like that,' might have been Taylor's first response when the film was screened. Agreeing to participate was perhaps the greatest mistake he ever made. With his pedantic, long-winded soliloquies, his homespun catchphrases and his malapropisms, he emerges as a cross between Alan Partridge and David Brent.

His support team, led by former Southampton manager Lawrie McMenemy, do not fare much better. Phil Neal, the long-faced parrot on Taylor's shoulder, is a dead ringer for Gareth from *The Office*. ('You're not the assistant manager – you're the assistant to the manager.') McMenemy hardly speaks throughout, his features frozen in the thousand-yard stare of a man facing execution in the morning.

However Taylor intended it to play, *Do I Not Like That* winds up as the darkest of black comedies, as hysterically painful to watch as anything John Cleese or Chris Morris has ever invented. One of the bleakest moments is Taylor's empty bravado when Norway score their second goal in Oslo. 'Now then,' he says, slapping his thighs. 'Now then. This is a test.' 'This is a real test,' replies Neal. 'This is a real, real test,' Taylor concludes, almost with satisfaction.

The decisive moment of Taylor's reign was England's visit to Rotterdam in October 1993. England needed a draw to keep any realistic chance of qualifying for the World Cup alive. Instead, they suffered 'Rotterdamnation'. This was the match when Channel Four's cameras caught Taylor abusing the officials, whom he accused of getting him the sack. It was perhaps the most accurate judgement he made in the whole documentary.

Early in the second half, Andy Sinton sent David Platt through on goal with a typical piece of Taylor football, a looping long ball from inside the England half. Platt would have been looking at a one-on-one against the goalkeeper if Ronald Koeman had not hauled him down on the edge of the penalty area. It was a blatant sending-off offence, according to new FIFA guidelines demanding a red card for any last defender who committed a professional foul. But the German referee, Karl-Josef Assenmacher, settled for a yellow, and compounded England's frustration by awarding a free-kick rather than a penalty.

Five minutes later, Holland were awarded a very similar free-kick at

> **'Welcome to Bologna on Capital Gold for England versus San Marino with Tennent's Pilsner, brewed with Czechoslovakian yeast for that extra Pilsner taste and England are one down.'**
> Jonathan Pearce's first ten seconds of radio commentary, Bologna 1993.

the other end of the field. Koeman took it – twice, thanks to Assenmacher's ruling that England had encroached inside ten yards – and curled it past David Seaman's left hand. 'Because it was Koeman and it was in Holland, the referee bottled the decision,' Gary Pallister recalled. Assenmacher was later disciplined by FIFA, and would never take charge of another international.

Taylor had one more formality to fulfil. A 7–1 win over San Marino might sound respectable enough, but the scoreline hardly conveys the embarrassment of conceding a goal to a bunch of part-timers after only *nine* seconds. Stuart Pearce was responsible, sending a weak back pass to Seaman which Davide Gualtieri ran onto. The press-box erupted in disbelieving hilarity. It was one last belly-laugh to end the farce of the Taylor years.

El Tel, the shady supremo

Taylor always did his best to be open and ingratiating with the notoriously unruly British press. But the players resented him for airing their failings in public, and even the reporters admitted that some of his stunts were over the top. He was like the trendy schoolteacher who tries to 'get with the kids', only to find that they are all throwing paper darts and letting off stinkbombs.

'We criticised him once for only speaking to the press for a brief time,' said Brian Woolnough of the *Sun*. 'The next time he came in with an alarm clock. It was meant to be funny. On another occasion, after England had drawn 2–2 with Holland at Wembley making us a bit wobbly for qualification, he walked into the press conference the following morning singing Buddy Holly's "Oh misery! What is to become of me?"'

Unfortunately for Taylor, he could not resort to the 'Show us your medals' fall-back available to former internationals. He lacked either the cachet that goes with a distinguished playing career, or the charisma to compensate. With his giant, aviator-style spectacles, he looked less like a professional athlete than a snooker player – perhaps even a relative of his namesake Dennis Taylor.

All of which made him a total contrast to his successor, former Spurs manager Terry Venables, a cheeky chappie from the East End with a gleaming smile and a 'hail-fellow-well-met' charm. Venables had been a successful player, emerging from East London at the same time as Greaves and Moore, and rising to captain Chelsea. His natural ebullience helped him ride out many a testy press conference with great aplomb.

> **'If Terry Venables is made England manager, it will be the first time the team has been coached from prison.'**
> Andrew Neil.

Venables should have been the ideal man for this 'impossible job'. He had the tactical nous, the communication skills, and the breadth of experience. But there is no manager so perfect that he cannot be laid on the rack of the popular press. In Venables's case, the fatal weakness lay in his murky business dealings. While Taylor's character was above suspicion, his successor had a whole chorus line of skeletons dancing in the closet. At least, that is what the *Daily Mirror* chose to tell us, almost every day.

When football managers find themselves on TV, they are usually starring on *Match of the Day*. Venables was different: in the space of one week in 1993 he had two current affairs programmes – the BBC's

Panorama and Channel Four's *Dispatches* – devoted to allegations about his business practice. Almost inevitably, Gascoigne was at the centre of the storm. Venables was accused of pocketing a portion of his £5.5 million transfer from Tottenham to Lazio the previous year.

Further claims would emerge over the next couple of years, surrounding everything from Venables's refinancing of Tottenham Hotspur to his Kensington nightclub Scribes West. Nothing was ever proven, not beyond contradiction. But the rumours did for him in the end, despite some impressive performances on the pitch. After two-and-a-half years in the job,

> **'Alan Sugar said to people he'd dance on my grave. And he's done it.'**
> Terry Venables on his hostile parting with Tottenham Hotspur.

Venables became the only England manager to quit with the public fully behind him.

Gascoigne and the art of mid-air refuelling

'I want to play good football but not fantasy football (playing well and losing),' was one of Venables's early statements on taking that job. His record – 11 wins and just one defeat in 23 games – suggests he achieved his aim, even if he sometimes had to submerge his attacking instincts to get there.

Facing Denmark in his opening fixture, Venables's first move was to recall Beardsley after three years in the wilderness. A modern-day Mannion if ever there was one, Beardsley drove the Danes to distraction with the patter of his tiny feet. But he was also 33, and approaching the end of a distinguished career. As Euro '96 drew nearer, Teddy Sheringham took over his role, striking up such a successful partnership with Alan Shearer that the two of them became known as the SAS.

Shearer went on to become one of England's finest modern frontmen, equalling Lofthouse's tally of 30 international goals. But what

> **'I'm on a see-food diet. That's when I eat everything I see.'**
> Paul Gascoigne.

is often forgotten is that in the lead-up to Euro '96, he suffered a debilitating loss of form, going 14 internationals without scoring and generally doing less in the box than David Blaine. Without a show of loyalty from Venables, he might never have started the tournament.

Venables's faith was also tested by Gascoigne, who was now on his third coming at the very least. During a pre-tournament tour to the Far East, a drinking scandal erupted when photographers captured the celebrations for Gascoigne's 29th birthday in Hong Kong. The players had indulged in a series of drinking games, one of which involved lying back in a dentist's chair and having tequila poured straight down their gullets.

On the flight home, more high-jinks resulted in a couple of smashed TV screens and broken arm-rests. According to some versions of the story, the damage was caused when a sleeping Dennis Wise fell out of the overhead locker where his giggling team-mates had stashed him. The *Sun* headline shrieked 'DISGRACE FOOL GAZZA', while the *Mail*'s Jeff Powell called for England to 'sling out Paul Gascoigne on his ear-ring. They must devise a way to play without this playboy relic.'

Venables declined Powell's advice, preferring to announce that the England squad would be taking 'collective responsibility' for their actions. This was the modern equivalent of Ramsey coming to the aid of Nobby Stiles in 1966. As the historian James Corbett writes, 'It was a master-stroke, and one that created a renewed sense of solidarity amongst the team.'

Euro '96, and a footballing Saturnalia

Five minutes can be a long time in football, as Graham Taylor found out in Rotterdam. Three years later, England's feisty Euro '96 campaign was kickstarted by a different kind of double-whammy.

England had opened their first home tournament in three decades without any great fanfare, earning a point with a 1–1 draw against Switzerland. A week later, they were leading the Scots 1–0 at Wembley when Tony Adams mistimed a challenge and conceded a penalty. But Gary McAllister's shot was weak, and easily saved by David Seaman.

Suddenly the action was up the other end, and Gascoigne was raging towards the Scottish goal like a man chasing a kebab van. As the ball was

Fixing the drinks: McManaman, Shearer and Redknapp do the honours – dentist's chair-style – for an exultant Gazza, Euro '96.

played neatly into his stride, he flicked it over the unfortunate Colin Hendry with his left boot, then hammered it into the net with his right. Gascoigne kept running, then threw himself down by the side of the Scottish goal for his team-mates to spray Lucozade into his mouth, dentist's chair-style.

TONY ADAMS
Caps 66   Goals 5

The rock in England's defence, Adams was also the latest in a long line of boozy English footballers stretching back through Bryan Robson and Bobby Moore. He had a habit of getting into fights in nightclubs, and in 1990 he smashed his car into a wall while *four* times over the legal limit, earning himself two months in gaol. Appointed England captain during Euro '96, Adams publicly confessed to being an alcoholic after a seven-week bender at the end of the tournament. He has been teetotal ever since, founding the Sporting Chance Clinic to help other addicts, and redirecting his obsessive personality to more civilised pursuits. 'He would come up

to me an hour before training, and start talking about Jean-Paul Sartre,' wrote Graeme Le Saux, when discussing the 1998 World Cup. 'He had gone from one extreme to the other: from a kind of out-of-control lager lout to an aesthete.'

Amazingly, things were about to get even better for England, who went into their final group match against the Dutch in bubbly spirits. The ancient Romans used to observe a festival called Saturnalia, when the masters served dinner to their slaves. And that is how it felt as the English players marmalised their Dutch opponents with a decent approximation of 'Total Football'. The score was 4–1, the pick of the goals created by Gascoigne and Teddy Sheringham, who worked the ball sideways across the penalty area for an unmarked Shearer to blast past Edwin van der Sar.

> **'How good Teddy would have been if he had been a yard quicker than my wife's tortoise Miles is a tantaliser.'**
>
> Matthew Norman salutes the class of Sheringham on his retirement, *Evening Standard*.

England were instantly installed as tournament favourites, according to both Dutch coach Gus Hiddink and the bookies. But in their quarter-final against Spain, the magic stubbornly failed to come.

Venables was missing one of his main men in the suspended Paul Ince, the self-styled 'Guvnor' who had emerged as a holding midfielder in the Alan Mullery class. Platt made a rather less intimidating stand-in, and as Brian Glanville observed, 'England's midfield seemed made of cardboard'.

> **'LET'S BLITZ FRITZ'**
>
> *Sun* headline on the morning of England's semi-final.

Still, with the help of a few lucky refereeing decisions, England staggered through the match to claim a 0–0 draw, then won the penalty shootout. This remains the only time they have come out on top in six attempts at this poor-man's lottery. After Stuart Pearce had buried a cathartic strike, Seaman saved from Miguel Angel Nadal – the so-called 'Beast of Barcelona' and uncle of Rafael, the 2008 Wimbledon men's singles tennis champion. England were through to the semi-finals of the European Championships for the first time in 24 years.

Seconds from disaster: Gareth Southgate places the ball on the penalty spot, Euro '96. A starring role in a Pizza Hut advert beckoned.

England pay the ultimate penalty

'ACHTUNG SURRENDER!' screamed the *Daily Mirror* headline on the morning of Monday 24 June, the day of England's semi-final against Germany. 'Please shut up,' thought everybody else. The players were quick to dissociate themselves from such mindless xenophobia. Paul Ince pointed out that they didn't regard 'the Germans as the enemy and don't like some people treating it as World War Three', while Venables called for the crowd to respect both teams' anthems. 'Insulting people's mother country is not funny,' he said.

The tone of the coverage was reminiscent of the England–West Germany encounter at the 1982 World Cup, which had turned out to be a complete flop. At least the 1996 version produced some compelling drama, starting in the fourth minute when a Gascoigne corner was flicked on by Tony Adams and buried by Shearer. The joy, for the FA International Committee, was mixed with consternation. Venables had asked them to guarantee his future before the tournament and they had declined, mainly out of concern over his shady business dealings. If his last act as England manager had been to lift the Henri Delaunay Trophy, the outcry would have been deafening.

The issue never arose. After 15 minutes, Stefan Kuntz broke free of his marker to stab in a low cross from Thomas Helmer, a centre-back who had ghosted forward to the edge of England's penalty box. Here was a clue to Germany's enduring success: they play controlled, risk-free football, but have the technique and flexibility to attack from anywhere on the pitch.

'Why didn't you blast it, dear?'
Gareth Southgate's mum.

The match now entered a sort of hard-running stalemate, which lasted until the 90 minutes were up. But in the first period of extra-time, the chances suddenly started flying around like confetti. Anderton hit the post from five yards out, and a sliding Gascoigne was inches away from tapping Shearer's low cross into an empty goal. At the other end, Kuntz did find the net, but his header was disallowed for an invisible push on Adams. And so it was penalties, again.

England were efficient, nailing all five of their spot-kicks. But so were the Germans, and they had history on their side. The contest went to sudden death; very sudden, it turned out. Central defender Gareth Southgate, England's next man, stepped up and placed his shot too close to Andreas Kopke. Andreas Möller coolly stuck the next kick past Seaman, whose horrific tutti frutti outfit was presumably intended to dazzle opposition strikers. On this occasion, it failed.

Southgate might have expected to escape the inquests by taking a romantic holiday in Bali with his wife. 'One day we found ourselves in an isolated Buddhist temple with lakes and volcanoes nearby,' he said later. 'It was magical but unfortunately I was spotted by a monk who came over and said: "You Gareth Southgate, you England penalty drama." I reckon he was one of those long-distance Manchester United fans.'

GOLDEN
BALLS

England's campaigns at Italia '90 and Euro '96 both ended in exactly the same way: a semi-final, a 1–1 draw against the Germans, and a tearful exit on penalties. Yet so much had changed in between.

In the course of those six short years, the domestic game had grown up and become respectable. It had subdued the hooligans, through the introduction of all-seater stadia. It had wooed a new audience, thanks to a new wave of glamorous European stars. And it had finally woken up to its own economic potential, via the triumphant launch of the Premier League. By the mid-1990s, the only terrifying charges seen at English football grounds were the ones mounting up on your credit card.

> **'Becks hasn't changed since I've known him. He's always been a flash cockney git.'**
> Ryan Giggs, 2003.

The middle-classes may have abandoned the game after the First World War, but now they came flocking back, reassured by cultural artefacts such as Nick Hornby's *Fever Pitch* – a book which made it possible to admit you liked football without immediately being classed as a troglodyte – and the BBC's satirical magazine show *Fantasy Football League*.

'Suddenly it was trendy to be a football obsessive,' wrote Graeme Le Saux, whose Channel Islands background made him one of the more cosmopolitan members of the England dressing-room. 'A lot of the successful bands of the Nineties were made up of football fans who were always making reference to the sport they loved … The Lightning Seeds did the theme tune for Euro '96 and the separation between footballers and pop stars became more and more blurred.'

At first, the one thing the BSkyB era lacked was a massive England icon to hang the marketing operation on. Then, on the first day of the 1996–7 season, a promising young Manchester United midfielder lobbed the Wimbledon goalkeeper from the halfway line. John Motson's commentary was prescient: 'David Beckham, surely an England player of the future, scores a goal that will be talked about and replayed for years.'

At this early stage, Beckham's crossing ability still exceeded his crossover appeal. But the real breakthrough came when he copped off with Victoria Adams, aka Posh

> **'The face of an angel and the bum of a Greek god.'**
> Gay magazine *Attitude* names Beckham its ultimate fantasy footballer, 1999.

Beckingham Palace meets Buckingham Palace: David Beckham picks up his OBE, November 2003. 'They are precisely the kind of people that one would dread as neighbours,' said Dame Barbara Cartland. 'They have lots of money but no class.'

Spice, in 1997. The pair became the first couple of the *Heat* generation. Each was an A-lister in their own right, and together they represented celebrity squared.

Known to his future wife as 'Golden Balls', Beckham would go on to become arguably the most successful sporting brand in the world. His handsome, slightly vacant façade made him a blank screen for corporate projection. He sold razorblades, sunglasses, suits and cars, setting new records with each endorsement deal along the way.

'[Beckham] has turned himself into a soccer virus,' wrote the cultural commentator Mark Simpson in 2003. 'One that has infected the media, replicating him everywhere, all over the world, endlessly, making him one of the most famous men that has ever lived. David Beckham, in other words, is a superbrand.'

Glenn Hoddle and his Hollywood honeymoon

As one of the glamour boys of the 1980s, not to mention the co-author of the execrable single 'Diamond Lights', England's new manager Glenn Hoddle fitted the mood of the moment. A man with a mirror in every room, he set new standards in sporting narcissism.

In his three seasons in charge of Chelsea, Hoddle had shown that he was an educated reader of the game. But when it came to people, he was practically illiterate. Venables would tailor his management style to the needs of each player, singling out the fragile Gascoigne for extra support. Hoddle's first concern, by contrast, always seemed to be himself. He loved to show off in training, and could be disdainful of his charges' ability. The mullet may have gone, but the lordly attitude had not.

> **'If he was an ice-cream, he would lick himself.'**
> Unnamed player on Glenn Hoddle.

'When Glenn joined in, he was unbelievable,' wrote Graeme Le Saux. 'His balance, his poise, everything ... Sometimes it seemed he was frustrated by members of the England team who were praised to the skies by the critics but ... did not possess his talent.'

The Hodfather: Terry Venables hands on the 'impossible job' to Glenn Hoddle at Lancaster Gate, 1996.

Hoddle's weaknesses, like those of his predecessors, would be ruthlessly exposed in the fullness of time. They always are, in this 'impossible job'. Yet his start was inspirational. Inheriting a more settled and successful set-up than any other England manager, Hoddle steered his side to home-and-away wins against Poland (an achievement that Alf Ramsey would have given his left leg for a quarter-century earlier). They then went to Rome, and chalked up the 0–0 draw they needed to top their World Cup qualifying group.

That match showed off the positive aspects of Hoddle's management. His three central midfielders – Gascoigne, Ince and Batty – ran the game masterfully, outdoing their hosts in those ancient Italian arts of diving and timewasting. Meanwhile Hoddle's opposite number, Cesare

> **'When you stepped offside with Glenn, there was nothing to do but accept your fate and hope that you returned in the next life as talented and perfect as him.'**
>
> Tony Cascarino, Chelsea and Republic of Ireland striker.

Maldini, wasted Gianfranco Zola – the Italians' most dangerous attacker – in a deep-lying role. Zola said afterward that he had spent the game 'running after Batty like a madman', when it should really have been the other way round.

The Italians have always been known for their defensive mindset, but this was excessive. Once England had claimed the necessary point, the local press savaged the home side's 'timorous' approach. 'We got out … without ever really having risked trying to win,' said the *Corriere dello Sport*, 'against a real team, much better organised than ours, which finished coming closer to a goal than ever Italy did in the ninety minutes.'

This was questionable, although the last five minutes had certainly produced more goal-mouth action than the rest of the game put together. Ian Wright drove a shot against the post, whereupon the Italians picked up the ball, broke clear, and carved out an even better opportunity for Christian Vieri at the other end. If Vieri had buried his header, rather than glancing it past the far post, England would have been condemned to the purgatory of play-offs. And the Hoddle honeymoon would have been over in a flash.

The white witch of Wokingham

After the match, one of Hoddle's aides came up with perhaps the greatest ever excuse for failing to score. Eileen Drewery, a former pub landlady with a bouffant hairdo, claimed that she had interceded with the Almighty to deflect Wright's shot onto the post. Had the ball gone in, she added, there would have been a riot.

Clearly, Mrs Drewery was not your common or garden FA

timeserver. Instead, she was a faith healer and self-proclaimed psychic, who had established a 'connection' – cue *Twilight Zone* music – with Hoddle while he was dating her daughter in the 1970s.

In his book, *My World Cup Story*, Hoddle said that he had chanced across Drewery's abilities by accident. 'I happened to be out of the game with a torn hamstring,' he wrote. 'When she told me she was going to do some absent prayer I looked at her really strangely … But she told me to see if the injury was any better in the morning – and it was.'

> **'Jesus was a normal, run-of-the-mill sort of guy who had a genuine gift, just as Eileen has.'**
> Glenn Hoddle on Eileen Drewery, 1998.

In the build-up to the 1998 World Cup, Drewery was given her own room in England's team hotel at Burnham Beeches. Some players went to her for emotional support. Others – like the injury-prone Darren Anderton – were hoping for ligament repair. Steve McManaman and Robbie Fowler, the two cheeky Scousers, wanted to know who would win the next day's 3.15 at Wincanton.

Contact with the fourth dimension was not compulsory. Hoddle left it up to his players to decide whether they needed Drewery's help. Yet the perception still developed that disbelievers would be discarded. As the Arsenal midfielder Ray Parlour put it, 'When she put her hands on my head, I asked her for a short back and sides. I never played for England again.'

> **'I hear Glenn Hoddle has found God. That must have been one hell of a pass.'**
> Comedian Jasper Carrott.

It was Hoddle himself who briefed the media about Drewery's role in England's World Cup preparations. The pressmen could hardly believe their luck. The England manager soon found himself

> ### 'Joining up with England is like being part of a religious cult.'
> Ascribed to Steve McManaman during the Hoddle era.

portrayed as a credulous crank, a superstitious nut-job, and – worst of all – a friend of Uri Geller. Even so, he stuck by his psychic sidekick, who seemed to occupy a more prominent place in his thoughts than any single member of the team.

'He used the press to promote Eileen Drewery,' said the journalist Rob Shepherd. 'He would either bring it up himself or when asked about it he would talk about it *ad nauseam* … If she had nothing to do with Glenn Hoddle, you might find her down the end of Brighton pier now.'

Gazza's last fling

In May 1998, England flew to the Spanish resort of La Manga, where Hoddle indulged his elephantine ego with a king-sized power trip. At the end of the week, he explained, he would be whittling down his squad to the 22 men who would go to France. Six would be flying home disappointed.

There was nothing especially radical in this. Ramsey had performed a similar operation at Hendon Hall all those years ago. But Ramsey had earned the respect and unquestioning loyalty of just about all his players; Hoddle, by contrast, was viewed with little warmth. And no-one especially enjoyed waiting by the pool to hear their fate, like so many university applicants on judgement day. It was 'a bit like a meat market,' said Beckham. 'You're in, you're out.'

Gascoigne, in particular, became stressed beyond endurance. Hoddle had recalled him after the wife-beating scandal, saying 'I accept that people are human.' But now Gazza's England career was back in the balance after 'kebabgate' – a photograph of him sharing a late-night snack with celebrity mates Chris Evans and Danny Baker. He must have guessed he was about to get the bullet because he stormed into Hoddle's room, interrupting Phil Neville's interview.

'I went over to his wardrobe and kicked in the door,' wrote

Gascoigne later. 'Then I overturned his table, smashing a pottery vase and sending it crashing to the floor. In the process I managed to cut my leg, so now there was blood all over the place as well ... I was about to start smashing all his windows, when David Seaman and Paul Ince burst in and managed to restrain me. Then they called for the doctor, who gave me a valium tablet to calm me down.'

It was a sad way for an England legend to leave the stage. Whatever his faults, Gascoigne had always put his body – and, arguably, his mind – on the line for his country. Few questioned the wisdom of the decision at the time, for Gascoigne's fitness was clearly on the slide. But Hoddle made a gross tactical error by relating the gory details in his World Cup diary – including the hilarious revelation that he had put a Kenny G record on in an attempt to lighten the mood. No wonder the dressing-room turned against him.

> **'I once said Gazza's IQ was less than his shirt number and he asked me "What's an IQ?"'**
> George Best, 1993.

The boy with wings on his feet

Whatever else you might say about Hoddle, his England team scored some scorching goals. They found the net seven times at the 1998 World Cup, and four of those were Goal of the Month material.

After Paul Scholes had set the tone in the opening match, sealing a 2–0 win over Tunisia with a right-footed curler, Anderton and Beckham kept the bandwagon rolling against Colombia. Rivals for the right wing, they matched each other with a ferocious near-post volley and a 30-yard free kick respectively. Hoddle's team had attacking options all over the pitch.

But there was no question about the champagne moment of England's World Cup. In the round of 16, they met Argentina in a contest that was freighted with emotional and historical baggage. The match turned out to be the biggest cliffhanger of the tournament. And it was graced by a goal that must be ranked among the finest in English football history.

> **'Michael Owen is not a natural goalscorer.'**
> Glenn Hoddle, 1998.

Michael Owen was the new sensation of the team, an 18-year-old striker with such supersonic acceleration that he routinely left defenders floundering in his slipstream. He had come on as a substitute in the group-phase game against Romania and equalised within five minutes. Now Hoddle was ready to pitch him in from the start, in preference to Teddy Sheringham. It was the best decision the manager ever made.

The game had only been going six minutes when Diego Simeone went down under pressure from David Seaman, and Gabriel Batistuta opened the scoring from the penalty spot. Owen responded speedily in every sense. Darting into the opposition penalty area, he staged one of the most dramatic falls since the Book of Genesis. It was true that Roberto Ayala had barely touched him, but then the same could have been said of Simeone's theatrics at the other end. What comes around, goes around. Or, in this case, goes to ground.

Shearer equalised nervelessly, finding the top left-hand corner from 12 yards. Five minutes later, the flying pipsqueak was at it again. Standing just inside the centre-circle, Owen received a neat little pass from Beckham, flicking the ball delicately into the acres of open space ahead of him. He then switched on his afterburners, streaking past the attempted challenge of Jose Chamot like a white-shirted comet.

By now, Ayala was thoroughly disconcerted, and defending so deep that he was in danger of getting the bends. As he dithered on the edge of the penalty area, Owen went past him with a body-swerve that looked like a Stanley Matthews video running at double-speed. Swinging to the right, Owen chipped a perfect cross-shot into the top corner. 'He is

> **'When I played I always loved to go out against English teams because they always gave you the ball back if you lost it. They still do.'**
> Johan Cruyff, former Ajax and Netherlands captain, 1998.

That good! Michael Owen exults after scoring a wondergoal to rank among the finest in England's history, St Etienne, 30 June 1998.

18 years and 198 days old,' crowed Jon Champion on the BBC commentary. 'Just think what he'll be like when he grows up.'

That made it three goals inside 16 minutes – and yet it was only the beginning of the evening's drama. Argentina hit back with an equaliser a few minutes before half-time, courtesy of a clever free-kick orchestrated by Juan Sebastian Veron. And then things got really interesting. It's time to talk about Becks.

Beckham earns his crown of thorns

Of all the players in the England squad, you would have expected Hoddle to bond with Beckham. The two men had a great deal in common, including a sublime right foot and a quarterback complex. Asked in 2007 whom he had modelled his game on, Beckham said 'Glenn Hoddle. I thought he was one of the world's best passers. He could put the ball anywhere he wanted and I tried to model my style on his – the passing, the crossing, the scoring goals.'

The admiration seemed mutual as Beckham started all eight of England's World Cup qualifiers. He was passing and crossing like his idol, while covering far more ground. But then Victoria arrived, and it was almost as if Hoddle was jealous. He became convinced that Beckham was irresponsible and over-emotional, and even left him out of the team during the early stages of the World Cup.

'He wasn't as focused and sharp as he might have been in our warm-up matches,' was the verdict in Hoddle's *My World Cup Story*. 'Fine, he's in love, but I think he lost his way a bit at the end of last season and his form suffered as a result.' For the first two games of the tournament, Darren Anderton was preferred on England's right wing.

Beckham finally won his chance when Ince injured an ankle against Romania. He was soon into his rangy stride, lubricating the midfield with a series of inch-perfect passes. And then came the free-kick against Colombia. This was a seminal moment for Golden Balls, who struck his shot with all the verve, curve and swerve he could muster. It was his first goal for England, and as Ken Jones wrote, it 'launched a phrase – "Beckham territory"'. In his autobiography *My Side*, Beckham wrote 'Part of me wanted to run over to the bench to Glenn Hoddle. *There you go. What do you make of that?*'

And so to Argentina. Beckham may have deserved an assist for Owen's spectacular goal, but any other contributions were overshadowed by his fatal indiscretion in the second half. The incident stemmed from a foul by Diego Simeone, Argentina's bruiser of a captain, who clattered into Beckham from behind.

Marching orders: Referee Kim Milton Nielsen sends off England's David Beckham for kicking out at Diego Simeone (second from the right). Gabriel Batistuta looks on.

Simeone then pretended to ruffle his hair, only to grasp it by the roots. Beckham flicked out a petulant boot, and Simeone went down as if struck by lightning. It was a cheap shot, and a feeble way to earn a red card. But that is exactly what Kim Milton Nielsen produced.

In his book, Hoddle could not resist an 'I told you so'. 'What happened against Argentina vindicated my judgement that David wasn't properly focused on the task early on in the tournament,' he wrote. Yet Graeme Le Saux felt that Hoddle's insensitive treatment of Beckham had set up a self-fulfilling prophecy. 'Hoddle had created this seething resentment in him,' Le Saux wrote, 'and laid the foundations for him to react the way he did to Simeone.'

Hoddle meets his destiny

Reduced to ten men, England were forced to fall back on what they did best: heroic, Spirit-of-Dunkirk-style defence. They were undeniably brave in adversity. It was a major feat to keep Argentina at bay for the remaining 40 minutes of normal time; to extend that defiance through extra-time was phenomenal.

> **'The biggest mistake I think I made was in not getting Eileen Drewery out to join us from the start.'**
> Glenn Hoddle, in *My World Cup Story*.

With 82 minutes played, Hoddle's men thought they had won the game when Sol Campbell powered a header into the net. But the goal was disallowed for Shearer's elbow into the face of the Argentine keeper Carlos Roa. And so it was penalties again – England's nemesis in three major tournaments during the 1990s. This time, Ince and Batty were the fall guys as Roa beat both their shots away. Beckham's absence had proved too big a handicap in the end.

England were out. And so, within a couple of months, was *Glenn Hoddle: My World Cup Story*. If the haste seemed indecent, so did some of the detailed content from inside the England camp, especially the account of Gascoigne's room-trashing rage on being excluded from the final 22. In November, when the players gathered for the first match since publication, there was a virtual mutiny. 'What is said in the dressing-room, stays in the dressing-room,' stormed their shop steward, Alan Shearer.

Hoddle's rampant egomania had prevented him from anticipating the trouble his diary would cause. Men who see themselves as the centre of the universe rarely stop to worry about distant planets. But he should surely have had better advice from David Davies, the FA's director of public affairs, especially as Davies had actually ghost-written the book. The man responsible for Hoddle's publicity had just dropped the biggest PR bollock since *Do I Not Like That*.

> **'If Hoddle is right, then I must have been a failed football manager in a previous existence.'**
> David Blunkett, Labour home secretary (2001–4), and blind from birth.

> ## '[Hoddle] became the first Englishman since Thomas Cranmer to be sacked for heresy.'
> Simon Barnes.

The press were only too eager to capitalise, since Hoddle had made enemies of them with his habit of deliberately handing out misinformation. The classic example came before the World Cup match against Romania, when he claimed that the injured Gareth Southgate would be fit to play. This was another policy Davies should have warned against, but Hoddle, typically, thought he was being clever. 'They say I'm too secretive, that it's wrong to throw them a few googlies,' wrote Hoddle in his book. 'But I say it's just being professional.'

The end, for Hoddle, was nigh. In the course of a long interview with *Times* football correspondent Matt Dickinson, he mentioned his belief that disabled people were paying for the sins of past lives. 'You and I have been physically given two hands and two legs and half-decent brains,' he said. 'Some people have not been born like that for a reason. The karma is working from another lifetime.'

The comment was not even at the top of the piece that Dickinson filed. For one thing, Hoddle had expressed the same views nine months earlier; for another, the religious convictions of the England manager must have seemed about as relevant as his preferred brand of tea. But Dickinson's editors wanted a 'write-off' to stick on their back page, and they promoted this oddball observation. Within two days, Tony Blair was among the voices calling for Hoddle's resignation. Within three, Hoddle had obliged.

1998 WORLD CUP FRANCE

Round One:

England 2 – 0 Tunisia
Shearer 43
Scholes 89

England 1 – 2 Romania
Owen 79   Moldovan 47
                     Petrescu 90

England 2 – 0 Colombia
Anderton 20
Beckham 29

Round Two:

England 2 – 2 Argentina (a.e.t.)
Shearer 10 (pen.)   Batistuta 6 (pen.)
Owen 16   Zanetti 45+
(Argentina win 4–3 on penalties)

Different manager (Glenn Hoddle), same sad story on penalty misses, as Argentina, England's other great jinx team, got the better of them in the second round.

'At my signal, unleash hell!'

In his 1979 autobiography, Kevin Keegan delivered a withering verdict on Don Revie's selection for a World Cup qualifier against Finland. 'He picked that football monstrosity, "an attacking team",' Keegan wrote. 'The extra strikers get in each other's way.'

This was a lesson that Keegan had apparently forgotten by the year 1998, when he began his brief spell as England manager. While he never went so far as to pick four strikers, as Revie had against Finland, he certainly put his faith in firepower. His playing career had been an exercise in positive thinking, and the same applied to the teams he sent onto the park. You could almost imagine him as Maximus in *Gladiator*, urging on his troops: 'What we do in life … echoes in eternity!' The trouble was that underneath his bombast, Keegan was not much of a strategist. His players tended to charge forward, battle-lust shining in their eyes, only to leave the compound unguarded at the rear.

'As a coach Kevin Keegan does not give tactical masterclasses,' wrote Jim White in November 1999. '"Go out and drop hand grenades," he tells Paul Scholes before the Sweden game. And when Scholes does a two-footed tackle and gets sent off in the first quarter, he reprimands him by saying "when I told you to go out and drop hand grenades, I didn't mean you should fire Exocets".'

Geordie messiahs: Kevin Keegan (right) with Alan Shearer, his successor as the darling of St James's Park, and the most dangerous English striker of the 1990s.

STUART PEARCE
Caps 78   Goals 5

THE BRITISH BULLDOG personified, 'Psycho' Pearce was the sort of player Graham Taylor admired: a trained electrician who had climbed the greasy pole after five years with non-league Wealdstone. In fact, no-one had a bad word to say about Pearce: the fans loved him because of the obvious pride he took in the three lions, while team-mates appreci-

ated his honesty and professionalism. Even when he missed the vital penalty in Turin, sending the Germans through to the final of Italia '90, the response was more sympathetic than scornful. Penalties apart, the classic Pearce moment dates back to the 1992 European Championships, when the cameras caught French centre-back Basile Boli head-butting him during a break in play. After the game, Pearce told the press that the resulting cut had been caused by an innocent clash of heads. 'It was time I lived up to my adage of living by the sword,' he wrote in his autobiography. A fax then arrived at the team hotel. 'It was from Boli, written in pidgin English, thanking me for my sportsmanship and wishing me well for the future.'

Keegan's training sessions were based on short, sharp five-a-side matches, the same technique he had learned from Bill Shankly at Liverpool. But he never had the ability – or even the desire – to co-ordinate his players in the manner of a Venables or a Hoddle. Like the thrilling yet vulnerable Newcastle side that had established his reputation, Keegan's England were permanently open at the back.

It was this lack of rigour that brought them down in his only tournament in charge – the European Championships of 2000. In their opening match against Portugal, England were 2–0 up inside 20 minutes. But Luis Figo then restored Portugal's self-belief with a 30-yard screamer, and their super-talented midfielders began pouring through the gaps in an under-organised defence. In the end, Portugal romped home 3–2.

England hit back with a rare competitive victory over Germany in Charleroi – 'HUN-NIL', according to the *Sun*. But the joy was tempered by the realisation that this was the worst German side in decades – a point proven when they faded out of the tournament without winning a single game.

Meanwhile England were searching for the draw with Romania that would have sent them through to the quarter-finals. Up by 2–1 at half-time, they really should have done the job with something to spare. But Keegan's team always felt like a bucket of water with a hole in the bottom. When Dorinel Munteanu volleyed the Romanians level in the 48th minute, England's confidence began draining away. Phil Neville revealed their fragile state of mind when he slid in needlessly on Viorel Moldovan on the right-hand side of the penalty area. The spot-kick sealed England's second 3–2 defeat in a week.

Keegan lasted just two more matches – a 1–1 draw in Paris and a 1–0 defeat at home to the Germans. Serenaded by cries of 'What a load of rubbish' on the way back to the Wembley dressing-room, he told the players he was resigning. There were echoes here of Ron Greenwood, who had been talked out of his own resignation threat, 20 years earlier, by none other than Keegan himself. This time, David Beckham was the dissenting voice. 'Kevin,' he said, 'We want you as England manager.' But it was no good. Keegan rushed into the showers and wouldn't come out.

'Keegan is a romantic,' wrote Ken Jones, 'and like all romantics he acts on impulse.' It was a fitting epitaph to his chaotic reign.

THE SVEN DEADLY SINS

'British is best,' the beef industry boasted, in a desperate attempt to downplay the impact of mad cow disease during the 1990s. The same theory had informed the choice of England manager for the past half-century, but as Kevin Keegan made his excuses and left, the citadel was finally crumbling. A country that had once exported coaches to the Continent by the boatload now found itself looking abroad for inspiration.

From the moment Sven-Göran Eriksson's appointment was confirmed, on 31 October, 2000, a not-so orderly queue formed to hack him, rake him and trip him up. For the next couple of months, a battalion of English tabloid reporters spent their weekends piling onto short-haul flights to Rome. Their monopoly on seats at Lazio press conferences was reminiscent of German towels on Mediterranean sun loungers. Even though Eriksson wasn't due to take office until the following summer, his lack of Premier League savvy was cruelly set upon. Joe Lovejoy wrote in *The Sunday Times* 'It was disturbing that,

> 'I don't know why everybody's making such a fuss about a foreign manager when it's having all those English players in the team which is the problem.'
> Comedian Jeremy Hardy on Eriksson's appointment.

when challenged to do so, the new manager was unable to name the Leicester City goalkeeper. We are hardly talking about an obscurity here; Tim Flowers may well play for England in Turin in 10 days' time.'

There was to be little respite over the following five years. In January 2006, the character assassination culminated in the nastiest sting of all, administered by the 'fake Sheikh' Mazher Mahmood on behalf of the *News of the World*. Eriksson was done for audibly fantasising (perhaps not in his usual way) about leaving his job and luring David Beckham to Aston Villa. Admittedly this wasn't the wisest move he ever made, but the trap had been cunningly baited. From the moment he thrust his slippers under the desk at Soho Square, Eriksson sparked a Machiavellian intrigue. As the man himself said, it could not and would not have happened in any other country.

> 'At last England have appointed a manager who speaks English better than the players.'
>
> Brian Clough on Sven-Göran Eriksson.

Eriksson certainly gave the scandal sheets plenty of material to work with. Bedroom farces would become as synonymous with his reign as desperate rearguards. In England, it seems, we can no longer distinguish between night and day, work and leisure, man and manager. All are inexplicably linked. When every passing glance is deconstructed, Alan Hansen-style, like a defensive mistake, what chance did an unlikely Lothario like Sven have? Moral spotlessness was suddenly a pre-requisite for the role. It was no longer win, and win in style. Now you had to keep the cleanest of sheets.

From turnip to Swede

In the very same week that the European Commissioner for Justice said we should all have the same EU passport, the FA invited Eriksson the Outsider across a threshold never breached before. He was now at the hub of our national sport and in office by January 2001. His salary was to be a wallet-

Camp controller: Sven-Göran Eriksson may have looked like Julian Clary's long-lost uncle, but he turned out to be a thoroughly red-blooded male. His nocturnal escapades would send shock and alarm (or Alam?) through the ranks of the FA hierarchy.

busting £3.6 million, a pay packet 10 times the size of his own country's co-coaches Tommy Soderberg and Lars Lagerback. England may not be the top football nation in the world, but by Jove, it is certainly the richest.

Such sums only fuelled the rage of English jingoists, whose nationalistic pride had already been stung by the influx of foreign mercenaries fleecing the Premier League. Swedes, after all, specialised in saunas, muppet chefs and flat-pack furniture. Yet here we were asking one to reassemble broken dreams. Eriksson himself had summed up the situation even before he had taken charge of his first match. 'If we don't get results, they will try to hang me. But if I was an Englishman, they would also try to hang me.' He was getting to know the culture already.

Still, some foreigners are more foreign than others, and the Scandinavians – like the Dutch – have that northern European stoicism that marks them out from the excitable Latin. Eriksson's curriculum vitae included experience of dealing with some of the best players on the planet, plus league titles in three different countries. He also had a natural affinity with English football, having spent part of his coaching education observing Bobby Robson at Ipswich Town and Bob Paisley at Liverpool.

Eriksson had made his name at Gothenburg with a strict 4-4-2 formation – the only shape, he soon discovered, that his English charges could possibly cope with. His one refinement was the use of zonal marking. 'Svennis would place us like chess pieces on the training pitch,' said Gothenburg midfielder Glenn Schiller. Almost every training exercise was designed to heighten the players' tactical awareness.

> **'How the rest of the world, who have chuckled for so long at our delusions of grandeur, must be laughing.'**
>
> Joe Lovejoy, in *The Sunday Times*, on Eriksson's appointment.

In his time with England, this was the lesson that Eriksson found hardest to impart. Overall, he was our best manager since Ramsey; certainly no-one else had led England to the quarter-finals of three successive tournaments. His selection was generally sure-footed, his tactics clear-eyed. But every time his team took the lead in a major competition, they insisted on dropping back to the edge of their own penalty area like so many human shields.

'Having worked in Italy, Eriksson expected his players to have some idea how to defend a lead,' says the tactical analyst Jonathan Wilson. 'Instead, they would put eight men behind the ball, drop deeper and deeper and try to re-enact the Siege of Mafeking. It remained the defining weakness that brought them down in every tournament.'

Arise, King Sven of England

To some, Eriksson's coronation was a European defeat comparable to the 1953 Magyar mauling or the 'hell of a beating' inflicted by the Norwegians in Oslo. To others, it was a fresh opportunity. Eriksson and his trusty sidekick Tord Grip spent January migrating around the Premier League grounds. Wherever they went, English footballers started laying on career-best performances.

> **'We've sold our birthright down the river to a nation of seven million skiers and hammer-throwers who spend half their lives in darkness.'**
>
> Jeff Powell in the *Daily Mail*.

Eriksson combined his European calm with a distinct lack of prejudice or favour to select a first squad chock-full of surprises. Unheralded left-back Chris Powell was Charlton's first England cap for 36 years. The young West Ham trio of Frank Lampard, Joe Cole and Michael Carrick had barely 60 summers between them. The north-eastern outposts of Middlesbrough and Sunderland provided Ugo Ehiogu and Gavin McCann respectively.

The initial impact was impressive, as Spain were comfortably seen off in Eriksson's first engagement at Villa Park. Just as in Glenn Hoddle's spell, it was the enigmatic Nick Barmby who got the new regime under way in style with the first of three unanswered goals, and England did not relinquish the momentum for months.

When Keegan walked out, England's position in the qualification stakes had been so bad that one school of thought had been to forget the next World Cup, name a caretaker manager, and start afresh for 2002 and beyond. But by August 2001, England had sealed World Cup qualifying victories over Finland, Albania and Greece, which put them in line for a play-off spot at the very least. The scale of their transformation would have impressed Gok Wan.

The results were as well received in Stockholm as they were in Stockport. 'Forty-two thousand people were at the arena when Mr Eriksson, the boy from Torsby in Sweden, was dubbed King Sven of England,' wrote *Aftonbladet* correspondent Peter Wennmen after the curtain-raising win over Spain. 'Since this is the football country that looks at everything in black and white, you can imagine how big Sven is here now.'

Don't mention the score

'How are England going to win in Germany? It hasn't happened for 100 years. I have no doubts whatsoever that Germany will quite clearly thrash England,' bragged Uli Hoeness, the former international striker. 'They will easily qualify for the World Cup with this match.'

Hoeness may have been a few years out (the correct figure was 36) but his point stood. Since 1966, Germany had morphed from England's weediest whipping-boys into their wartiest bogeymen. Fortunately, Eriksson had no ancestral hang-ups to cling to. In his final address before

I'm sorry, I'll read that again: the Munich Olympiastadion spells out a scoreline that had most English supporters pinching themselves. This match would remain the high point of Eriksson's reign.

kick-off, he reminded his young team that they were capable of upsetting any opponent. And so it proved as England staged a Septemberfest in Munich. The match represented a 'Where were you moment?' comparable to Wembley 1966 or Headingley 1981.

Despite going 1–0 down to a collector's item – an international goal from Addams Family extra Carsten Jancker – England's spirit did not buckle. They had a purpose about them, and a pattern too. The first three goals were laid on by a series of delicate knock-downs, cushioned by headers softer than babies' bottoms. Midway through the second half, Michael Owen completed England's first hat-trick against the Germans since Sir Geoff Hurst. Another incisive pass allowed Heskey to sidefoot a salt-rubbing fifth. Germany 1 England 5.

Eriksson watched this virtuoso display unfold from the sidelines, occasionally clenching his fist in the mildly embarrassed manner of a parent at school sports day. It was merely reward for sticking to the principles that Englishmen knew best. Up until the arrival of Jose Mourinho, the Premier League had always been won by teams employing a 4-4-2 formation. Now Eriksson's team were proving the value of this bread-and-butter system on the international stage.

> **'I had forgotten all about it within three days. It was a day when everything came right for Michael Owen and England while we were extraordinarily unlucky.'**
>
> Oliver Kahn, Germany's captain and goalkeeper, on England's 5–1 win.

'The tinkering of formations – which I personally fell foul to – can only apply when a team have the confidence to believe they are good enough to take on the rest of the world simply on ability alone,' said former manager Graham Taylor in the aftermath. He also added a word of caution: 'England are not there yet just because they destroyed a moderate Germany.'

Nevertheless, the result was a cue for celebration in the next day's newspapers. 'SVENSATION!' roared the *Sunday Mirror*. Even Franz

Beckenbauer was impressed. 'I have never seen a better England team and I have never seen an England team playing better football,' he said. 'They had pace, aggression, movement and skill. It was fantasy football with England on a high.' With confidence coursing through their veins, England were suddenly favourites for automatic qualification.

David Beckham, England's wandering star

The renovation of Wembley had left Eriksson as the only England manager without a permanent base. Yet the travelling circus worked to his advantage when Greece flew in for the decisive qualifying match, which would be played at Old Trafford. The choice of venue proved inspired as David Beckham, the fallen idol of the last World Cup, delivered the greatest performance of his career in front of the adoring Manchester faithful.

Beckham had suffered in silence as he was booed around the Premier League throughout the 1998–9 season. Against Greece, he took the chance to etch his name into England folklore for all the right reasons. The fluency of five weeks earlier had drained away, and England went a goal down when Angelos Charisteas fired a cross-shot across Nigel Martyn. Then, with 67 minutes gone, Beckham slalomed past two challenges, won a free kick, and deposited the ball onto the head of Teddy Sheringham.

> 'He can't kick with his left foot, he doesn't score many goals, he can't head a ball and he can't tackle. Apart from that, he's all right.'
> David Beckham, as seen by George Best.

England were level for all of two minutes, until another defensive muddle let in Demis Nikolaidis. The fans scarcely dared watch during an excruciating finale in which Beckham huffed, hustled and harried, producing more wattage than the rest of the team put together. Attacks from other areas of the field proved disjointed. As Andy Cole once admitted of his frontline interaction with Sheringham, 'It's fair to say that we don't have Sunday lunch together.' But with Germany unable to break down the Finns in Gelsenkirchen, England needed just one goal to send themselves through.

The moment of destiny arrived at the very death, after Sheringham was clambered on 25 yards out. 'I was feeling exhausted and a little desperate that it had to go in,' Beckham said. 'I'd been taking free-kicks all afternoon and it wasn't like me not to hit the target and make the goalkeeper work. Every time I missed it I was just waiting for another chance, and another one and another one. I knew that it was our last chance ...'

The left leg bowed in trademark style, the right foot struck the ball, and the clock ticked onto 92:42; for a split second time stood still. So did goalkeeper Antonios Nikopolidis as the ball arced over the defensive wall and into the top corner. As relief raged around the stadium, Beckham stood there receiving the adulation of the Stretford End. Arms aloft, bedecked in white, he was the angel of the North-West.

Heart of oak, feet of clay

Beckham's entry to the post-match media conference was greeted with a standing ovation from the assembled press corps. 'That's something that never happens,' he reflected in his autobiography. 'Thinking back to after France 98, it's not something I'd ever have imagined happening to me. I hope those guys know how good they made me feel that afternoon.'

Beckham's goal completed the slow process of redemption. Pictured with a noose around his neck in 1998, he was now installed with a halo. If anything, the ups and downs had only boosted his burgeoning popularity. Manchester United would soon discover this to their cost. In negotiating a new deal, they had to factor in his image rights.

Nowhere was Beckham's profile higher than in the Far East, England's destination for the World Cup in June 2002. Yet when he broke a metatarsal, in a Champions League tie at Old Trafford in April, the initial diagnosis suggested that he would miss the entire tournament. It was ironic that the injury was inflicted by an Argentine exile named Aldo Duscher,

> ## 'They are treating me like an assassin, but I didn't kill anyone.'
> Aldo Duscher, the man who broke David Beckham's metatarsal.

because the draw had already revealed that Argentina would be England's most powerful rivals in the so-called group of death.

Beckham's metatarsal joint suddenly became the focus of all the nation's sporting hopes and fears. Every newspaper had its own tame podiatrist on call, supplying weekly prognoses and anatomical diagrams. Two months before the tournament, Beckham abandoned his bed to sleep in an oxygen tent that simulated conditions at 10,000ft. Whether it was the extra red blood cells, or the *Sun* front page calling for a mass experiment in faith healing ('BECK US PRAY'), he did report fit for the first match against Sweden on 2 June. The fact that he only managed 63 lacklustre minutes was shrugged off as a minor detail; like some exfoliated *El Cid*, Beckham was an indispensable figurehead, a man capable of inspiring the team by his mere presence.

Of eastern promises and freaky free kicks

David Seaman was the outstanding performer against Sweden, beating out a couple of threatening shots to salvage a scrappy 1–1 draw. After that, England's World Cup was all about David Beckham, the new Captain Marvel. In the much-hyped clash with Argentina, the pre-tournament favourites, he found himself stepping up to take the crucial penalty. Those melodramatic script-writers had been at it again.

This match was full of echoes of St Etienne. Once again, Owen terrorised the Argentinian defence. And once again, Beckham was goaded by his old nemesis Diego Simeone, who tried to distract him as he walked up

> ## 'Bangers with Batistuta. Cornflakes with Crespo!'
> Hysterical, unintelligible commentary from John Motson during England's 1–0 win over Argentina, 2002.

> **'You look at Sven and you think ... he's a pharmacist ... he should be saying, "Here's your pile ointment."'**
> Frank Skinner on Eriksson, 2004.

to the spot. But he steeled himself and struck the ball low and hard; not a great penalty, if truth be told, but still good enough to beat Pablo Cavallero, who failed to commit himself in either direction.

Beckham had nothing left to prove to the English fans, not after all his whole-hearted efforts over the previous six years. But he clearly had something to prove to himself. 'In those few seconds after the ball settled in the back of Argentina's net, I could see flashbulbs fire off around the ground,' he wrote, with a rare flourish. 'As each little explosion died against the blur and colour of the stands, it took everything that had happened, everything that had been said or written since my red card in Saint Etienne, away into the night sky with it.' His penalty proved to be the only goal of the match. The Argentines did not even make it through their group.

Back home, football was riding the crest of a wave. When Eriksson's men beat Denmark 3–0 in the first knock-out round, even the sceptics were engulfed by a powerful surge of hope. England's next opponents were Brazil, the only team with a 100 per cent record thus far. They had a formidable line-up of creative forwards: Ronaldo, Rivaldo, Ronaldinho, Risorgimento (sorry, I made the last one up). Yet when matchday came, England made the more confident start. They even took the lead in the 23rd minute, when a horrible error from Lucio gifted the ball to Owen right in front of goal. If they could only hold firm in defence …

Beckham's decision to pull out of a challenge was arguably the *El Nino* moment which culminated in Brazil's place in the final. When Roberto Carlos slid in for a tackle, England's captain leapt out of the way, claiming in his autobiography that 'I jumped in the air to let his momentum take the ball over the touchline.' Others reckoned he might have been protecting his fragile left foot. Either way, Carlos kept the ball in play and instigated a magnificent, flowing break. Ronaldinho escorted the ball through midfield like a dispatch rider, and within ten seconds Rivaldo had steered home from 15 yards.

Worse was yet to come. Five minutes after the interval, Ronaldinho's ugly-beautiful free kick gave Brazil the lead. Hit from 40 yards, the ball dipped late in its flight like a wounded bird. Seaman could only flap his own arms in despair. 'At the time, I was certain it was a fluke,' wrote Beckham. 'Watching it again, I'm not so sure.'

Stranded Seaman: Ronaldinho's doodlebug of a free-kick falls into the net behind England's devastated goalkeeper, and Brazil are on their way to another World Cup triumph.

English hopes were briefly renewed ten minutes later, when Ronaldinho was sent off for a rash challenge on Danny Mills – a role reversal if ever there was one. But in the final half-hour, they never even raised a threat against Brazil's ten men. 'We seemed to lack the urge and intelligence to win it and that really disappointed me,' commented the watching Bobby Robson.

There should have been no shame in being outplayed by Brazil's shimmering superstars. And yet something was missing in England's second-half performance. Where was the passion, the drive, the sheer bloody-mindedness that had carried them through so many scrapes in the past?

Perhaps we were finally seeing the negative side of Eriksson's management. At half-time, he had offered his usual impassive façade. But this was one moment when England could have used a little Keegan-style ranting. Defender Gareth Southgate summed up the team-talk in withering fashion. 'When we needed Winston Churchill,' he said, 'we got Iain Duncan Smith.'

2002 WORLD CUP SOUTH KOREA

Round One:
England 1 – 1 Sweden
Campbell 24   *Alexandersson 59*

England 1 – 0 Argentina
Beckham 44 (pen.)

England 0 – 0 Nigeria

Round Two:
England 3 – 0 Denmark
Ferdinand 5
Owen 22
Heskey 44

Quarter-final:
England 1 – 2 Brazil
Owen 23   *Rivaldo 45+2, Ronaldinho 50*

In the first of Sven-Göran Eriksson's two World Cups in charge of England, his team put on a dogged display to advance to the quarter-finals, where they were simply outclassed by a stylish Brazil, the eventual champions.

Red hot Swedish

While the intrusion into Eriksson's private life could hardly be justified on public interest grounds, there was a certain fascination to the saga. The idea of this weak-chinned bank manager bedding a succession of lovelies seemed totally implausible. It was as if your pet rabbit had suddenly developed a taste for steak.

First up was Ulrika Jonsson. In October 2003, the *Daily Mirror* revealed that the former hostess of *Gladiators* had become closely acquainted with Eriksson's jousting stick the previous summer. And it wasn't long before Eriksson was on the prowl again. His next conquest was Faria Alam, a secretary at the FA who had also been knocking off the organisation's chief executive, Mark Palios. After revealing this bizarre ménage, the *News of the World* threw in another juicy titbit, claiming that the FA had

> **'He is what John Major would be if he swallowed a bucket of Viagra.'**
>
> Paul Hayward on Eriksson, *Daily Telegraph*.

Easy, tiger: Sven-Göran Eriksson looks ready to pounce on his Italian *inamorata* Nancy Dell'Olio.

> **'FA officials gave Faria Alam a severe grilling, which was a relief, because she thought she might get a roasting.'**
> Comedian Dara O'Briain.

tried to offer them the Eriksson story in exchange for their silence on Palios. Sports administrators are like mobsters: they always look after their own.

Alam proceeded to give the *News Of The World* a memorable kiss-and-tell in which she ridiculed Eriksson's official girlfriend, Nancy Dell'Olio, as a 'drag queen'. She also said that she and Sven had dined on seafood and champagne, at which point he had cleared the dinner table and loaded the dishwasher before leading her upstairs and performing like 'a master of love'. She made Eriksson's approach to the boudoir sound as methodical and rigorous as his coaching routines.

The media had no excuse for savaging Eriksson over his sexcapades. He was not a married man anymore, and neither did he attempt to pose as some sort of paragon. The worst he should have suffered was a little light ribbing about his indirect approach play. Yet certain sections of the press acted as if they were suffering from Svennis envy. From the way they tore into his reputation, they could have been writing about the local vicar.

Suggestions that Eriksson's list of lovers might ruin his relationship with the players were laughable; if anything, his charges probably looked at him with newfound respect. In any case, the game had wider problems to worry about. In the

> **'The England fans will be talking about their 1–0 win over France in Lisbon for many years to come.'**
> ITV commentator Clive Tyldesley, moments before Zinedine Zidane scored two goals from dead-ball kicks in England's Euro 2004 group match with France.

autumn of 2003, four players were caught up in a 'roasting' scandal. The allegations centred on the word of a 17-year-old convent schoolgirl who had supposedly been involved in an orgy in Room 316 of London's Grosvenor House Hotel.

While the case never came to court, it certainly sold a few newspapers along the way. 'At one point,' leered a breathless headline, 'she was having sex with three men at once.' We've heard of passing triangles, but this was ridiculous.

Roonaldo makes his bow

In June 2003, David Beckham left Manchester United for Real Madrid – a move that presaged a gentle yet unmistakeable decline. By Euro 2004, a fiery young talent named Wayne Rooney had stepped into Beckham's boots as England's leading man. Perhaps this might explain his similar susceptibility to metatarsal damage.

Rooney had made his *Match of the Day* debut as a 16-year-old, ending Arsenal's 29-game unbeaten record with a Beckhamesque bender at Goodison Park. It soon became clear that he possessed a Promethean talent. 'Rooney has what no amount of age or experience can bestow,' wrote Paul Hayward in the *Daily Telegraph*, 'an instinctive sense of where the goal is and how to get there fast ... [he is] a player for tomorrow – but he deserves his garland through fire today.'

> **'Rooney, in a word, saved Eriksson's skin.'**
> Brian Glanville on Euro 2004.

England's overall performance at Euro 2004 must rank as their best in a tournament under Eriksson. Some of their football was spicier than Keith Allen's *Vindaloo*. Rooney bagged a pair of braces against Switzerland and Croatia to bring up a quarter-final against Portugal, the tournament hosts. And when Owen netted with a predatory flick of the boot just three minutes in, they had one foot in the semis. Unfortunately, Rooney soon needed one foot in plaster. What had appeared to be an innocuous tangling with Portugal centre-back Jorge Andrade turned out to be the first metatarsal break of his career.

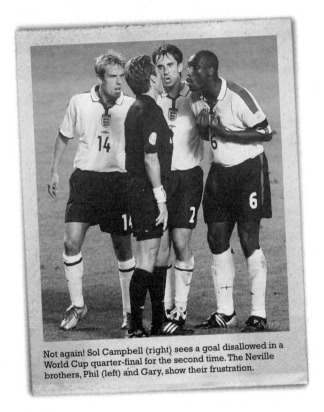

Not again! Sol Campbell (right) sees a goal disallowed in a World Cup quarter-final for the second time. The Neville brothers, Phil (left) and Gary, show their frustration.

Such moments alter matches. Without their offensive spearhead, England became introverted. After hanging on grimly for most of the match, they lost concentration with just ten minutes to play and allowed the unheralded Tottenham striker Helder Postiga to head Portugal's equaliser. Just seconds before the end of normal time, Sol Campbell thought he had scored the winner, only for the goal to be denied because John Terry had impeded the goalkeeper. Those looking through Union Jack glasses could see no infringement. Those looking for omens recalled Campbell's disallowed effort against Argentina in 1998.

Extra time in Lisbon produced another twist as Rui Costa's fine strike was cancelled out by Frank Lampard's opportunist finish five minutes later. Such drama merely heightened the pain, however, as for the fourth time in the space of seven major tournaments, England went out on penalties.

Beckham sliced the first over the bar, which caused consternation in the aftermath, not least for the fact that the ball appeared to wobble a nanosecond before impact. Rui Costa provided further proof that reputations count for little from 12 yards. But all the other Portuguese marksmen were successful. 'Were there mistakes in selection?' Eriksson considered. 'Absolutely not. I think those XI were the best and they will not change much before 2006.'

Of fake Sheikhs and career breaks

At the point when Sven-Göran Eriksson was booted out of the England job, he had lost only three competitive matches. And on each occasion, wrote David Beckham, 'It was only a break of the ball or one mistake or being on the wrong side of a referee's decision ... that made the difference.'

In any normal line of work, Eriksson could have claimed constructive dismissal. But he was dealing with the weird world of English football, where morality is deemed every bit as important as results. Already a wounded animal after his dalliances with Ulrika and Faria, Eriksson was now brought down by his taste for wonga. His acquisitiveness should hardly have been a surprise, considering that he had already broken the payscale for international coaches. But as the author and journalist Simon Barnes pointed out, there had been a conspiracy to undermine him from the very beginning.

> '**I know Sven has a roving eye, he's like a seagull, he can wrap his wings around people.**'
> FA executive director David Davies.

'Most columnists on the sports pages of English newspapers have more or less consistently taken a Sven-must-go line from the first moment that this was tenable,' Barnes explained. 'To write such stuff certainly makes you look tough, hard-minded and controversial. The truth, in fact, is the exact opposite. From an actuarial point of view, it is more likely that an England team will lose a major tournament than that they will win one.'

In January 2006, Eriksson was asked out for crab claws and lobster by Mazher Mahmood, an undercover journalist posing as an Arab sheikh. The inspiration for the stunt was clearly derived from the Revie affair, though Eriksson did not go so far as to walk out on England. Instead, he offered indiscreet observations on a few of his players, and declared that he might be interested in managing Aston Villa if the price was right.

None of this should have been particularly surprising. To quote Barnes again, 'the whole business was nothing more than a practical joke'. Still, as far as the FA were concerned, it was a case of three strikes and you're out. Eriksson had previously been connected with the managers' jobs at both Manchester United and Chelsea. Now he would pay for his perceived disloyalty. In fact, everybody would. Along with the termination of his contract – which was announced after the second instalment of Mahmood's 'exclusives' – Eriksson received a golden handshake amounting to several million pounds.

> **'If Sven-Göran Eriksson was a US president he would be impeached.'**
> James Lawton in the *Independent*, February 2005.

Throughout his tenure, he could barely hide his bemusement at the regular media intrusions into his personal life. 'I have great difficulties in understanding that with this England job you should be a saint,' he said. 'You shouldn't earn a lot of money or have a private life and should absolutely not listen to other great possibilities in life. If I have ambition in life, I will listen to other jobs as well. You should be allowed to do that even if you're England manager.'

Live by the anorak, die by the anorak

England's footballers entered the World Cup in Germany in the knowledge that this would be their last assignment under Eriksson. Teams playing under soon-to-depart coaches perennially fail; one only has to recall the effect Sir Alex Ferguson's expected retirement had on Manchester United

BADEN BADEN
(Germany)
Population 54,000

THE LIFE OF THIS GERMAN spa resort normally centres on its baths – though not when the English WAGs (alias wives and girlfriends) came to town during the 2006 World Cup. At times, it seemed as if there were more photographers in the local designer boutiques and hairdressers than there were at the football grounds. *The Guardian*'s Marina Hyde referred to the 'set pieces' of this bizarre existence: most notably 'the group exit from the hotel and the boarding of the bus to take them to an England game, which feels like it should be taking place in the slo-mo style already dubbed Reservoir Wags.' Still it made a nice change for the media to be ganging up on a gaggle of fragrant party chicks. Fifteen years earlier, they would have been throwing a brick through a window in the hope of starting a riot.

in 2001. And so it was with England in 2006. Ultimately, the nation got the performance her prurient press deserved.

Since the Greeks' efficient yet unspectacular success at Euro 2004, other countries had forsworn style in the search for substance. Eriksson's tactics in Germany were a case in point. His approach was so conservative that many felt he was squandering one of the most talented England squads in living memory.

'Eriksson was an exponent of Swedish direct play who had swallowed the Italian manual on negativity,' wrote Paul Hayward in the *Daily Mail*. 'He was a refugee from *Serie A* in the Nineties. He eulogised these England players then locked them in a cage. Their attacking spirit was neutered by a leader who encouraged them to boot long balls out of defence and who made negative substitutions.'

2006 WORLD CUP GERMANY

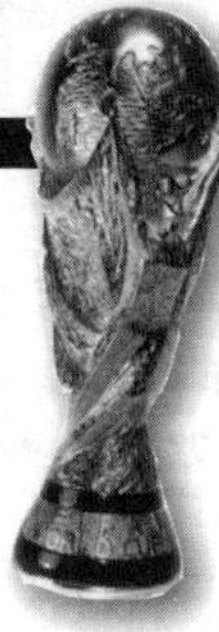

Round One:
England 1 – 0 Paraguay
Gamarra (o.g.) 3

England 2 – 0 Trinidad & Tobago
Crouch 83
Gerrard 90

England 2 – 2 Sweden
Cole 34   *Allback 51*
Gerrard 85   *Larsson 90*

Round Two:
England 1 – 0 Ecuador
Beckham 60

Quarter-final:
England 0 – 0 Portugal (a.e.t.)
(Portugal win 4–3 on penalties)

Return of the penalty shoot-out nightmare, as England converted just one of their first four spot-kicks at the first knockout stage. Eriksson resigned, and English football entered a dire period of underachievement reminiscent of the 1970s.

The team maintained a dysfunctional feel in spite of its creative components. Steven Gerrard and Frank Lampard, midfield mastodons of the Premier League, repeatedly failed to gel. Beckham, top of *La Liga*'s assists list the previous season, lacked mobility if not spirit. And although Joe Cole's displays suggested a solution to the age-old problem of the left flank, his eagerness to cut inside limited the attacking threat. In the heat of a sultry German summer, the crème de la Prem simply curdled in the sun.

Frustrated supporters felt that the English players were slumbering through the tournament, only jolting awake when events turned against them. Perhaps their best performance came in the 2–2 draw against Sweden, when Owen tripped and tore his cruciate ligament in the third minute. His team-mates managed to lift themselves, whereupon Cole scored one of the goals of the tournament with a looping, dipping volley from 30 yards.

But in the next match against Ecuador – a generous draw in the last 16 – Eriksson's men returned to the underwhelming, functional football that had earlier brought results against Paraguay and Trinidad & Tobago. With no fluency in their passing or combination, it fell to Beckham to carry them through with a vintage free kick – his 17th goal in England colours.

The fates now dictated a quarter-final rematch against Portugal. Just as Argentina had targeted Beckham in 1998, so the Portuguese knew they had another dormant volcano on their hands in Rooney. The point was proven when Ricardo Carvalho hauled his man down on the half-way line, and Rooney replied with a forceful boot to the *cojones*. The red card was hard to dispute, as replays suggested far more vicious intent than there had been in Beckham's 'attack' on Simeone. As one wag (not WAG) had it, 'The real question was not whether Rooney's foot would stand up to a tackle, but whether Carvalho's tackle would stand up to Rooney's foot.'

Deprived of their talisman's services, England were undermanned but also invigorated. For a while, it seemed that this petulant kick in the bollocks might double as a kick up the arse. Yet, for all England's industry, they could not penetrate the steely poise of the Portuguese back-line. A 0–0 draw threw them back on their collective Achilles heel: the penalty shoot-out.

With a tearful Beckham joining Rooney on the sidelines, ruled out by an ankle injury, there were new anti-heroes from the spot in Lampard, Gerrard and Jamie Carragher. The only Englishman to score in the 3–1 reverse was the undoubted man of the match, Owen Hargreaves.

Dropping a bollock: Wayne Rooney's attack on Ricardo Carvalho's testicles could hardly have been more blatant. Referee Horacio Elizondo steps in.

England returned home to one of the most downbeat receptions of recent years. 'What excuses can be made for these tosspots?' demanded the former cabinet minister David Mellor. And so Eriksson departed, taking some small consolation from the fact that the FIFA rankings now considered England the fifth-best team in the world, up from 17th when he arrived. At his best, he had led them with insight, patience and wisdom. Yet the big-tournament jinx remained, and the closest this 'golden generation' ever came to a major final was while fiddling with their PlayStations.

> **'What excuses can be made for these tosspots?'**
> David Mellor on England's exit from the 2006 World Cup.

THE WALLY WITH THE BROLLY

It is a shame, from England's point of view, that Jose Mourinho failed in his efforts to bring Steven Gerrard to Stamford Bridge. If he had succeeded, we might have discovered the answer to the great unsolved question of English football. Can Gerrard and Frank Lampard both be accommodated in the same team?

This was the burning issue during Steve McClaren's time as manager, and he never came to grips with it. As Eriksson's deputy for the previous few years, he should have understood that Lampard and Gerrard both want to be James Bond. At club level, they have licence to roam – which works as long as they have a Felix Leiter character to clean up behind them. Together, they just get in each other's way.

The most effective solution was to drop one of them, and call up a holding midfielder instead. Circumstances forced McClaren down this road in September 2007, when Lampard tore a thigh muscle in training. Aston Villa's Gareth Barry was granted a short

> **'I'd like to welcome Steve McClaridge.'**
> Manchester United chairman Martin Edwards introduces Steve McClaren as Alex Ferguson's deputy at Old Trafford, 1999.

stint as Gerrard's left-hand man, and England promptly recorded successive 3–0 wins over Israel and Russia in the space of four days. The chemistry was unmistakeable. As Brian Glanville wrote, 'Gerrard had a midfield partner who could complement him rather than duplicate him.'

On 21 November, Slaven Bilic's Croatia came to Wembley. Here was the moment of truth for McClaren, who needed only a draw to reach the finals of Euro 2008. Yet he seemed to forget everything he had learned

Gimme shelter: Steve McClaren, the shortest-serving manager in England's football history, takes refuge from the rain under an FA umbrella. A shower of vitriol was soon to follow.

two months earlier. With qualification on the line, he returned to his lop-sided 4-4-2 formation, hitching Lampard and Gerrard together in the most uncomfortable partnership since Prince Charles and Lady Di.

Croatia won the game 3–2, through two fine goals and one epic howler from rookie goalkeeper Scott Carson. They were good value for it, too, surging through the middle of the pitch with pacy counter-attacks and delightful ball-skills. England could offer little but one rapier-like pass from substitute Beckham, which Peter Crouch buried with aplomb.

This really was a dark and stormy night for English football, and the driving rain provided us with a defining image: the hapless figure of McClaren sheltering under a red-and-blue umbrella. It just looked wrong, somehow. England's finest were rushing hither and thither like firefighters after a bomb blast, and their boss was impersonating Gene Kelly. The *Daily Mail* headline nailed it: from this moment on, McClaren was destined to be remembered as 'the wally with the brolly'.

> **'He thinks he's Goldmember.'**
> Verdict by countless bloggers on Steve McClaren, who became manager of Holland's FC Twente in June 2008 and immediately took on a bizarre Dutch accent.

PHIL NEVILLE
Caps 59 Goals 0

A COMPETENT Premier League battler, the younger Neville sibling has never once forced himself into a first-choice position for the national side. Perhaps that is because he spent the first decade of his career as Manchester United's Polyfilla, holding the cracks together at full-back or across the midfield as Alex Ferguson required. As many as 23 of his 59 appearances have come as a substitute, yet he stands high up the list of England's most-capped players, ahead of Gascoigne, Greaves, Haynes and Hoddle. There, somewhere, lies a deep indictment of the English game.

Fabulous Fabio or Crappy Capello? Only time will tell ...

It was hardly as if the Croatian débâcle came out of the blue. England had been misfiring all year, at one point scoring just one goal in five successive matches. It seemed for a moment that Israel had handed them a 'get out of gaol free' card by beating Russia 2–1 in Tel Aviv. But then McClaren went and blew it all over again.

> **'It's like replacing Captain Mainwaring with Field-Marshal Montgomery.'**
>
> Mark Perryman, England fans' figurehead, on the transition from McClaren to Capello.

A draw at Wembley should not have been too much to ask, especially when you consider that the Croatians had nothing to play for. The trouble was, they also had nothing to lose. England, by contrast, seemed almost paralysed with anxiety. Carson's attempt to stop Nico Kranjčar's speculative shot made Peter Bonetti look like Securicor.

Some coaches are clever at picking teams. Others are good at motivating their players. McClaren, apparently, was neither. When it came down to it, he was an over-promoted No. 2 – a much-admired technical coach who had limited experience of making the big decisions. His appointment to the main England job represented the Peter Principle run wild.

'You'll be sacked in the morning,' sang the crowd at Wembley, with some relish. They were right, too. The boy from the bootroom had failed, and a chastened FA now began making eyes at Fabio Capello, one of the giants of Italian football. Determined to land a big fish, they dangled the lure of a £30 million contract for four-and-a-half years' work. Yes, that's thirty *million* pounds. The sense of desperation was palpable. As Patrick Barclay wrote in the *Sunday Telegraph*, 'Most of the major football nations aspire to win the World Cup. England's ambition is to become the first to buy it.'

Capello took the job. How else would a 61-year-old with no active employment respond? Yet he might have had second thoughts a few days later, when a paparazzo long lens captured an image of him on the beach with his wife. (Of course, the only reason McClaren had been entrusted with the job in the first place was because 'Big Phil' Scolari had been freaked out by the instant frenzy of media intrusion. After a brief dalliance with the FA in the summer of 2006, the outgoing Portugal coach withdrew in a panic over the posse of reporters camped in his front garden.)

Capello felt like the right man, even if he came at the wrong price. His coaching record – which included seven *Scudettos* with three different

> **'In the Premier League only 35% of the players are English. In Italy it's about 72% [Italians]. I'm worse off than anyone.'**
>
> Fabio Capello gets his excuses in early.

clubs – was awe-inspiring. And after the listlessness of their recent performances, England clearly needed a manager with real credentials. Their latest qualifying campaign was shaping up like one of those reality TV shows in which an inspirational leader turns a bunch of spotty slackers into a choir, or a brass band, or a sailing crew. Or even, God willing, a world-class football team.

'Most of the major football nations aspire to win the World Cup. England's ambition is to become the first to buy it.'

Patrick Barclay in the *Sunday Telegraph*.

GIORGIO DE CHIRICO

Not an Italian striker, but Fabio Capello's favourite surrealist painter. De Chirico's canvases tend to be dark and brooding, with a hint of suppressed violence. A little like Capello himself, some might suggest. During a BBC Radio Four discussion of Capello's £17 million collection of modern art, one pundit expressed concern about de Chirico's titles. '*Enigma Of An Autumn Afternoon* sounds like a stalemate at Wembley with Frank Lampard in the wrong position.' And as for *Melancholy of Departure* …

Melancholy of Departure,
De Chirico 1916

INDEX

Adams, Tony 42, 289, 290, 293
Adamson, Jimmy 183
Ademir 137
Alam, Faria 325–6, 329
Alcock, Charles 17, 19, 20, 28, 45
Allison, George 107, 186, 227
Anderson, Viv 257
Anderton, Darren 293, 299, 301, 304
Andrade, Jorge 327
Arlott, John 117
Armfield, Jimmy 187
Ashman, Ron 236
Assenmacher, Karl-Josef 284
Astle, Jeff 215, 219, 222
Athersmith, Charles 40
Atkinson, Ron 281
Ayala, Roberto 302
Azevedo, João 133
Baden-Powell, Robert 33
Bahr, Walter 143
Baily, Eddie 126, 145, 149, 232
Baker, Danny 300
Bakhramov, Tofik 204, 207
Ball, Alan 191, 192, 193, 197, 202,
    204, 216, 222, 228, 240, 242
Bambridge, Charlie 24–5, 26, 27, 28,
    38, 39
Banks, Gordon 160, 189, 190, 201,
    222, 223, 224, 225, 226, 228, 231
Barclay, Patrick 338, 340
Barker, Jack 97
Barmby, Nick 316
Barnes, John 257–9, 260, 265, 267,
    272
Barnes, Simon 307, 329, 330
Barotis, Lajos 179
Barry, Gareth 335
Barthez, Fabien 93
Bass, Alan 193
Bassett, Billy 39–40, 45, 51, 59
Bastard, Segar 27
Bastin, Cliff 77, 91, 92, 96, 99
Batista, Sergio 265
Batistuta, Gabriel 302
Batt, Peter 216
Batty, David 297–8, 306
Baxter, Jim 208

Beardsley, Peter 262, 280, 287–8
Bearzot, Enzo 247
Beasley, Pat 112
Beckenbauer, Franz 117, 191, 202, 225,
    227, 228, 318–19
Beckham, David 45, 53, 92, 277, 294–
    6, 300, 301, 302, 303–5, 311, 313,
    319–21, 322, 327, 328–9, 332, 333,
    334, 336
Beckham, Victoria 295–6, 304
Beenhakker, Leo 272
Bell, Colin 242
Bennaceur, Ali 264
Bentley, Roy 137, 149
Berthold, Thomas 275
Best, George 177, 234, 301, 319
Beverley, Joy 173
Bilardo, Carlos 265
Bili , Slaven 335
Blair, Tony 110, 307
Bletchley, Edward 205
Blissett, Luther 257, 258
Bloomer, Steve 34, 58–61, 64, 70, 72
Blunkett, David 306
Bohr, Hansen 54
Bohr, Harald 54
Bohr, Niels 54
Boli, Basile 310
Bonetti, Peter 160, 225–6, 227, 231,
    338
Bonnel, Jean 196
Bonsor, Alexander 13
Borghi, Frank 140, 145
Botham, Ian 268
Bowen, Dave 190
Bower, Alfred 73
Bowles, Stan 212, 214, 236, 240–1,
    245, 260
Brabazon of Tara, Baron 174
Brabrook, Peter 171
Bradford, Joseph 73
Bradman, Don 83, 117
Bradshaw, Tom 'Tiny' 86
Brand, Chris 76
Brehme, Andreas 275
Bremner, Billy 208
Bridges, Barry 194

Brolin, Tomas 281
Brooking, Trevor 245–6, 250, 252
Buchan, Charles 75, 78–9
Busby, Matt 79
Butcher, Terry 260, 268–70, 274, 275, 276
Butler, Bryon 215, 264
Butler, Frank 181
Buzanszky, Jeno 156
Byrne, Johnny 193
Byrne, Roger 164, 167, 189
Callaghan, Ian 192
Cameron, Rhona 277
Campbell, Charles 22
Campbell, Nicky 231
Campbell, Sol 306, 328
Capello, Fabio 240, 338–40
Carey, Johnny 114
Carlos, Roberto 322
Carr, Billy 23
Carragher, Jamie 333
Carrick, Michael 316
Carrott, Jasper 299
Carson, Scott 160, 336, 338
Carter, Raich 121, 131
Carvalho, Ricardo 333
Cascarino, Tony 298
Castignolla, Camilla 100
Catton, James 27, 34, 37, 44, 49
Cavallero, Pablo 322
Chamberlain, Sir Austen 90
Chambers, Harry 73
Chamot, Jose 302
Champion, Jon 303
Channon, Mick 239, 242
Chapman, Frederick 55
Chapman, Herbert 73, 78–9, 96, 187
Charisteas, Angelos 319
Charles, Gary 278
Charles, John 193
Charlton, Bobby 113, 165, 166, 174–5, 182, 183, 189, 190, 192, 196, 197, 198, 202, 217, 219, 225, 227, 229, 245, 247
Charlton, Jack 121, 190, 193, 199, 201, 208, 270
Chenery, C.J. 14
Cherry, Trevor 240
Chivers, Martin 232

Churchill, Winston 91, 110, 122
Clarke, Allan 231
Clemence, Ray 248, 249
Clemenceau, Georges 74
Clement, Dave 281
Clough, Brian 230, 231, 244, 313
Cobbold, John 189
Cobbold, W.N. 30, 36
Cockburn, Henry 134
Cohen, George 190, 193
Cole, Andy 320
Cole, Charlie 159
Cole, Joe 316, 332, 333
Coles, Frank 111
Compton, Denis 117, 120
Connelly, John 192, 194
Connery, Sean 196
Connolly, Patrick 122
Cooke, Harry 83
Cook, Theodore 71
Cooney, Bryan 270
Cooper, Henry 236
Copping, Wilf 97–9, 118
Corbett, James 207, 209, 218, 219, 257, 288
Costa, Flávio 138
Costa, Rui 328, 329
Coulter, Phil 224
Cowan, Jamie 46
Coward, Noël 88
Crampsey, Bob 23
Crayston, Jack 98
Croker, Ted   239, 267, 268
Crompton, Bob 57, 58
Cronje, Hansie 253
Crouch, Peter 337
Cruyff, Johan 241, 302
Cullis, Stan 108, 109, 110, 116, 117–18, 119, 120, 130, 131, 136, 148–9
Currie, Tony 212, 214
Czibor, Zoltan 152, 157
Dattilo, Generoso 144
Davies, David 306, 307, 329
Davies, Donny 133
Davies, Hunter 232
Davies, Pete 248, 263, 268, 276
Davies, Russell 267
Dean, Bill 84

Dean, William 'Dixie' 74, 81, 91, 94, 106, 112, 122, 123, 164
Delgado, Rogelio 263
Dell'Olio, Nancy 325
Derwall, Jupp 247
Dexter, Ted 164
Dickinson, Matt 307
Didi 167
Diem, Carl 64
Dobbs, Brian 41
Docherty, Tommy 186
Domarski, Jan 231
Douglas, Bryan 174
Downing, David 183, 229
Doyle, Sir Arthur Conan 67
Drake, Ted 96, 97
Drescher, Ludvig 55
Drewery, Eileen 298–300, 306
Drewry, Arthur 139, 144
Dunn, Arthur 42–4
Dunn, Jimmy 113
Duscher, Aldo 320–1
Eastham, George 191
Edwardes, Charles 43
Edwards, Duncan 164–6, 167
Edwards, Martin 335
Edworthy, Niall 172, 255, 269
Ehiogu, Ugo 316
Ekstrom, Johnny 269
Eriksson, Sven-Göran 120, 312–34, 335
Ettori, Luc 260
Eusébio 200
Evans, Chris 300
Everaldo 222
Fenwick, Terry 261, 262, 265, 272
Ferdinand, Rio 257
Ferguson, Sir Alex 330–1, 335, 337
Ferguson, John 26
Ferraris, Attilio 97–9
Ferrier, Bob 175, 176
Figo, Luis 311
Finn, Ralph 161, 163
Finney, Tom 128, 131, 133, 134–5, 145, 151, 159, 170–1, 191
Flo, Jostein 283
Flowers, Tim 313
Foulke, William 47, 56
Forrest, James 39

Fowler, Robbie 299
Francis, Gerry 242
Franklin, Neil 117, 131, 133, 136
Freeman, J.H. 86
Fry, C.B. 31, 35, 36, 38, 42
Gaetjens, Joe 128, 143, 144
Galeati, Giovanni 145
Gallacher, Hughie 74
Gardner, Robert 12–13, 15
Garrincha 181–2
Gascoigne, Paul 71, 74, 83, 212, 213, 270, 272, 275–6, 277–8, 282, 287–9, 291, 292, 293, 296, 297, 300–1, 306, 337
Gauld, Jimmy 197
Gee, Charlie 94
Geller, Uri 300
George VI 110
George, Charlie 212, 213–14, 229
Gerrard, Steven 131, 165–6, 332, 334, 335, 336
Gerson 220
Gibb, William 14
Gibson, Alfred and Pickford, William 13–14, 26, 34, 41, 57, 58
Gibson, Colin 283, 325
Giggs, Ryan 60, 113, 294
Giller, Norman 140, 182
Ginola, David 277
Glanville, Brian 72, 73, 80, 96, 127, 128, 143, 159, 188, 193, 221, 237, 256, 268, 270, 291, 327, 335
Goebbels, Josef 110
Goldberg, Isaac 52
Goodall, John 34
Göring, Hermann 108
Gosling, R. Cunliffe 45
Goulden, Len 108
Grace, W.G. 13
Graham, George 55, 78
Gray, Andy 158
Grayson, Edward 29, 32, 40
Greaves, Jimmy 35, 131, 176–9, 182, 184, 185, 190, 193, 194, 196, 197, 244, 249, 286
Green, Geoffrey 134, 142, 145, 154, 155
Greenhoff, Brian 240
Greenwood, Ron 154, 244–7, 248,

249, 250, 251, 252, 254, 311
Grip, Tord 316
Gualtieri, Davide 285
Gullit, Ruud 35
Hackett, Desmond 195
Haffey, Frank 178
Haller, Helmut 201
Hamilton, Ian 277–8
Hammond, Derek 20–1
Hansen, Alan 24, 313
Hapgood, Eddie 96, 105, 110, 111, 115, 117
Hardaker, Alan 231
Harding, John 60
Hardwick, George 135
Hardy, Jeremy 312
Hardy, Sam 75
Hargreaves, Owen 333
Harris, Ron 'Chopper' 213
Harris, Stanley 57
Hartle, Roy 113, 153
Hateley, Mark 258, 260
Havelange, João 207
Haynes, Johnny 164, 167, 171, 174, 175, 177, 178, 179, 188, 337
Hayward, Paul 325, 327, 332
Hector, Kevin 232, 233
Hegan, Kenneth 73, 75
Helmer, Thomas 293
Henderson, Sir Nevile 104–6, 108
Hendry, Colin 290
Herberger, Sepp 100, 167
Herkenrath, Fritz 171
Heron, Hubert 24–6
Heskey, Emile 318
Hibbert, William 103
Hiddink, Gus 291
Hidegkuti, Nandor 154, 157, 158–9, 160, 162, 230
Higuita, René 93
Hill, Jimmy 188
Hitler, Adolf 90, 103–6, 136, 146
Hobsbawm, Eric 51
Hoby, Alan 160
Hoddle, Glenn 34, 246, 247, 255, 260–1, 265, 296–307, 308, 311, 316, 337
Hodge, Steve 262, 263
Hoeness, Uli 317

Hogan, Jimmy 73, 101–3, 113, 147
Holt, Richard 54
Homer 20, 31
Honeyball, Lee 250
Hornby, Nick 71, 294
Howe, Don 167, 171–2, 260
Howell, Leonard 12
Hudson, Alan 212, 214, 215, 229
Hufton, Ted 83
Hughes, Charles 256
Hughes, Emlyn 220, 233, 244
Hunt, Roger 131, 204
Hunter, Norman 194, 213, 216, 229, 231, 233
Hurst, Geoff 54, 193, 197, 198, 199, 201, 203, 204, 226, 228, 318
Hyde, Marina 331
Ilgner, Bodo 276
Ince, Paul 292, 297, 301, 306
Jacks, Brian 236
Jackson, Alex 86
Jackson, N. Lane 28–30, 32, 33
Jair 137
Jairzinho 221, 222
Jakob, Hans 108
James, Alex 77, 86, 107
James, Brian 40, 46, 57, 107, 147
Jancker, Carsten 318
John Paul II, Pope 93
Johns, Hugh 204
Johnson, Ben 253
Johnson, Samuel 149, 186
Johnson, Tommy 94
Johnston, Harry 158–9
Jones, Bryn 107
Jones, Ken 98, 127, 148, 172, 194, 220, 226, 231–2, 267, 304, 311
Jones, Vinnie 98, 118
Jones, W. Unite 25
Jonsson, Ulrika 325, 329
Joy, Bernard 77
Kahn, Oliver 318
Kay, Tony 197
Keane, Roy 198
Keegan, Kevin 215, 232, 233, 236–8, 239, 240, 241, 243, 246, 247, 249, 250–1, 252, 255, 308–11, 312, 316, 324
Keith, John 94

Kelly, Robert 73, 85
Kelso, Robert 36
Kenrick, Samuel 27
Kenyon-Slaney, Captain William Slaney 12, 14, 17–18, 21, 22, 35
Keough, Harry 143
Kevan, Derek 169, 174
Kinnaird, Arthur 15–16, 20, 28, 69
Knievel, Evel 79
Kocsis, Sandor 152, 157–8
Koeman, Ronald 284
Kopke, Andreas 293
Kranj ar, Nico 338
Kuntz, Stefan 293
Kuper, Simon 110, 111
Lagerback, Lars 314
Lampard, Frank 131, 316, 328, 332, 334, 335, 336, 340
Langenus, John 90
Langton, Bobby 131
Lato, Grzewgorz 231, 233
Laudrup, Michael 255, 256
Law, Denis 178, 208
Lawton, James 271, 330
Lawton, Tommy 105, 109, 111–12, 115, 116, 118, 121, 131, 133, 134, 135, 136, 170, 176
Leake, Alec 60
Leandro 258
Lee, Francis 221, 228
Leitch, Sam 175–6
Le Saux, Graeme 290, 294, 296, 305
Liddell, Billy 142
Lillelien, Bjorge 249–50
Linde, Ceve 148
Lindley, Tinsley 30–1, 35, 36, 37, 38, 39, 43, 52
Lindsay, Alec 237
Lineker, Gary 35, 253, 257, 260, 262–3, 265, 268, 275, 276, 281
Lintott, Evelyn 71
Livingstone, Robert 24
Lloyd, Marie 70
Lofthouse, Nat 35, 132, 149–53, 157, 174, 287
Lorant, Gyula 156
Lorenzo, Peter 172–4
Lovejoy, Joe 266, 312, 315
Lucio 322

Lund, Tom 249
Macadam, John 111, 112, 116
McAllister, Gary 289
McDonald, Colin 171
McDowall, Les 162
McIlvanney, Hugh 198, 214, 227
MacKinnon, Angus 26
McBride, Peter 58
McCann, Gavin 316
McClaren, Steve 335–7, 338, 339
McColl, R.S. 38
McCracken, Bill 118
McKinstry, Leo 203, 226
McLintock, Frank 213
McManaman, Steve 299
McMenemy, Lawrie 284
McMullen, Jimmy 86
McNeill, Terry 255
Magee, Thomas 74
Maldini, Cesare 297
Mangnall, Ernest 53
Mannion, Wilf 131, 132, 133, 134, 136, 138, 143, 247, 287
Maradona, Diego 253–4, 259, 263, 264–6
Marsh, Rodney 212, 215, 246
Martin, Bill 224
Martyn, Nigel 319
Matthews, Stanley 30, 74, 91, 97, 104, 106, 108, 109, 112, 113–15, 116, 117, 118, 119, 120–2, 129, 131, 133, 134, 136, 137, 138, 139–40, 141, 144, 148, 161, 162, 163, 170, 182, 185, 191, 302
Mazzoni, Tomas 139
Mears, Joe 175, 205
Meazza, Giuseppe 95, 97
Meeham, Thomas 73
Meisl, Willy 56, 78, 80, 99–101, 122, 148, 157
Mellor, David 334
Menti, Romeo 134
Mercer, Joe 112, 113, 116, 117, 119, 131, 236, 238
Meredith, Billy 58, 60, 185
Merrick, Gil 154, 157, 159, 160, 161, 163
Milburn, Jackie 110, 144, 186
Miller, Karl 278

Millichip, Bert 272
Milligan, Spike 205
Mills, Danny 323
Moldovan, Viorel 311
Möller, Andreas 293
Montgomery, General Bernard 109
Monti, Luisito 96
Moore, Bobby 117, 166, 179, 184, 186, 189, 190, 193, 194, 196, 201, 204, 209, 216, 217–18, 219, 222, 228, 229, 231, 233, 237, 272, 286, 290
Moore, Brian 201
Morais, João 197
Mortensen, Stanley 119, 123, 133, 134, 138, 139, 140, 141, 143
Morton, Alan 74, 85–6
Mosforth, William 24, 26
Motson, John 295, 321
Mourant, Andrew 238
Mourinho, Jose 318, 335
Mullen, Jimmy 140, 143, 149
Muller, Gerd 226
Mullery, Alan 216, 219, 225, 226, 228, 291
Munteanu, Dorinel 311
Murphy, Jimmy 164
Mussolini, Benito 90, 92, 96, 99, 136
Nadal, Miguel Angel 291
Neal, Phil 256, 284
Neil, Andrew 286
Netzer, Gunther 228–9
Nevill, Captain W.P. 65, 66–8
Neville, Phil 300, 311, 337
Newbolt, Sir Henry 48–9, 68
Newton, Keith 225
Nicholson, Bill 167, 183, 232
Nielsen, Kim Milton 305
Nikolaidis, Demis 319
Nikopolidis, Antonios 320
Norman, Matthew 291
Nottage, Jane 279
Oakley, W.J. 42
O'Briain, Dara 326
Olivieri, Aldo 95
Olsen, Egil 283
Olsen, Jesper 255
Orwell, George 50, 99
Osgood, Peter 228

Osim, Ivan 216
Owen, Michael 301–3, 304, 318, 321, 322, 327, 333
Owen, Syd 155, 160
Padilla, Clara 217–18
Paez, Fito 254
Paine, Terry 192
Paisley, Bob 315
Palios, Mark 325–6
Pallister, Gary 283, 285
Palmer, Carlton 280, 283
Pantling, Harry 73
Parker, Paul 272, 275
Parlour, Ray 299
Parola, Carlo 132
Peacock, Alan 181
Pearce, Jonathan 285
Pearce, Stuart 272, 276, 285, 291, 310
Pelé 113, 132, 181, 197, 200–1, 221, 222, 223
Pellizzari, Tommaso 258
Pentland, Fred 102
Perry, Bill 120
Perryman, Mark 338
Peskett, Roy 136
Peters, Jan 241
Peters, Martin 189, 191, 192, 193, 197, 198, 202, 203, 225, 228
Pickles 205
Platt, David 270, 274, 284–5, 291
Polgar, Alfred 101
Postiga, Helder 328
Powell, Chris 316
Powell, Ivor 123
Powell, Jeff 226, 234, 242, 288, 316
Pozzo, Vittorio 97, 134, 172
Preston, Thomas 90
Priestley, J.B. 41–3
Pumpido, Nery 254
Puskás, Ferenc 52, 117, 146, 152, 154, 155–6, 157, 159–60, 230
Ramallets, Antonio 145
Ramsey, Alf 130, 145, 159, 160, 184–97, 199, 200, 203–4, 206, 209, 213, 214–15, 216, 218, 219, 220, 225, 226, 227–8, 229, 230, 233, 234, 236, 244, 246, 253, 254, 279, 288, 297, 300, 315
Rattín, Antonio 198

Raynor, George 102
Reep, Charles 256–7
Renny-Tailyour, Lieutenant Henry 14–15
Rep, Johnny 241
Revie, Don 162, 213, 234–6, 238–42, 243, 244, 308, 330
Rhodes, Cecil 26
Rivaldo 322
Rivelino 221
Roa, Carlos 306
Roberts, Herbie 82
Robinson, Jack 38, 56, 58
Robson, Bobby 174, 248, 252, 254–7, 258, 260, 261, 262, 263, 265, 267, 268, 269, 270, 272, 273, 274, 276, 279, 315, 323
Robson, Bryan 92, 249, 252, 260, 261, 272, 290
Rocco, Nereo 179
Ronaldinho 160, 322, 323
Ronaldo 322
Rooney, Wayne 327, 333, 334
Roose, Leigh Richmond 70
Rose, Henry 94
Rothschild, Baron 50
Rous, Stanley 93, 102, 106, 108, 119, 129, 130, 145, 207
Rowe, Arthur 147
Sadler, Dave 226
Sadler, John 261
Saldanha, Joao 217
Sansom, Kenny 255, 263
Schiller, Glenn 315
Schoen, Helmut 229, 247
Scholes, Paul 301, 309
Scolari, Phil 339
Scott, Alan 200
Scott, Laurie 135
Seaman, David 160, 285, 289, 291, 293, 301, 302, 321, 323
Sebes, Gusztáv 103, 152, 155–6
Seed, Jimmy 75
Seeler, Uwe 226
Sexton, Dave 154
Shackleton, Len 131, 168, 170–1
Shankly, Bill 123, 311
Shaw, George Bernard 55

Shearer, Alan 281, 287, 290, 293, 302, 306, 309
Shepherd, Rob 283, 300
Shepherdson, Harold 194, 203, 233
Sheringham, Teddy 247, 287, 291, 302, 319, 320
Shilton, Peter 160, 231, 253–4, 260, 263, 264–5, 270, 274
Simeone, Diego 302, 304–5, 321, 333
Simon, Jacques 196
Simonsen, Allan 256
Simpson, Mark 296
Sinclair, Trevor 117
Sindelar, Matthias 99–101, 157
Sinton, Andy 284
Skinner, Frank 322
Slater, Bill 167
Smith, Alan 280
Smith, Billy 86
Smith, G.O. 34, 37–8, 39, 42, 52, 59, 64, 75
Socrates 246
Soderberg, Tommy 314
Southgate, Gareth 293, 307, 324
Spiksley, Fred 39, 45
Sprake, Gary 239
Sproston, Bert 104
Steen, Rob 184, 212, 214
Stefano, Alfredo di 178
Stein, Brian 257
Stephen, Sir Andrew 233
Steven, Trevor 262, 275
Stiles, Nobby 34, 191, 196–7, 200, 201, 216, 246, 288
Stokoe, Bob 235
Storey, George 77
Storey, Peter 228, 229
Strachan, Gordon 24
Stringfellow, Olga 275
Stubbes, Philip 18
Swan, Peter 182, 197
Swift, Frank 122, 134, 135, 160, 163
Sykes, Eric 205
Tagg, Ernie 240
Taylor, D.J. 27, 39
Taylor, Edward 73
Taylor, Graham 256, 258, 279–87, 286, 287, 289, 310, 318
Taylor, Tommy 164, 167

Terry, John 328
Thatcher, Margaret 248, 267
Thomas, Geoff 280
Thompson, Sir Harold 233, 244, 248
Thompson, Peter 192
Thoreson, Hallvar 249
Thring, Revd Edward 17
Tolkien, J.R.R. 109
Tomaszewski, Jan 230, 231
Tomlinson, Alan 50
Tomsett, Pete 76
Trivi, Dobrivoje 216
Tunstall, Frederick 73
Tyldesley, Clive 326
Ungar, Stu 29
Valdano, Jorge 263
van Basten, Marco 272
van der Sar, Edwin 290
Varley, Nick 133
Vava 182
Veitch, Colin 55, 57
Venables, Terry 252, 254, 286–8, 291, 293, 296, 297, 311
Veron, Juan Sebastian 303
Vieri, Christian 298
Vignes, Spencer 70
Villa, Ricky 12
Waddle, Chris 265, 272, 276, 280
Wadsworth, Samuel 73
Wagg, Stephen 92–3
Wall, Frederick 45, 89
Wallace, Dougie 118
Walsh, Bradley 304
Walsh, Paul 257
Walters, A.M. and P.M. 34, 43
Waring, 'Pongo' 106
Watkin, Sir Edward 76
Waugh, Evelyn 99
Weber, Wolfgang 203
Wells, H.G. 50
Wenger, Arsène 78
Wennmen, Peter 317
White, Jim 309
Whitfield, June 205
Whittaker, Spen 101
Widdowson, Samuel 30
Wilkins, Ray 246, 260
Williams, Bert 142, 143
Wilson, George 73

Wilson, Harold 218, 226
Wilson, Jonathan 26, 103, 159, 233, 257, 315
Wilson, Ray 179, 190, 196, 201, 208, 261
Winner, David 17–18, 97, 150, 258
Winterbottom, Walter 80, 128, 129–30, 131, 135, 137, 139–40, 141, 144, 146, 148, 155, 156, 158, 160, 161, 162, 163, 167, 168, 174, 175, 177, 183, 186, 188, 244
Wise, Dennis 288
Withe, Peter 257
Wodehouse, P.G. 88, 106
Wolstenholme, Kenneth 156–7, 158, 199, 204
Woodcock, Tony 247, 259
Woodward, Vivian 52–3, 54, 55, 61, 65, 70, 71, 72, 91, 146–7, 255
Wooldridge, Ian 178
Woolnough, Brian 286
Worthington, Frank 212, 213, 214, 229, 236
Wreford-Brown, Charles 21
Wright, Billy 117, 126, 131, 134, 135, 136, 141, 143, 147, 149, 154, 157, 161, 165, 166, 172, 173, 174, 176, 178, 179
Wright, Ian 298
Wright, Mark 272
Yashin, Lev 170–1
Zamora, Ricardo 93–4, 145
Zarra, Telmo 145
Zatopek, Emil 193
Zidane, Zinedine 83, 326
Zizinho 137
Zola, Gianfranco 297–8
Zwartkruis, Jan 241

PICTURE CREDITS Pages: 2-3 Bob Thomas Sports Photography, Bob Thomas; 10-11 Popperfoto, Bob Thomas; 16 Popperfoto, Bob Thomas; 19 Popperfoto, Bob Thomas; 25 Popperfoto, Bob Thomas; 32 Popperfoto, Bob Thomas; 37 Hulton Archive, Reinhold Thiele; 44 Popperfoto, Bob Thomas; 47 Hulton Archive; 56 Hulton Archive, Charles Hewitt; 59 Popperfoto, Bob Thomas 60; Hulton Archive, A. R. Coster; 63-4 Popperfoto/Getty Images; 66-7 The Art Archive, Imperial War Museum; 76-7 Hulton Archive, Central Press; 83 Popperfoto, Bob Thomas; 87 Hulton Archive, H. F. Davis; 95 Hulton Archive, Central Press; 98 Hulton Archive, Central Press; 100 Popperfoto; 104 Hulton Archive, Keystone; 107 Popperfoto, Bob Thomas; 112 Hulton Archive, J. A. Hampton; 114 Hulton Archive; 116 Popperfoto; 118 Hulton Archive, Reg Birkett; 121 Popperfoto, Bob Thomas; 124-5 Popperfoto, Rolls Press; 132 Hulton Archive, Keystone; 141 Popperfoto; 142 Hulton Archive, Central Press; 150-1 Popperfoto; 152 Hulton Archive, Keystone; 162 Hulton Archive, *Evening Standard*; 168 Hulton Archive, Douglas Miller; 169 Popperfoto; 170 Getty Images Sport, Hulton Archive; 173 Hulton Archive, Raymond Kleboe; 180 Popperfoto; 181 Popperfoto; 185 Hulton Archive, Robert Stiggins; 195 Hulton Archive, Keystone; 198-9 Hulton Archive, Central Press; 202 Hulton Archive; 205 Hulton Archive, Reg Speller; 206 Hulton Archive, Central Press; 207 Hulton Archive, *Evening Standard;* 208 Hulton Archive, Dennis Oulds; 210-1 Bongarts; 213 Hulton Archive, Arthur Jones; 218 Popperfoto, Rolls Press; 220 Hulton Archive, Keystone; 223 Popperfoto, Rolls Press; 224 Hulton Archive, Keystone; 230 Bob Thomas Sports Photography, Bob Thomas; 232 Getty Images Sport, Getty Images; 235 Hulton Archive, Central Press; 237 Bob Thomas Sports Photography, Bob Thomas; 243 Bob Thomas Sports Photography, Bob Thomas; 245 Bob Thomas Sports Photography, Bob Thomas; 251 Bob Thomas Sports Photography, Bob Thomas; 259 Bob Thomas Sports Photography, Bob Thomas; 262 Bob Thomas Sports Photography, Bob Thomas; 264 Bongarts; 269 Getty Images Sport, David Cannon; 271 Bob Thomas Sports Photography, Bob Thomas; 274 Getty Images Sport, Billy Stickland; 283 News Group Newspapers Ltd; 289 Bongarts, Mark Sandten; 290 Bongarts, Mark Sandten; 292 Bob Thomas Sports Photography, Bob Thomas; 295 Getty Images Sport; 297 Getty Images Sport, Stu Forster; 303 Popperfoto; 305 Bob Thomas Sports Photography, Bob Thomas; 307 Getty Images Sport, Ross Kinnaird; 309 Getty Images Sport, Laurence Griffiths; 310 Bob Thomas Sports Photography, Bob Thomas; 314 Getty Images Sport, Stuart Franklin; 317 Getty Images Sport, Ben Radford; 323 Getty Images Sport, David Cannon; 325 Tim Graham Photo Library, TG Stock; 328 Getty Images Sport, Laurence Griffiths; 331 FilmMagic, Niki Nikolova; 334 AFP, Volker Hartmann; 336 AFP, Adrian Dennis; 339 AFP, Carl De Souza; 340 Private Collection, The Bridgeman Art Library © DACS 2008

ACKNOWLEDGEMENTS

This book would not have been possible without the patience of my editor Richard Milbank, the tirelessness of my researcher Richard Gibson, and the forbearance of my lovely wife Belle. Others who have provided expert advice and assistance include Mike Dash, Jonathan Wilson, Alan Smith, Martyn Smith, Richard Holt, Matt Taylor, Tony Collins, Richard Hobson, Derek Pringle, Nick Hoult, Tim de Lisle, Jim Holden, Gideon Haigh, Will Paul, Cath Green, Peter and Susie Hill, my brother Jon and my father Robin. Thank you all. And thank God for the British Library.

If you find yourself wanting to explore the subject in further detail, I would recommend James Corbett's superbly comprehensive *England Expects*, plus two books with narratives that kick in around 1950: Ken Jones's eye-witness view *Jules Rimet Still Dreaming* and Niall Edworthy's witty and caustic *The Second Most Important Job in the Country*. For the early stuff, Brian James is excellent on *England v Scotland*.

Simon Briggs
De Beauvoir Town
17 September 2008

First published in Great Britain in 2008 by Quercus

This paperback edition published in 2009 by
Quercus
21 Bloomsbury Square
London
WC1A 2NS

A CIP catalogue record for this book is available
from the British Library

ISBN 978 1 84916 071 1

10 9 8 7 6 5 4 3 2 1

Printed and bound in Great Britain
by Clays Ltd, St Ives Plc
Design by Hugh Adams